THE CLASSICS
OF WESTERN
SPIRITUALITY

THE CLASSICS OF WESTERN SPIRITUALITY
A Library of the Great Spiritual Masters

President and Publisher
Kevin A. Lynch, C.S.P.

EDITORIAL BOARD

GERTRUDE of HELFTA
THE HERALD OF DIVINE LOVE

TRANSLATED AND EDITED BY
MARGARET WINKWORTH

INTRODUCED BY
SISTER MAXIMILIAN MARNAU

PREFACE BY
LOUIS BOUYER

PAULIST PRESS
NEW YORK • MAHWAH

Cover art: MOTHER PLACID DEMPSEY is a Benedictine nun of the Abbey of Regina Laudis in Bethlehem, Ct. A sculptor and painter, she began doing book illustration over 30 years ago when a member of her community asked her to do the cover for a translation of another of St. Gertrude's writings. Mother Placid says that "the cover for this volume, while taking inspiration from the forms and feeling found in Germanic manuscripts of St. Gertrude's time and particularly influenced by the beautiful illuminations of the Thuringia Saxony region, is, beyond all else, an attempt to give expression to the characteristically personal, experiential, feminine response of St. Gertrude, the intensity of which was expanded and modulated by the pervading ethos of her deeply monastic sensibility. The Christ crucified on the cover of this book expresses above all else the Divine-human love which was St. Gertrude's lived experience of Christ, both in himself and in his members. Doing this cover has been especially meaningful to me because the nun who, 30 years ago, started me in book illustration by that first work on St. Gertrude was Mother Columba Hart, O.S.B., the great medieval scholar and translator whose works *Hadewijch of Brabant* and *Hildegard of Bingen* (posthumously completed by Jane Bishop) have appeared in this series of The Classics of Western Spirituality. With profound respect and affectionate gratitude I dedicate the artwork of this book to her."

BX
4700
.G6
A3
1992

Copyright © 1993 by Margaret Winkworth

Library of Congress Cataloging-in-Publication Data

Gertrude, 1256–1302.
   [Legatus divinae pietatis. English]
   The herald of divine love / Gertrude of Helfta ; translated and
edited by Margaret Winkworth.
    p. cm. — (The Classics of Western spirituality)
   Includes bibliographical references and index.
   ISBN 0-8091-0458-X : (cloth) — ISBN 0-8091-3332-6 (pbk.) :
   1. Gertrude, the Great, Saint, 1256–1302. 2. Christian saints—
Germany—Biography. 3. Mystics—Germany—Biography.
I. Winkworth, Margaret, 1900–   . II. Title. III. Series.
BX4700.G6A3 1992
248.2'2'092—dc20
[B]
                                          92-20663
                                            CIP

Published by Paulist Press
997 Macarthur Boulevard
Mahwah, New Jersey 07430

Printed and bound in the United States of America

Contents

CONTENTS

CONTENTS

CONTENTS

CONTENTS

Translator of this Volume
MARGARET WINKWORTH describes herself as "an elderly house-
wife of no education." Her translations from the German, published in
Vienna, Basel and London, include *The Mind and Work of Paul Klee* by
Werner Haftmann (London: Faber and Faber, 1954). She lives near St.
Cecilia's Abbey on the Isle of Wight in order to enjoy the Liturgy and
the Chant. She was received into the Catholic Church on the feast of
the Epiphany 1956—the 700th anniversary of the birth of St. Gertrude the Great. Her husband, the late William Wilberforce Winkworth, MC, FSA, was a direct descendant of William Wilberforce the
Emancipator, and his great-aunts were Susanna and Catherine Winkworth, translators of German hymns and the German mystics.

Author of the Introduction
SISTER MAXIMILIAN MARNAU was born in London in 1956 of
Austro-Hungarian parents (her father is the poet, novelist and translator Alfred Marnau). After studying Classics and Theology at Oxford
and Cambridge she entered St. Cecilia's Benedictine Abbey, where she
made solemn profession in 1988.

Author of the Preface
Born in Paris in 1913 and brought up as a Protestant, LOUIS
BOUYER prepared for ministry in the Lutheran church. From the
first he was interested both in the mystical tradition and in the ecumeni-
cal movement. At the beginning of the Second World War, he was
received into the Catholic church and became a member of the French
Oratory, influenced both by Saint Philip Neri's pastoral ideal and
Newman's vision of a theology inseparable from spirituality. He has
taught for many years, both in France and around the world, especially
in North America. The author of more than fifty books of theology
and spirituality, Father Bouyer has been especially concerned with
biblical meditation, the Christian Fathers and the spirit of the liturgy
of the church. He now spends most of his time in retirement at the
Benedictine abbey of St. Wandrille in Normandy, but still lectures for
one semester every year at the University of San Francisco.

DEDICATION

To His Holiness Pope John Paul II

Preface

Born in Protestantism, I was early attracted to the mystical tradition, which I discovered first mainly through that apparently extreme form—Quakerism. Nevertheless, I felt that something was lacking from the basic experience of biblical meditation, so essential for all Protestants—how to make our own, here and now, the biblical religion as the religion of the Word made flesh. By this I mean how we are to take the whole of our created being, together with the world we live in, into the wonderful exchange of the creator with his creature.

Soon I came to realize that this is what is taking place in the liturgical tradition, as maintained by the Lutheran churches who are faithful to their origins, or by that part of Anglicanism that wants to get back to the ideal of the Caroline divines, as was the case with the early Oxford movement of John Henry Newman and his friends. Contacts with Benedictine monasticism, especially where it has been most faithful to its own tradition, deepened and broadened this into a decisive experience for me.

It was then that for the first time I came across Saint Gertrude through Dom Guéranger's translation of her *Spiritual Exercises*. There I came to realize that we had that mystical life which is not an absorption of the soul into a philosophical, metaphysical, abstract mysticism, but an assumption into what the biblical authors, especially Saint Paul, explicitly describe as the life of the Christian taken up into the mystery of Christ, the only mystery which is genuinely that of God made man to make of man the child of God, within the body ("mystical" par excellence) of Christ: the only son of God made the son of man. I believe I have good reason to think that the book called *The Herald of Divine Love*, here translated and offered to the public, was understood

1

by Gertrude in a way quite similar to this. Thus, she is able to present her book, even to modern readers, in so persuasive a way.

Learned and highly critical German authors of the last century believed in the existence of two radically different kinds of mysticism in the medieval church: an abstract mysticism, essentially philosophical, that of Meister Eckhart and his disciples and followers; and, on the opposite side, what they contemptuously called "the mysticism of the nuns," precisely that of Gertrude and her sisters, halfway between Cluny and Citeaux. Now that Hadewijch of Antwerp has been rediscovered, and it is clear that the mysticism of Eckhart, vulgarized by Tauler and finally decanted by Ruusbroec, has its roots in the feminine mysticism of the thirteenth century in Flanders (itself clearly a development from those German contemplative nuns so disparagingly treated by some nineteenth-century scholars), it is obvious that the supposed opposition between a "high" and a "low" mysticism is merely a misconception of both. Eckhart's spirituality, whatever may have been his enthusiasm for a Neoplatonism more or less happily Christianized, is not a mere metaphysical abstraction in its deep core, nor is the "mysticism of the nuns" just sentimental and naively erotic.

Throughout the development of the continuous, although many-sided, mystical tradition we have complementary and inseparable aspects of an interior experience: that of the most intimate union of the total human being with the depths of a Godhead that is pure unselfish love. This is the experience of very different kinds of believers—men or women, learned or not, technically "religious" or lay—always an experience most personal and absolutely transcendent, the experience of that most intimate union Saint Paul described to the Colossians as "Christ in you, the hope of glory" (Col 1:27). In other words, it is the mystery of Christ not only "with us," but "in us" through the Spirit.

This is what Gertrude's *The Herald of Divine Love*, with its fine Introduction by Sister Maximilian, will enable us to make our own through what the Second Vatican Council described as "an actual and personal participation" in the prayer, the "service," of the whole church.

Foreword

The present translation of the *Legatus Memorialis Abundantiae Divinae Pietatis* (*Legatus* for short) has been made from the 1875 Latin edition of Paquelin collated with the 1412 MS now in the Staatsbibliothek, Munich (CLM 15,332) and generally follows the critical edition of *Sources Chrétiennes* (see Bibliography).

Included in this volume are Books 1 and 2 complete, and Book 3 with the omission of certain chapters of lesser interest or importance, or which contain duplication of material found elsewhere.

I am deeply indebted to the monks of Wisques, Quarr, and Solesmes for their unfailing courtesy and helpfulness and for the loan of books and in particular to the late Dom Pierre Doyère and Dom Hubert Dauphin for their encouragement and help. I wish also to express my heartfelt gratitude to the Rt. Rev. Fr. Abbot Aelred Sillem of Quarr for his invaluable advice and support.

I am also grateful to Dr. C. H. Talbot, who read my translation at an early stage and made valuable suggestions; to Anthony Levi, without whose encouragement the work would never have been begun; and to Fr. James Walsh, S.J., without whose infinite patience and labor in revising my text it could never have been completed or prepared for publication. To these and many others who gave encouragement and help my thanks are due. I wish also to record my gratitude to Dom Cipriano Vagaggini, who gave me much valuable support before I had even attempted to carry out my project.

Introduction

Gertrude's Origins and Early Life

Gertrude is not concerned to tell us about herself, except that she was totally unworthy of the graces with which she was showered by the Lord. However, she does share the concern of the prophets and of many mystics not only to describe but also to date with meticulous care the actions of God. Here is a typical prophetic introduction: "Now it came to pass in the thirtieth year, in the fourth month, on the fifth day of the month, when I was in the midst of the captives by the river Chobar, the heavens were opened and I saw the visions of God. On the fifth day of the month, the same was the fifth year of the captivity of king Joachin, the word of God came to Ezechiel . . ." (Ez. 1:1–3). There are several other comparable passages in the same book and in the other prophetic books. It is a concern to authenticate, perhaps; to mark the importance of the event, certainly; to divide one's life between "before" and "after," in many cases. Paul was to do the same thing in his description of his conversion on the road to Damascus and surely the evangelists Matthew and Mark intended something of the sort when they wrote their genealogies of Jesus. The "before" and "after" in that case, of course, refer to the whole history of the world.

Mechthild of Magdeburg, Gertrude's older contemporary, specifies that her first touch by the Holy Spirit occurred in her twelfth year; Hildegard dated with precision the beginning of her mystical life; and Gertrude is no exception. She says: "I was in my twenty-sixth year. The day of my salvation was the Monday preceding the feast of the Purification of your most chaste Mother, which fell that year on the 27th of January. The desirable hour was after Compline, as dusk was falling." That fixes the year as 1281; since, as she tells us elsewhere, she was born on the feast of the Epiphany, January 6, the date of her birth was 1256. She will always date her most important experiences of divine grace with the same care, but she gives us no further information about her external life thereby. The date of her death is uncertain; it was a November 17, and, judging from the approximate date at which the *Legatus* ceases, it seems to have taken place in 1301 or 1302.

Her origin, about which nothing at all is known, seems to have been something of a mystery even in her lifetime. There is no record of her family name in the monastery's archives, otherwise so careful to list the noble families from which its nuns came. Gertrude herself says nothing about her family except for implying that her parents were long dead at the time of writing (Bk. 2 ch. 16). (Perhaps she did not know this for certain herself?). It seems also that her birthplace was distant from Helfta: "I have exiled her from all her relatives, so that there should be no one who would love her for the sake of ties of blood" (1:16).

It was not unusual for monasteries to receive children as oblates; the custom went back to the days of St. Benedict himself. Mechthild of Hackeborn, Gertrude's confidante and fellow visionary, began her monastic life at the age of seven, according to the Prologue to the record of her revelations (*Book of Special Grace*), though such was not the intention of her mother, who had brought her on a visit to her sixteen-year-old sister Gertrude, already a nun of the monastery. This Gertrude, incidentally, was to become abbess three years later; it is with her that our Gertrude was frequently confused in the martyrologies. The mistake is perhaps not surprising given the shared name, the fact that they were contemporaries, and that both were particularly close to Mechthild of Hackeborn, one by blood, the other by spirit. That it is a mistake is certain, however; our Gertrude was never abbess and outlived Abbess Gertrude by several years.

It may well be that Gertrude's entry to the monastery at the extraordinarily early age of four ("in her fifth year," says her biographer) was due to the death of her parents. However that may be, she certainly had no further contact with her family, and her upbringing from her earliest childhood was completely monastic. She was one of those of whom it can be said that rather than leaving the world, she never knew it—at least firsthand. That did not prevent a certain worldliness in her life, as she was later to lament.

The presence of these child oblates in the monasteries made it necessary for education to be provided within the walls; it is clear that this education was excellent at Helfta. Gertrude, Mechthild, and the author or authors of Books 1 and 3–5 of the *Legatus* are thoroughly familiar with scripture, which is hardly surprising, but they are also well-read in the Fathers of the Church, notably Augustine and Gregory the Great, and in the more contemporary spiritual writers such as Richard and Hugh of St. Victor, William of St. Thierry, and above all, Bernard. But it is evident that the training at Helfta went beyond these sacred bounds. Gertrude is obviously well-versed in rhetoric, and her Latin, if not classical, is fluent and can be very graceful. Her biographer says that "as soon as she was admitted to the school, she showed such quickness and intelligence that she soon far surpassed in learning and knowledge all the children of her own age, and all other companions as well. Gladly and eagerly she gave herself to the study of the liberal arts." That these studies were not religious is clear from the later comment that "through her excessive attachment to secular studies, up to that time (the time of her "conversion") she had neglected to adapt the highest faculties of her mind to the light of spiritual understanding. By attaching herself with such avid enjoyment to the pursuit of human wisdom, she was depriving herself of the sweet taste of true wisdom."

Her interest in studies did not disappear after her conversion; it merely took a different direction, being applied exclusively to the scriptures and the things of God, and to cooperating with the action of the Holy Spirit within her. She was no less eloquent in speech than in writing, insists her biographer, and even the devil paid her a backhanded compliment on the subject when he appeared to her as she was reciting her Office (3:32).

Gertrude's Conversion

Gertrude herself saw her life as sharply divided in two by her conversion experience at the age of twenty-five, which is referred to by her biographer at 1:1 and described in detail by Gertrude herself at 2:1. It took the form of an apparition of the Lord as a youth inviting her to close union with himself. Gertrude's spirituality is always spousal, and this vision is no exception. It was followed by others, of greater or lesser importance for her spiritual life—that on the vigil of the Annunciation and that on the Sunday of *Esto mihi* are two major ones—and, as she confesses herself, was not followed by a total and irrevocable change of lifestyle. She claims that "my mind wandered away or sought pleasure in temporal things for hours or days at a time—yes, alas, and even weeks" and that when on one occasion the Lord withdrew the consciousness of his presence from her, she failed to desire to find it again or even to notice its disappearance.

However, the event marked a break with her former life radical enough to be called a conversion. Despite her constant insistence on her unworthiness, her negligences, and even her wickedness, as well as her statement that she had formerly been living in a "land of unlikeness" to God, we must not imagine that Gertrude had been living a life which could be described honestly as sinful. At no point in her writings does she give any indication of the spiritual struggles we find in an Augustine or even in a Teresa of Avila. Sin, even in the form of laxity, was never attractive to Gertrude. Her abiding faults were largely what one might call sins of surprise, such as impatience. The Lord assured those who consulted him that other traits of hers which might appear like imperfections in fact stemmed from virtues: her zeal in his service sometimes seemed like harshness toward others; her freedom of spirit like flightiness or inconstancy. The total lack of the attractiveness of sin is expressed by the similitude in 3:4, in which attachment to fleshly pleasures and self-will is compared to flower gardens but rather uninviting ones! This was surely always so.

The conversion was a genuine one, but it was not a conversion from sin to virtue. It was simply a conversion from a life lived in a monastery and following a monastic rule, and so having God for its object but permitting other interests and motivations, to a life totally centered upon and given up wholly to God. Henceforth there was nothing in Gertrude's life but God; all she did was for God's sake. It is not impossible that the outward difference was not very great; the inward difference was infinite. The closest comparison is perhaps with Mechthild of Magdeburg who says: "I, unworthy sinner, was greeted so overpoweringly by the Holy Spirit in my twelfth year when I was alone, that I could no longer have given way to any serious daily sin." She had not been a sinner in the usual sense before that experience, any more than Gertrude had been before her conversion. Mechthild says herself: "All my life before I began this book and before a single word of it came from God into my soul, I was the simplest creature who ever appeared in the spiritual life. Of the devil's wickedness I knew nothing, nor of the evil of the world, and of the falseness of so-called spiritual people I had no idea."

INTRODUCTION

Gertrude's Life in the Monastery

After her conversion, as before, Gertrude seems to have lived the ordinary regular life of the monastery. Her days were made up of the Divine Office, *lectio divina* (which is, as we shall see, not quite the same thing as spiritual reading), and work. We are told that she wrote spiritual works and explanations and simplifications of scripture; she probably worked at copying manuscripts, and she may even have taught in the school, as we know Mechthild of Hackeborn did. We see her spinning, and at least once helping the other nuns with some manual work outside the monastery. She was also assistant chantress to Mechthild of Hackeborn, who is invariably referred to in the *Legatus* as "Dame M. the chantress" and whose exceptional voice earned her the name "The Nightingale of God."

Gertrude's health, at least in her later years, was poor, and the amount of manual work of which she was capable must have been greatly reduced. She was frequently unable to assist at the Office in Choir, or, if able to be present, could not follow the conventual movements. She was also prevented at times by her state of health from being as available as she would have liked to those who came to seek her spiritual counsel. Perhaps this last is the only point in which her external life differed from that of the other nuns. It is obvious from the whole *Legatus*, especially Book 3, that Gertrude was a much sought-after spiritual adviser, not only of her sisters in the monastery, but also of people from outside. A question which clearly recurred frequently was that of the reception of holy communion, in which Gertrude was very much less restrictive than was usual at the time. She would seem to have been a reassuring spiritual adviser, though certainly never a lax one, and her humility as well as the instructions which she received through Mechthild of Hackeborn (1:16) and others ensured that she did not say anything but what she truly believed to be inspired by the Holy Spirit. Hand in hand with her role as spiritual adviser went that of intercessor. Religious, and especially contemplative nuns, receive constant requests for prayer, but it was recognized as Gertrude's special gift. She in her turn would beg prayers for herself.

It speaks well for Gertrude's sisters that her exceptional single-mindedness, her virtues, her uncompromising way of correcting those who fell short, and her fame as a holy and skilled director and intercessor did not lead to envy or resentment. There were those who did not heed her advice, even taking pains to do precisely the opposite of what she suggested, and we do get the occasional echo of difficulties in that area. But she never experienced the persecution so many holy people—most especially mystics or visionaries from the Old Testament prophets to Mechthild of Magdeburg and Hadewijch, and in later times John of the Cross and Bernadette—did experience, and which the Lord himself had said would be the lot of his disciples. Helfta was, there can be no doubt, a fervent and observant monastery; both the *Book of Special Grace* and the *Legatus* give ample evidence of that. It was also—for the two go together—a joyful place. And it seems to have been a beautiful one too, from Gertrude's descriptions and from what we can still judge today.

Perhaps this is the point to mention the question of whether Helfta was a Cistercian or a Benedictine monastery. The question itself is a little misleading, as the distinction was not then as clear-cut as it is today. Helfta, like many other monasteries of nuns following the Rule of St. Benedict at the time, was very much influenced by the Cistercian customs (Bernard is the main influence on Gertrude's spirituality and even on her style), but it did not actually belong to the Order of Cîteaux. At the beginning of the thirteenth century the General Chapter of Cîteaux forbade the acceptance of any more monasteries of nuns into the Order, because the monks were overburdened by the large number of nuns already under their care. Helfta, founded in the mid-thirteenth century, could not have been officially Cistercian. Whether the nuns wore a black "Benedictine" or a white "Cistercian" habit we cannot know, but it is worth noting that both Gertrude and Mechthild are almost universally represented in black. The spiritual directors of the monastery were neither Benedictines nor Cistercians but the Dominicans of Halle; perhaps that was one of the motives which led Mechthild of Magdeburg, that lover of St. Dominic, to choose Helfta as a retreat in which to end her life.

Gertrude's Writings

Gertrude's main manual occupation was writing. Her biographer tells us, "She compiled several books full of the sayings of the saints. . . . She composed several prayers 'sweeter than honey and the honeycomb' and many other spiritual exercises." She also produced simplified versions of difficult scriptural passages, and some of her spiritual counseling may have been carried out in writing: "She labored

INTRODUCTION

tirelessly at collecting and writing down everything that might be of use to others, without expecting any thanks, desiring only the good of souls. She imparted her writings to those most likely to profit by them." Perhaps these were collections of extracts from the writings of others, perhaps her own.

Of these writings only Latin works survive, though she also wrote in German, her native tongue. Of the spiritual exercises mentioned above, some may have found their way into the *Legatus*, which is a very disparate work (only Books 1 and 2 having any real structure, though Book 4, following as it does the liturgical year from Advent to the Dedication, has a certain superficial order). A collection of *Spiritual Exercises* has survived, which has, generally speaking, been the most popular part of Gertrude's writings. It consists of seven long chapters treating in a liturgical and often very practical way such subjects as "The renewal of baptismal innocence," "Spiritual conversion," "On the love of God," and "Preparation for death." The work known as the *Preces Gertrudianae* (*Gertrudian Prayers*) is a later compilation, made up partly of extracts from the writings of Gertrude and partly of prayers composed in her style. Other books of extracts have also appeared in various forms, for example, the Gertrudian *Liturgical Year*.

It is almost certain—although this is not mentioned in the *Legatus* either by Gertrude in Book 2 or by the authors of the other books— that Gertrude was the author of a part of the revelations of Mechthild of Hackeborn, the *Book of Special Grace*. The style and thought are not unlike Gertrude's, though that may just represent the Helfta style; in addition, we know that Gertrude and Mechthild were close spiritual friends. Gertrude confided in Mechthild, as we know from the *Legatus*; it is more than likely that the reverse was also true. It was not until Mechthild was fifty years old that she could be persuaded to make her revelations public, and they are written in the third person, by two of her sisters. That one of these was Gertrude is suggested by the remark that there was never Mechthild's equal in the monastery. At that time Gertrude's fame was at its height both within and without the monastery, and it is hard to imagine that anyone but Gertrude herself would have made such a statement.

The most important of Gertrude's works, however, is the one from which this present translation is made, the *Legatus Memorialis Abundantiae Divinae Pietatis* (*Legatus* for short), the *Herald of the Memorial of the Abundance of Divine Love*, or book of her own revelations. It can be roughly divided into three unequal parts. The first is the core of the

INTRODUCTION

work, Book 2, which is properly entitled "The Memorial of the Abundance of Divine Sweetness." It is the only one of the five books written by Gertrude herself, "in her own hand," the short prologue insists. It was begun on Maundy Thursday eight years after her conversion, that is, in 1289. The prologue tells us that it was begun "under a most violent impulse of the Holy Spirit." Gertrude actually began it, it seems, while standing waiting with the community while holy communion was being brought to a sick person; she was not even permitted the delay required to go and sit at a writing desk! The whole book, with the exception perhaps of the final chapter, reads as if written under a similar violent impulse. This is not to say that it was composed at one sitting; we are told that it was written at intervals, and that at least some was written only twenty years after Gertrude's conversion. But Gertrude herself stresses that she could only write the work when she was inspired to do so. Probably the inspiration was almost as irresistible as the original "violent impulse."

Books 3, 4, and 5 were written by another nun, or possibly more than one, during Gertrude's lifetime and probably at least in part at her dictation. Perhaps she, like Mechthild of Magdeburg when she dictated the seventh book of her revelations, was by then prevented from writing by her poor health. It is striking that there is no description of Gertrude's death, but only of her own presentiment of it and of the form which it would take, while Mechthild of Hackeborn's revelations contained a detailed description not only of Mechthild's death but also of her apparitions and instructions to another person (almost certainly Gertrude). It is likely, then, that the compiler of these books did not feel herself competent to add anything to what she had been told by Gertrude. In this she resembles the amanuensis of Mechthild of Magdeburg, who took down what Mechthild dictated and seems to have added nothing to it.

Finally there is Book 1, written after Gertrude's death as an introduction to the whole collection. It has been suggested that it was written by Gertrude's confessor, but it is far more likely that the author was another Helfta nun, possibly the author of Books 3, 4 and 5. She has the distinctive Helfta style; she claims to be neither clever nor experienced—would a Dominican priest, confessor for many years to a large monastery, do that?; she speaks of "our" monastery; and her relationship to Gertrude and Gertrude's life looks very much more general than that of a confessor would be. Book 1 contains Gertrude's biography. Again we are told nothing of her death; one can only assume that there was nothing unusual about it, which would be typical of her. She was not "singular," and her mystical experiences do not appear to have been, in general, very noticeable. The biographer is concerned to relate only the external events relevant to her spiritual life; it is not possible to reconstruct Gertrude's *curriculum vitae* from it. It also contains a description of her virtues and of her intimacy, ever growing, with God. It includes the testimony of certain other persons, some identifiable, some not, who received revelations about her or graces through her counsel or intercession.

As in the case of Mechthild of Magdeburg, it took a direct and irresistible command from God to persuade Gertrude to write down her experiences. Mechthild constantly echoes Paul's "woe to me if I do not preach the Gospel!"; and Gertrude was told sternly by the Lord: "Know for certain that you will never leave the prison of your flesh until you have paid the last farthing that you are keeping back"—that is, until she had written down all the favors which she had received and which she was so reluctant to communicate. She says:

> You, my God, know all my secret thoughts; you know that I am compelled by a force which is external to me, and indeed is against my will, to commit these things to writing. I consider that I have profited but little from your gifts and so I cannot believe that they were meant for me alone, because in your eternal wisdom you cannot be misled. That is why, Giver of gifts, you who have so freely loaded me with gifts unmerited, I ask you to grant that at least one loving heart reading these pages may be moved to compassion, seeing that through zeal for souls you have permitted such a royal gem to be embedded in the slime of my heart.

Gertrude's Unworthiness

There are several passages of this sort. Gertrude's awareness of the exceptional nature of the graces she had received did not lessen but increased her humility and her consciousness of the gulf between God and his creature. She constantly insists upon her unworthiness, her negligence, even her wickedness. Considering what we are told about her virtues and her fervor, and the conclusions we must draw about the innocence even of her "pre-conversion" life, what are we to make of a passage like this: "Oh how I wish, a thousand times I wish, that all the sea, turned into blood, were to pass over my head, so that the sink of utter vileness in which your inconceivable majesty has deigned to choose to dwell might be overwhelmed by the purifying flood!"? Or her reference to "committing a multitude of faults and, alas, grave sins," or her hope that "no one may be found who makes worse use of God's gifts, or who gives greater scandal to their neighbors, than I do"? Her besetting sins, as we have seen, are impatience and perhaps a certain harshness and intolerance with the lukewarm (directed, more often than not, against herself), and no doubt she does have that in mind. But that would not be enough to justify such strong language or such a constant insistence upon her unworthiness. She herself confesses that even before her conversion she was preserved from committing the sins into which, she insists, she would naturally have fallen. So what does she mean?

However it may seem to us, this is neither exaggeration nor a pathological state of guilt. Gertrude does not feel guilty in the unhealthy sense; she trusts absolutely in the Lord, through whose death and resurrection all her guilt is washed away. We will find the explanation in her own words. Referring to the time of her conversion, she comments: "At that time I became so deeply aware of so much in my heart that might offend the perfection of your purity, and all the rest in such disorder and confusion that it was no fitting dwelling for you who wished to make your abode in it." That is the point; it is the contrast between God's absolute, infinite, immaculate purity and perfection, and the condition of one of his limited, imperfect creatures, wounded and stained by original sin, and, even if not by what most of us would consider actual personal sins, certainly by faults and negligences. No creature can respond worthily to the Creator, and that is the sort of thing Gertrude most laments: "I offer you my laments for the very many infidelities and sins which I have committed in thought, word, and deed . . . but *especially* for being so unfaithful, careless, and irreverent in the use of your gifts." "How mightily," she cries, "the torrents of your honey-sweet divinity overwhelm my nothingness, miserable little worm that I am, crawling about on the parched sands of my negligence and defects!"

We are attached to our low state and our laxness; it is much easier to remain in these parched sands than to try and raise ourselves up to God; and even if we do try, the contrast seems hardly, if at all, diminished. Gertrude says: "For although God exercises his omnipotence in the act of creation, yet the soul which he has made (although it is beautiful in his image and likeness) in as far distant from him as is the creator from the creature." It is unthinkable that a creature favored even with lesser graces than Gertrude's (even, for example, that grace offered to everyone, of receiving the body and blood of Christ in holy communion) should ever cease to thank God, ever cease to strive to her utmost to make return, to respond to his love and to the free gift of the dignity he has given to her—"Oh, the dignity of this minutest speck of dust that has been lifted up out of the mud and taken as a setting for the noblest gem of heaven!" exclaims Gertrude. And yet, it is the universal human experience that things do not work like that. Human adaptability is not always a good characteristic. Most of us become quite used to things which are, in fact, inestimable marvels, and cease even to advert to them; Gertrude admits that this happened to her even in the case of the most wonderful graces. The saints, though this does happen to them, cannot take it for granted; their own failure to respond distresses them acutely, and the closer to God they are the more they will see it, feel it, and suffer. That is why the saints are convinced that they are the greatest sinners. There is even a certain objective truth in it, since the Lord himself said that more is required of one to whom more has been given. St. Benedict in his *Rule* instructs the monk to consider himself always as a bad and unworthy workman and to believe in his heart that he is the vilest and the last of all. How can that be difficult for one who compares himself only with God?

An example of the freedom Gertrude draws from this conviction is her attitude to the reception of holy communion. We hear frequently in the *Legatus* of people who felt themselves unable to go to holy communion because of their general sinfulness, or some fault which they had committed, or simply because they felt themselves insufficiently prepared. Gertrude herself is aware that she is never sufficiently prepared. But her biographer explains:

> She always communicated gladly and confidently, trusting in God's mercy. So little did she esteem her own labors, holding them to be worthless, that if she forgot to recite the prayers and other devotions by which people usually prepare to receive communion, she did not abstain from communicating, considering that all human efforts compared with the excel-

15

lence of that free gift are like a tiny drop of water in comparison with the immensity of the ocean.

Indeed, this consciousness of our nothingness is actually a source of joy. Paul said not only that God's power is perfected in weakness but that he specifically chooses the weak to confound the strong, so that it may be clear that the transcendent power is from God and not from us. Gertrude says that many times in various ways. One of the best examples is at 2:23: "As gold gleams more brightly when it is contrasted with other colors, and the greatest contrast is with black, because that is the color that least resembles gold, so it is with me. For the blackness of my ungrateful life contrasts with the divine splendor of your incomparable benefits to me."

If Gertrude was surprised at first that God should choose to heap his favors upon "the least of human creatures, the one lacking every endowment of fortune or grace, despicable in her life and conduct," and was certainly reluctant to publish those favors, yet she was not really surprised that he did expect her to publish them.

> She used to say that the graces which she (unworthy and ungrateful) received from the Lord in his excessive bounty were, because of her own vileness, as if hidden under dung as long as she kept them to herself, but when she revealed them to others, these treasures became like gems set in gold. . . . She thought herself to be so entirely unworthy of all God's gifts that she could not believe that they were meant for her alone, but thought, rather, that they were for the salvation of others.

She obviously gave the matter much thought and came to the conclusion that in fact all this was intended for her benefit also. She was, she decided, so lacking in merits that the Lord could not think of any way to save her except by using her as an instrument to lead others to merit. "In your merciful love," she says, "you do not want me to perish. On the other hand, in your admirable justice, you could not allow me to be saved with so many imperfections. At least you have provided for me that by my sharing in the gain of many, the share of each might increase . . . in this way you relieved my miserable poverty by giving me a share in the victory of others."

16

INTRODUCTION

Gertrude's Character

Enough has been said above to give the impression of a thoroughly and genuinely humble person with, however, no complexes about her own inadequacy. Her biographer devotes a whole chapter to Gertrude's trust and confidence in God, which is indeed central to her whole spirituality and to her character. "Her soul was always in such a state of serene confidence that neither tribulations nor loss, nor hindrances of any kind, nor even her own faults, could cloud or shake this firm confidence in the loving mercy of God."

We are given a pretty complete character sketch in Book 1. Since it is cast in the form of a list of virtues, a chapter to each virtue, we may feel it is a little one-sided, and yet the picture we get from Gertrude herself (quite unconsciously, of course) is not so different from that of her admiring biographer. Humility and trust shine throughout Book 2, as do the overriding desire for the glory of God and her preoccupation with charity, expressed both in prayer and in action. The biographer, generally speaking, mentions the virtues one would expect: purity and chastity (Gertrude herself mentions among God's gifts her ability to "wash away all the stains of fleshly and ephemeral pleasure in the fountain of God's cleansing love"); humility, fidelity (Gertrude would disagree with this one, but her very distress over her supposed failures rather supports the testimony of the biographer); hatred of sin; discretion; and charity. An attractive detail is that this charity extends itself not only to God and to others, but also to animals. Her detachment from all things, including the gifts of God, is also remarkable and will be discussed in more detail below, as it is an essential part not only of her character but also of her spirituality. So is her zeal for souls.

However, there are two points which are perhaps more surprising. The first is that the picture we receive of the less perfect side of her character is not confined to vague generalities or to her own laments. We see her weak points, and they are just the same as our own—none of the "heroic" sins which by their very enormity seem to give particular scope for repentance and conversion. Hers were the everyday sins and faults into which we find it hard to imagine a saint falling. We have seen that she could be more harsh and severe than might appear absolutely necessary; Mechthild was surprised by that and so was another, unnamed sister. The Lord excused her on both occasions but did not say that she was blameless. Gertrude accuses herself more than once of giving way to anger and makes it clear that impatience was one of her besetting sins: "How seldom have I consented to practice this virtue (of patience) or rather, I have never practiced it as I ought." She laments that she is capable of "treating others so coldly, so discourteously, and even wickedly." There is no doubt that she was fundamentally abandoned to the will of God, and yet we do sense a certain resentment when she relates (twice) that she was left alone by the infirmarians when she was ill. And she tells us in some detail, and without apology, that when the Lord seemed to be dealing with her in a way less exalted than usual, giving her some recommendations which she felt were below her, she was not at all pleased. She was quite capable of complaining to him when his will did not seem to accord with hers or of trying to persuade him to change his mind. She is no doubt referring to the question of making her special graces public when she says that she sometimes pretended not to know what the Lord wanted—how familiar this self-inflicted blindness is to the rest of us!—but it shows that she too was capable of doing it. Perhaps more unexpected still is the fact that she really does seem to have fallen into a certain laxness or negligence at times. A certain person, at her request, asked the Lord "why it was that, although she had lived so long in the presence of God, she seemed to be living in such a negligent way." The person probably took Gertrude at her word, but the Lord, although explaining why he was never offended with her, does not deny the accusation of negligence. She could be less than attentive to the Divine Office, as she confesses (and that is an accusation which the devil chose to level at her also). Of course, all this adds up to very little. The faults are not serious ones and her consciousness of them, her repentance, and the increase of humility which they bring her more than outweigh them, as the Lord frequently says. But it does show that we are dealing with a person of flesh and blood who, despite the extraordinary graces she was granted, had the same struggles as the rest of us.

The second surprising point is this: When the Lord was asked by a certain person (Mechthild?) what it was that pleased him most in Gertrude, he replied, "Her freedom of heart." Then,

> this person, most astonished and, so to speak, considering this an inadequate answer, said: "I should have thought, Lord, that by your grace she would have attained to a higher knowledge of your mysteries and a greater fervor of love." To which the Lord replied: "Yes, indeed, it is as you think. And this is the result of the grace of the freedom of her heart

which is so great a good that it leads directly to the highest
perfection. I have always found her ready to receive my gifts,
for she permits nothing to remain in her heart which might
impede my action."

It is clear that freedom of heart (*libertas cordis*) to the Lord does not
mean quite what we might today take it to mean. It is not unwilling-
ness to be bound, desire for independence, or anything of that sort. It
is certainly not laxness in monastic observance on the pretext of following the spirit rather than the letter. It could be divided into two closely
related characteristics which between them do indeed sum up Gertrude to perfection. *Libertas cordis* is, first of all, purity of heart; it is the
opposite of what James calls double-mindedness (James 1:8 and 4:8).
Nothing but God is allowed into that heart—God, and what he decides to put in it. It is totally available to him and so he can do with it
whatever he pleases. *Libertas cordis* is Gertrude's exclusive concern with
the will and the glory of God; nothing, however good or attractive,
may distract her from that. *Libertas cordis* is also freedom of heart in the
sense of untrammeledness. Gertrude is always open to the voice of
God. Her own assumptions, opinions, and desires simply vanish before it. That leads her to great detachment, confidence, freedom from
anxiety, and often what we would call broadmindedness. We have
mentioned the way in which she encouraged people to go to holy
communion even if they felt unworthy or unprepared. An event which
shows a similar attitude, and which obviously surprised her companions, is related at 1:10: After an accident, her first reaction was joy at
the prospect of dying. That amazed her companions, who asked her
whether she was not afraid to die without the sacraments of the
church. Her response was characteristic:

I desire with all my heart to be fortified by the sacraments of
salvation, but I consider that the will of my Lord and what he
has ordained are the best and most saving preparation. Therefore I will go to him gladly in whatever way he wants,
whether my death be sudden or long foreseen, knowing that
his mercy will not fail, for without it I know that I cannot be
saved, whether death is long foreseen or sudden.

The Lord obviously approved of her attitude and encouraged her
to freedom of this kind when she seemed more cautious than usual, or

when she was doubtful about praying for certain souls who, she feared, were destined to be damned, as well as when she voiced the conventionally pious desire that the eucharist should be her last food. Mechthild of Magdeburg did so too, but did not receive the reply that Gertrude received; namely, that it really makes no difference. The Lord did not want Gertrude to have any sort of preoccupation; he thoroughly approved of what, to Mechthild of Hackeborn, seemed like flightiness—the way in which Gertrude at once did whatever came into her head if she believed it to be his will. It is "abandonment to Divine Providence" and the "sacrament of the present moment" five centuries before de Caussade.

Gertrude's Literary Style

Libertas cordis in many ways sums up Gertrude's literary style also. She is an enthusiast and fundamentally has only one theme: God's goodness, love, and generosity. A general description of her style is hardly necessary; a glance will tell the reader what it is like. It is to a great extent the Helfta style: descriptive, pictorial, laden with adjectives, comparisons, similes, metaphors, and various other rhetorical devices, with a tendency to give everything a spiritual significance, whether numbers, shapes, materials, or any other detail. The style of the *Book of Special Grace* bears a great similarity to that of the *Legatus*, especially—because of their nature—to the books not penned by Gertrude herself. The theology, the attitude, the type of language, the use of scripture, of the liturgy, and of other authors is very much the same. Book 2 of the *Legatus*, however, while obviously belonging to the same family, is distinctive. One could hardly fail to notice the affective nature of the style, the exuberance, the breathlessness, one might almost say. There is a sense that the author can hardly contain herself. She can, however, be extremely precise and almost academic, and this dual character of her writing is another point of similarity with the prophet Ezekiel.

At first glance her writing may appear a little childish; full of images, superlatives, and heaped-up adjectives; with ideas repeated several times in very similar words and in long coinages not unlike those found in modern German. It has been remarked that Gertrude's style is very Teutonic, and in this way at least that is true; it is true also of her long and tortuous sentences. She does not actually lose track of her grammar, as the apostle Paul did at times, but then she was not dictating at speed as he was (on the contrary, she would have said, she was being dictated to). This is less marked in the *Spiritual Exercises*, not surprisingly; they are more carefully composed, and, while dealing with the things of God, are not an attempt to express the inexpressible, that is, the experience of God's irruption into the life of his creature. But Gertrude is childlike rather than childish. Children telling a story try to get across not merely the events but their reaction to them; what the events were like *to them*. They are deeply involved; everything seems to them new and exceptional; they try to evoke in their hearers the response which the events evoked in them. This is why children expect their hearers to react to what they tell them.

That is precisely what Gertrude does. What she is trying to tell us is, in fact, not just new and exceptional but impossible to convey. One must never lose sight of the fact that Gertrude is not writing down her ideas, her spirituality, or indeed anything that originates with herself. She is trying to convey the experience of the relationship between the infinite transcendent God and his very unworthy little creature. The style is hers, the setting and the similitudes are adapted to a particular medieval nun with particular interests. As she frequently repeats, God adapts himself to suit places, persons, and times. But the whole is still something that totally transcends her, and she intends this to show. She would have been more than pleased, for example, to be told that she had a completely inadequate vocabulary. Indeed, she tells us so herself: "I began to consider within myself how difficult, not to say impossible, it would be for me to find the right expressions and words for all the things that were said to me, so as to make them intelligible on a human level, without danger of scandal." Mechthild of Magdeburg made a similar comment about her own writing. But Gertrude goes further than that. Perhaps we would hardly feel surprise if she, so unworthy, could not express all this, but "to tell the truth, it seems to me that no one, even possessing the eloquence of every tongue" could have convinced her that such experiences were possible, let alone describe them. "Although the knowledge of angels and men were to be worthily combined, even that would not suffice to form one single word that might accurately express even a shadow of such sovereign excellence."

Why wonder, then, if for want of an entirely new language, she multiplies the language she does possess to its highest power, so that we, who have not shared her experiences, find it occasionally a little wearisome. The deficiency is not in Gertrude but in language itself. And although it is a fairly limited vocabulary, it is very much a whole and works together to convey a very consistent picture and atmosphere. Gertrude (and here I include the parts dictated but not written by her) is remarkably successful in depicting the Lord as she knows him, and herself and other creatures as she knows them. Her favorite words—sweet, benign, kind, tender, overflowing, abundance, deign, unworthy—are not random or repetitive. She is painting a picture of one whom she knows well and familiarly, who has certainly adapted himself to her understanding, but who is unchanging within that framework.

It is unfortunately inevitable that any English translation of Gertrude which is more than a paraphrase will give a slightly misleading impression of her language. There are several related reasons for that. First, there are many words which are quite normal in Latin but which, when rendered with any accuracy into English, are strange or stilted. There is no real translation for *dignari* except "to deign," but *dignari* is a common and natural Latin word while "to deign" is one which would never be used in normal English speech. *Pius* is a problem familiar to every schoolchild who struggles to translate the *Aeneid*: What is one to do with "pius Aeneas"? And what, in the case of Gertrude, is one to do with *pius* when used of God? "Pious" obviously means something quite different. Usually one must fall back on "good" or "loving," which impoverishes the vocabulary; in addition, one would like, ideally, to retain a single English word for the Latin one throughout. *Benignus* is another common Latin word rarely usable in English; "benign" does not have the same flavor. "Benevolent" or "kind" express it better, but the first is not a usual English word and the second has been cheapened by overuse. Superlatives and diminutives are always a problem. English does not use them in quite the same way as Latin does, because it needs a phrase where the Latin simply employs a suffix. Either one faithfully renders all Gertrude's superlatives (and she is addicted to them) and produces a prolix, repetitive, and unnatural version, or one sacrifices strict verbal—or rather grammatical—accuracy to good English and readability.

The list is endless, but one must remark on the greatest problem: the word "sweet." Gertrude does use *dulcis*, and fairly often, but she also uses a whole host of compounds which can be translated either literally as "sweetly flowing," "mellifluous" (which more often than not is not really what she means), or simply as "sweet," which is what

22

she means. Thus the impression is given that she is even more repetitive than she in fact is. When Gertrude thinks of sweetness she does not have in mind something sugary or insipid. Sweetness is something strengthening and satisfying—one thinks of the sweetness of honey—as is evident, for example, from the description of the saints receiving the sweetness flowing from the Lord at 2:19: they are avid not for pleasure but for the very life and strength of God. "Sweet" in English has another sense too. It may mean "gentle" or "soft" (*suavis*). English has no general equivalent for *suavis;* either we must use "sweet" again, or vary the translation which is, generally speaking, a pity. That is the word Keats was trying to express in *The Eve of St. Agnes* by "*sooth* jellies," that is, smooth, soothing. Gertrude frequently uses *suavis* of the Lord and his gifts to her. Sometimes we have chosen to express only one element of the word, but usually we have concluded that "sweet," being all-embracing, is the closest to what Gertrude wished to say.

Gertrude's Images and Similitudes

When we come to Gertrude's images and similitudes—and these are a very important part of her manner of teaching and expression—we discover a similar phenomenon. They can be of great beauty, such as the comparison of free will to a golden tube through which humans can draw from the heart of God, or this description of a soul returning from action to contemplation: "I may at once return to you, my universal Good, in the interior of my soul, like water which, when no longer restrained by obstacles, falls with full force into the abyss!" Another example is the way in which she expresses the fact that the cross of Christ makes life not more difficult but easier: she depicts the Lord using it as an instrument with which to part the thorny hedges blocking his path. Gertrude calls the Lord "the best of teachers," and she would protest that her similitudes originated with him. They are certainly often extremely enlightening. Whether or not inspired by the Lord, she was an excellent teacher herself. Why, for example, did the Lord allow her to keep her defects? "Just as a field covered with dung becomes more fertile, so she, through knowledge of her own wretchedness, will derive from them [the defects] the fruits of more exquisite graces."

She explains the manner in which God accommodates the abundance of his graces to what he knows a particular soul can take under the image of a downpour of rain which is too much for a frail little flower; a weak soul can only receive God's grace in small, measured doses. And why is it that God sometimes seems to place a soul which is very small and not advanced in an exalted position? "When a mother wants to do some embroidery with silk or pearls, sometimes she puts her little one in a higher place to hold the thread of pearls or help her in some other way." And what good can reception of God's grace do to someone who is not aware of it? Gertrude points out that a sick person does not feel or look cured as he swallows the medicine, but the doctor knows what the effect will eventually be.

One could make a long list of these didactic comparisons, but two more must suffice here. The first perhaps illustrates Gertrude's *libertas cordis* even better than it does the point she had set out to explain. If one were a servant supporting an old or infirm king, it would be absurd to go away and let him fall on the pretext that one had originally been ordered to go and serve at table. She understands, and makes us understand, that through excessive rigidity we may actually find ourselves going against the wishes of the person we intend to serve and obey. And if we must be supple in the service of God, we must also realize that he will not always follow what we think is best for us. Gertrude makes this point in a comparison which shows her sense of humor and her penetrating understanding of how blind we can be in matters spiritual. It is an answer to the ubiquitous question of why God does not answer our prayers. One imagines the Lord giving this reply with a smile on his face:

> When the queen is spinning and says to her servant, "Give me the thread which is hanging down over my left shoulder" (thinking it is so, since she cannot see behind her back), and he, seeking to obey her command and seeing that the thread is hanging down over her right shoulder and not her left, takes it where he finds it and gives it to his lady, deeming this more advisable than to fulfil her orders literally by pulling a thread out of the left side of her gown.

It must be admitted that the similitudes and images are not always so successful. Sometimes they are rather hard to visualize, such as the one at 3:73 which depicts a person climbing out of a nest on three supports. Sometimes they are extremely involved or contain such shifts of emphasis as to make the point unclear. Sometimes, too, their oddity makes them unclear. What exactly had Gertrude in mind at 2:15 when she spoke of a cloud as if of steam emanating from the walls, ceiling, and floor of a room? At times a comparison, acceptable as an idea, may become slightly ridiculous by being treated at too great length, for example, the bath of confession at 3:14. One must bear in mind that Gertrude is very simple in the best sense of the word and is not concerned with euphony but with accurate expression of what she has understood. So she can, without any sense of incongruity, speak of her motives as a lamb not merely immolated but cooked on the fire of her heart; or of leaving the wine cellar of contemplation with—literally—the belch of drunkenness, so that others may benefit from the scent of the wine. She has no idea that her image of the sacred host, consumed by the Lord, reappearing through the wound in his side, and becoming a sort of plaster to stick his wound to hers, might be a little unattractive; or that her picture of the festering wounds of his left side in 3:74 (omitted in this edition) is, in its length and detail, unnecessarily gruesome.

This is perhaps as it must always be. The externals of the prophetic and mystical experiences are to some extent describable, but the underlying contact with God is not; the description will inevitably fall short of the complete reality in the soul of the prophet or mystic and will not infrequently sound a little odd.

Gertrude's Use of Other Writings and of the Liturgy

Since Gertrude spent so much of her time copying, studying, pondering, and praying the scriptures, it is natural that her own writings are saturated in them. She does not, it is true, give the impression that Bernard does—and Benedict in certain chapters of his *Rule*—of being little more than a collection of scriptural citations and reminiscences, but there is a basically scriptural attitude and flavor. As her biographer puts it, she wrote "in such an admirable style that all scholars unanimously approved of it and took delight in the way in which it harmonized with the honeyed eloquence of Sacred Scripture." In general her use of scripture is straightforward; she is not much given, in this area, to allegorizing. The references to scripture fall into three categories: straight quotations, sometimes presented as direct citations with references given; quotations, longer or shorter, woven into the text, sometimes signalized, sometimes not; and finally, the echoes and reminiscences. We have tried to give references for the more obvious and certain of these, but it would be impossible to catch them all. What is a reminiscence of a particular passage of scripture and what is simply a scriptural way of looking at things and expressing them? It is certain that Gertrude herself was not always aware that she was quoting or using a biblical phrase or idea. She—and the authors of the other books—often quotes both scripture and the liturgy from memory.

It is perhaps worth remarking at this point on the very Benedictine concept of *lectio divina*, which will explain the way in which Gertrude uses the scriptures and certain other authors, most notably Bernard. *Lectio divina* (literally "divine reading" or perhaps "holy" or "godly" reading) is not the same as "spiritual reading" as the phrase is generally understood. It is distinctive not so much in its object as in its approach. In practice the main object of *lectio divina* is the scriptures and the Fathers of the Church, but it would be possible to apply the technique of *lectio divina* to a text that was basically unspiritual. *Lectio divina* is a slow, meditative reading, a "chewing over" the text, never very far from prayer. Indeed, it is sometimes impossible to say where the *lectio divina* stops and the prayer starts. To the early monks of the desert, accustomed to learning long passages of scripture by heart and mulling over them as they worked (this is the origin of *lectio divina*), the question would be meaningless. A text read in this way, especially if, as in the case of scripture and certain personal favorites (for Gertrude, Bernard's homilies on the Song of Songs) it has been so read repeatedly, becomes part of a person's thought, spiritual make-up, very existence. A chapter like 1:5, which is in part almost a mosaic of Bernard's homily 37 on the Song of Songs, is not plagiarism, nor is Gertrude's constant, usually unacknowledged, quotation or echo of that work, or indeed of scripture. One might be even more inclined to accuse Bernard himself of "plagiarizing scripture"! It has become part of her thought and her prayer—for her, the two are one—and is genuinely hers. It is the way in which the Lord communicates to her and so the way in which she communicates to us.

She does occasionally quote Bernard or Augustine, or scripture with references, as "authority," but that is not her normal way of going about things. She might have been faintly amused by her zealous editor's "marginal citations." One could say that for Gertrude the Lord is sufficient authority; her language is his language, whether one means by that direct inspiration or simply the effects of *lectio divina*. Speaking of her language and "what is related in the book" in general, her biographer says:

> One must not suppose that . . . it was simply the result of her natural qualities, or the liveliness of her intelligence, or what it pleased her to imagine, or, indeed, that it was composed as a result of her industry in words or the fluency of her eloquence; far from it! It must be firmly and unhesitatingly believed that all this proceeded from the fount of Divine Wisdom and was a gift of infused grace from the Spirit who breathes where he wills, to whom he wills, and how he wills, according to the person, the time, and the place.

Perhaps the liturgy shows itself even more formative in Gertrude's writing than scripture. Of course, such comparative terms are somewhat misleading, since the liturgy is made up very largely of scripture. The psalms are the most important element of the liturgy, and it is the psalms, with the New Testament, which we find most in her writing. It is interesting to note that when she is quoting from memory, it is often not the actual words of scripture she uses but the liturgical adaptation. This happens to all whose life is based on the liturgy; a text sung again and again becomes so familiar that one is astonished to discover that one was not, as one had thought, quoting scripture verbatim at all.

Again, the use of liturgical texts falls into three categories: the straightforward, acknowledged quotation, quite often with the precise liturgical reference, given usually because the date was an important one in her spiritual life. Then, in the text woven into Gertrude's there are some texts, for example, the Office of St. Agnes and the ceremony of profession and consecration, which recur constantly; Gertrude obviously lived perpetually with these texts. Finally, there is the general reminiscence, sometimes more and sometimes less recognizable or consciously quoted.

Something analogous to the *lectio divina* assimilation process discussed above takes place in a Benedictine with regard to the liturgy, especially perhaps in a cloistered Benedictine nun whose main work is the celebration of the liturgy. By dint of constant prayerful repetition day by day and year by year, the liturgical texts become part of one's mental and spiritual furniture—one will quite automatically formulate one's own personal prayer and one's dealings with God and the things of God in terms of the psalms, collects, and so on. That is reinforced by the fact that the liturgy is generally sung; in Gertrude's day, and still in ours in some places, sung in Gregorian Chant. Gregorian Chant is a unique form of music. It does not consist of melodies composed for words, or words adapted to fit a melody; the music grew naturally from the Latin text and is perfectly one with it, imprinting both words and music—a whole—indelibly in the mind and soul. Gertrude was a chantress, replacing Mechthild of Hackeborn during the illnesses and after the death of the latter, so this process must have been particularly effective in her.

Gertrude is transformed by a "Benedictine" knowledge of the liturgy in her reader; the echoes, connections, and allusions, when recognized, make her writings incomparably richer. There is no short-cut to acquiring this knowledge, and it is unlikely that most of her readers will now possess it, but to read her with little or no knowledge of the liturgy is to miss a great deal. For this reason we have tried to give particularly full notes in this area. An example may be found in Book 3, chapter 70, where the whole chapter takes on a deeper meaning if one realizes the connection with the ceremony of monastic profession, pointed to only by the use of the verb *suscipio* (see note 107). Other examples are Book 2, chapter 6, and the beginning of Book 3, chapter 30, with their echoes of the Christmas liturgy.

Fortunately, the recent liturgical reforms in the Catholic church do not seriously affect our understanding of Gertrude's liturgical life. Some Mass chants and some prayers are now used at different dates, and liturgical seasons are sometimes differently named or to a small extent differently arranged, but on the whole what she says is familiar today. Indeed, in some cases prayers which were used in her day and later fell into disuse have been restored. The monastic houses which still celebrate the Divine Office in its entirety according to the monastic rite will, essentially speaking, be celebrating it as Gertrude did at Helfta. The parts of the Mass sung today from the Roman Gradual would be perfectly familiar to her, even if the Missal itself now contains some elements which she would not recognize.

Gertrude's Spirituality

Gertrude is not really a classic because of her style, whatever one may think of it. It is distinctive, of great energy and inventiveness, and can be very clear and beautiful. She is, perhaps, a great teacher, but she is not really a great writer. She probably gave comparatively little thought to her literary style—in the *Legatus* at least—and she certainly had no interest in literary success or acclaim. The same applies to an even greater extent to the author or authors of the other four books.

Rather, it is in what she has to say that her importance lies, and that is not simply, or largely, because she is a representative of thirteenth-century Benedictine monasticism or of a certain mystical tradition. That has importance, and it is rewarding to read Gertrude in conjunction with her great predecessors and sources, Bernard, Hugh and Richard of St. Victor, William of St. Thierry or her great contemporaries or near-contemporaries in that era of flowering of women mystics: Hildegard, Julian, and the two Mechthilds. Gertrude, though not embarrassed by her sex as was Mechthild of Magdeburg, was not greatly concerned with it; the spousal mysticism is equally to be found in male mystics.

Her real importance, what she would have considered to be her only significance, the real gift which the Lord has given us through her, is that in the *Legatus* we have a detailed record of God's dealings with a soul, the personal relationship to which the Creator is willing to stoop with his creature. It is a picture of the Lord as she knew him, including not just his character, his goodness, and his love, but also the manner of his dealings with mankind.

It would be possible to put together a remarkably complete exposé of Catholic theology and spirituality from the *Legatus*. Gertrude is an excellent theologian, and however affective her visions and her reactions to them may be, she is never deflected from her accuracy in this area. One need only recall her vision of the Lord dipping the host in the heart of God the Father and bringing it out again colored red as if stained with blood. It is typical of Gertrude that she is not simply taken up by the beauty of the image, or content to think vaguely that it must somehow express the unity of the Trinity. She is surprised and protests: "Very much at a loss, she asked herself what this might signify, since red is the symbol of suffering, and God the Father could never be marked by any trace of the red color of suffering." No answer is given. This is what she saw, and she is convinced that it was a vision from God, but she cannot explain it and is concerned that her readers should realize the difficulty and not be misled.

We find almost every point of Catholic doctrine at least touched upon in this work. This is, however, not the place for a detailed study of Gertrude's theology; we will confine ourselves to indicating the most important themes in her spirituality and theology. It is evident from the most cursory reading of the *Legatus* that the central theme of her spirituality, as of the Gospel, is love. As her biographer says, "The Lord chose her as a special instrument to show forth the secrets of his love." That she certainly does; all else is either to serve that theme or is incidental. The very title of the book shows it: *Herald of the Memorial of the Abundance of Divine Love* (the word translated here as "love" is *pietas*, love of the tenderest and most self-giving kind). Love is present in all its aspects; primarily God's love for us, resulting, through his gift, in our love for him and for our neighbor (these two are one, as the Lord pointed out). Gertrude sees that all these flow from the mutual love of the Persons of the Blessed Trinity.

The Blessed Trinity

Gertrude, when speaking of her relationship of love with God, generally seems to be speaking of it as a relationship with the Second Person of the Trinity, the Son, Jesus the God-Man. That is natural and is certainly how it began. And yet, if one looks more closely, the Blessed Trinity itself is at the center of her life, and the Blessed Trinity not as a vague concept but as a living, loving, and beloved reality— three Persons, each with his own characteristics (notably power, wisdom, and goodness, her "shorthand" for the Trinity) and each with his own special relationship to Gertrude, but one God, who first loved her and is the object of her love. Her doxologies are superb. The reader cannot fail to notice them, but here is a single example: "With the sweetly melodious harp of your divine heart, through the power of the Holy Spirit, the Paraclete, I sing to you, Lord God, adorable Father, songs of praise and thanksgiving on behalf of all creatures in heaven, on earth and under the earth; all which are, were, and shall be." To which Person does the "divine heart" belong? At this stage in her spiritual life (perhaps only shortly before her death) she hardly knows.

Everything is in the name of the Trinity; not only doxologies but also verbal signs of the cross (see Bk. 2, note 37) abound. She begins her work: "May the depths of uncreated wisdom call to the depths of infinite power, worthy of all admiration, to extol that marvelous goodness which, through your overflowing mercy, has flowed down into the depths of my misery." *Wisdom*—God the Son; *power*—God the Father; *goodness*—God the Holy Spirit; *mercy*—the way in which God's love must inevitably manifest itself toward sinful humanity; *misery*—humanity's condition without God. Here, in a single sentence, is all of Gertrude's spirituality. There is a similar "sign of the cross" at the start of chapter 6, but there the Spirit is designated as Love.

The way in which Gertrude looks at the Trinity is a perfect illustration of the fruitful tension in which our limited human minds must try to keep the two concepts of three Persons and one God. She is very conscious of the three Persons and can speak of them as three distinct individuals. There are two similar examples of that in Book 3. The first is the threefold blessing in chapter 23, in which she is presented by her guardian angel in turn to Father, Son, and Holy Spirit to receive remission of her sins, each Person forgiving the sins she had committed against his particular characteristic—power, wisdom, and goodness again. Her different relationship to each of the Persons is brought out: she is the daughter of the Father, the sister of the Son, and the betrothed of the Spirit. It is worth noting that she does not receive these remissions and blessings until the Son has interceded for her with the Father to supply for all her shortcomings by "making over to her all his most holy life on earth." That is an essential idea to which we will return.

Then there is the threefold profession in chapter 70, one of the most delightful chapters of the book. She professes the wisdom of the Son, the power of the Father, and the goodness of the Spirit in disposing her life in exactly the right way. In this case it is the Son himself and not an angel who conducts her from Person to Person. Parallel with these passages, however, are the very many in which Gertrude, although aware of and referring to the Persons separately, is really thinking of the Trinity as a unity. In 2:11 she begins by addressing the Son: "Your precious body and blood." Then, with no apparent change of object, we discover that she is speaking to the whole "resplendent and ever tranquil Trinity"; then, again, she seems to be addressing the Son; and finally, the Trinity again, though there may be a reference to the Father intended in the word "power" in the last paragraph. We note here an interesting detail: she sees the whole Trinity as making reparation for our sins, whereas it is normal to attribute that to the Son alone. Gertrude is quite right. The whole Trinity acts together in all its external works; the distinction is only in the relations within the Trinity.

Such passages in which Gertrude slips from one Person to another and from one Person to the whole Trinity recur constantly; they can be found as early as 2:5, and we are reminded that this is a mystery too sublime for us to express in any clear way. We shall see it, though we shall never fully comprehend it *as it is*, only in our heavenly homeland. Gertrude can hardly contain herself and longs for this vision: "May I breathe my last breath in the protection of your close embrace, with your all-powerful kiss! May my soul find herself without delay there where you are whom no place circumscribes, indivisible, living and exulting in the full flowering of eternity, with the Father and the Holy Spirit, true God, everlasting, world without end!" It is Christ, the Son, for whom Gertrude chiefly longs, but he is inseparable from the Trinity. He is in a sense its mediator to us, as is expressed at 1:3: "The full force of my heartbeats I am keeping within myself until the hour of her [Gertrude's] death; at that moment she will feel from them three great effects: the first will be the glory to which the Father will call her; the second, the joy with which I shall receive her; the third, the love in which the Holy Spirit will unite us."

The Language of Love

God is love; the Holy Spirit is specifically the love of the Father and the Son; this, surely, is what Gertrude means when she calls herself the betrothed of the Holy Spirit. But as we have said, it is most natural to look upon God the Son, the God-Man Jesus, as the "other half" of a spousal relationship with God. And this Gertrude does indeed do. Beginning from the vision which inaugurated her conversion and her spiritual life properly so called, in which a sort of betrothal is enacted, Jesus is constantly seen as her spouse, her beloved, kissing her, embracing her, and uniting her to himself. The terms in which this is expressed, taken sometimes from the Song of Songs, sometimes from the Book of Esther, and sometimes simply from the language of human love, may at times disconcert us and cause us some discomfort. The similitudes can be quite general, but they can also be quite detailed and unashamedly erotic. The bridegroom, comments the Lord, "can take more pleasure in the bride in private than in public"; he prefers to see her hands and neck naked than covered by gloves and necklaces; he prefers to be alone with her in the nuptial chamber (not just anywhere!) where they can "delight one another with the charm of intimate converse and tender embraces." One cannot deny the erotic nature (which most certainly did not occur to Gertrude!) of the descriptions of two of her spiritual experiences: the wound of love and the vision "face to face."

Others have reacted with the same circumspection to the language of the spousal mystics, some of whom are considerably more explicit in their language than is Gertrude. The sixteenth-century Carthusian editor of Gertrude, Lanspergius, who was himself surely used to such language, felt it advisable to warn his readers that "it is necessary to approach this book with a pure and upright heart, and not in a spirit of idle curiosity; full of longing for holy things, one will discover in it, like hidden manna, a hidden life, the source of ineffable joy." But if it seems to us that Gertrude's language represents a sublimated or veiled sensuality or eroticism, perhaps a few points should be remembered. There can be no doubt that such a thing never entered her head. Her heart, we are told, was so pure that it could have been placed on the altar with the reliquaries. That is obviously true. She is following a time-honored tradition, which began with the Old Testament prophets—notably Hosea—and with the first interpreters of the Song of Songs and was taken up in monastic spirituality. Following Bernard especially, she saw the relationship of God and his people, or God and the soul, in terms of more or less erotic love. Bernard, when criticized, replied that "the language of love sounds strange to those who do not love, who do not understand it; but it is the language spoken in the courts of heaven, where love reigns." It is, after all, quite reasonable to express the relationship thus. The union of marriage is the closest natural one of which the human being has experience. The union of God and the soul is immeasurably closer, but we have nothing else to compare it with. Indeed, we may say that in a sense the union of marriage is precisely an image of the union of God and the soul. Paul says something very similar; to him the union of God and the Church is the great mystery of which the marriage union is the image (Eph. 5:25–33). Rather than saying, then, that the experience of the mystics imitates the human erotic, can we not say that the reverse is true? It is the union with God that is the original, and the human union that is the imitation, just as the marital union of Adam and Eve was an image of the creative act whereby God created each one of them, body and soul, and created them in relationship to himself. Paul would have agreed, and so, I think, would Gertrude.

INTRODUCTION

The Sacred Heart

Our Lord, then, is Gertrude's spouse; he is the king, and she the queen. We need not see a reference to worldly court life in comparisons such as this; Gertrude would have known very little about it and her references to it are always very vague. The thought behind them is more biblical than secular (the Book of Esther evidently appealed greatly to her). It is simply intended to stress the natural majesty of God and the supernatural majesty which he has chosen to bestow upon his creature. However, the relationship is not an equal one, except insofar as he deigns to consider it so. God first loved us, so Gertrude concentrates on his love and not hers (she feels indeed that hers is so paltry and out of proportion to his that she would hardly dare mention it except from that angle). Thinking of his love, she thinks of what is traditionally the seat of love: the heart.

Gertrude and Mechthild of Hackeborn are known particularly for their part in the devotion to the Sacred Heart of Jesus. They did not invent it, but were instrumental in giving it form and making it explicit. This is a devotion, as we see very clearly in both, to the actual physical heart of the incarnate Son of God. This heart is part not only of his humanity but also of his divinity, since the human nature is hypostatically united to the divine nature, that is, the two natures are united in a single person (Greek *hypostasis*). It therefore contains the love not only of the man Jesus of Nazareth but also that of the Second Person of the Blessed Trinity; the two cannot be separated. Gertrude speaks of "the wound of your divine heart, tabernacle of divine faithfulness and infallible truth." The litany of the Sacred Heart is not just a beautiful devotional composition, but theologically accurate and informative. It was taken to a large extent from the writings of Gertrude and Mechthild. The heart of Jesus was formed by the Holy Spirit in the womb of the Virgin Mary, certainly. It is a created thing, but it is "substantially united to the Word of God," that is, the second Person of the Blessed Trinity.

It is in speaking of the Sacred Heart that Gertrude most clearly expresses her deep awareness of the humanity and divinity of her beloved. When she sees her soul as a tree fixed in the wound in his side, the sap she draws from his heart is "the virtue of the humanity and divinity of Jesus Christ." When her soul is drawn like wax into his heart, it emerges marked with the seal of the whole Trinity. There is a lovely image at 2:9 in which a crystalline stream flows from the Sacred

INTRODUCTION

Heart, colored in gold and rose, representing the divinity and the humanity. They are distinct but inseparable and, typically, a conclusion is drawn about the relationship of Gertrude to the Lord: "Just as the gold and rose colors gleam through the purity of the crystal and are enhanced by it, so will your intentions be pleasing, seen through the cooperation of the gold of my divinity, and the perfecting power of the patience of the rose of my humanity."

To Gertrude the essential point about the Sacred Heart is that it is the instrument of the union between God and humankind, not just God the Son but the whole Trinity. It is, to use her expression, the harp of the Trinity, its instrument of communication within itself and to creatures. It is the Sacred Heart which draws creatures to God:

> Just as you stretch out your hand when you want to take hold of something and, when you have taken it, you draw it back toward you, so, languishing with love of you, when you are distracted by exterior things, I stretch out my heart to draw you to myself and again, when, your inmost thoughts in harmony with mine, you recollect yourself and again attend to me, then I draw back my heart again, and you with it, into myself, and from it I offer you the pleasure of all its many virtues.

It is a reciprocal action; we are drawn into the heart of God, and from that heart we draw all divine virtues. Gertrude shows that by depicting it as a two-way flow through a golden tube, which is our free will.

We are used to the concept of indwelling—God dwelling in the soul, as her biographer says he did in a special way in the soul of Gertrude—but this too is reciprocal. The Lord invites her into his heart and depicts his body as her monastery. One of Gertrude's notable spiritual experiences was the exchange of hearts, recorded for example at 2:23; another was the piercing of her heart, but she also pierced his: "Each word that she sang appeared like the sharpest spear, thrown from her to pierce the heart of Jesus Christ, and filling it with ineffably sweet delight." Her heart melts him so that it distills into her soul. Several times she describes the way in which he brings his heart close to hers by drawing her to the "wound of love," which to Gertrude always means the wound in the side.

Gertrude can speak of the Sacred Heart in a very symbolic way, sometimes difficult to visualize, for example, as half of a chalice, of which the other half is her own heart, or as something which is at once a harp and a lamp. But she also speaks of it as the physical, flesh and blood heart of the man Jesus, pierced by the soldier's lance. Its heartbeats can be heard. The pulsations certainly have a symbolic significance, but they are absolutely real.

Suppletio

The Sacred Heart is also our advocate, as the Lord tells Gertrude at 3:7; it is the expression of God's mercy. It is natural that Gertrude, with her acute consciousness of God's goodness and greatness and humanity's unworthiness, should lay great stress on his mercy. In her thought this takes two characteristic and related forms: first, the unshakable belief that for God the will is accepted for the deed. The fact that we are not capable of doing good of ourselves is a cause not for depression, much less for despair, but for joy at God's generosity, because—and this is the second point—he supplies what we lack. This idea of God's supplying for us is a favorite one in both Gertrude and Mechthild of Hackeborn and is closely bound up with the devotion to the Sacred Heart. The Latin word is *suppletio*, "supplying." The Lord tells Gertrude: "Behold, here is my heart, the sweet instrument of the adorable Trinity. I hold it in front of the eyes of your heart; it will supply all that you lack, faithfully making up for all you entrust to it." He has made himself Gertrude's servant, which is in line with his own words in the gospel: "The Son of man is come not to be ministered unto but to minister." It is really a work of the whole Trinity, each Person taking his own part. Gertrude prays: "I implore you [the Father] in union with the efficacious prayer of your beloved Son, in the virtue of the Holy Spirit, to amend my faults and supply for all my sins and defects."

God's love is his only motive for doing this; it is its own explanation. He makes us pleasing to himself because he loves us, and he loves us not because of our goodness but because of his own. One of Gertrude's expressive comparisons is used to demonstrate this idea. Told that the Lord claimed she was pleasing to him because she found him always pleasing, she protested that "after all, the sublime perfection of your works, my Lord, cannot displease me; that proceeds not from my virtue but from your perfect sanctity." He replied that his love makes him choose to see that as a virtue: "When the characters in a book seem too small to be read easily, one uses a magnifying glass to make the writing appear larger; it is not the book which has wrought this change, but the lens. Even so, in the abundance of my love, I make up for whatever defect I may find in you." He does approve of and accept the works we do for him and in his honor, but he prefers us to be forced by our weakness to have humble recourse to his mercy. He is ready at all times to make reparation and to supply as soon as we desire it. Gertrude very often refers to the practice of offering the life, prayer, and merits of Christ to make amends for our own. But it is not necessary to do that; he will do it himself, as she tells us in a brief but lovely chapter on the subject (3:40).

Suffering

Of course, the Lord has already made the great act of reparation in his passion and death. Gertrude has a devotion to his wounds, to the crucifix, and even to the passion, but not, one might say, in a realistic way. She is, of course, aware that he suffered in mind and body. She prays: "I offer you the prayer to which the extreme anguish of your agony gave such urgency, as the sweat of blood bore witness." Yet the suffering itself is not central in her thought. The above quotation goes on to lay far greater stress on his purity and love, and his wounds in general are seen as symbolic of love or of victory: they are jewels, decorations, or marks of honor. The cross too is often symbolic and in the depiction of the crucifixion thoughts of suffering are not generally primary. She is quite right again. The essential element in Christ's saving passion is not the pain but the love and obedience which led him to endure the pain. We shall see that this is the important thing about human suffering also. Christ suffered and we are to follow him, and suffering is important in Gertrude's spirituality—naturally, since she herself suffered a great deal physically in one way or another. But it is marked by her usual sensible approach and is really an aspect of the all-important self-abandonment to divine providence.

Suffering, she says, "is the truest sign of divine election and is like the espousals of the soul with God." The point is not an unhealthy desire to suffer for the sake of it, but rather a desire for conformity with Christ and a recognition that suffering can be an excellent instrument for bringing one's own will into harmony with God's and one's whole being into union with him.

INTRODUCTION

If one is visibly unable to do anything but sit or lie and suffer, it is impossible to fall into vainglory; one must inevitably concede that any good work is done by God and not by oneself. The Lord compared this to resting quietly in the nuptial chamber with him; he stresses that he looks on us with greater love and mercy the more conscious we are of our own utter dependence on him. Suffering does not necessarily bring out the best in a person, but when it does have positive results they can be really striking—an increase in patience and humility, says Gertrude, and she was not a patient person by nature. The Lord told her several times that suffering had increased her capacity to receive graces or had sanctified her soul. He goes into some detail on this at 2:15:

> When the body is afflicted and touched by suffering, it is as though the soul were bathed in air and sunlight which comes to it from the suffering member, and this imparts to it a marvelous clarity. The more intense the pain or the more general the suffering, the more the soul is purified and clarified. This is especially true of afflictions and trials of the heart. When these are borne with humility, patience and other virtues, they lend a wonderful luster to the soul the nearer, the more effectively and the closer they touch it.

That is, of course, the essence of it—the dispositions in which suffering is borne or, indeed, chosen. God likes us to choose the bitterer thing, for his love (3:14); to do it for any other reason would be meaningless. Gertrude refers several times to the value of praising and thanking God in adversity; that, even more than the severity of the suffering, gives it a great splendor and makes it pleasing to God. There is an unusual idea which occurs twice in the *Legatus* and which seems to have surprised Gertrude herself at first, though it is very characteristic of her cheerful and free spirit: that it makes little difference whether one has chosen the suffering or simply had it inflicted upon one. Even suffering in dreams brings merit to the sufferer. This is strongly expressed at 3:69. Gertrude was surprised that the Lord considers it meritorious to be patient in sufferings which are unavoidable; surely, she asked, it is more so to be patient in sufferings which could perhaps be alleviated? No, replied the Lord: "There is the same difference between the two kinds of sufferings as there is between two colors, both perfect and both considered so beautiful that it is hard to know which to choose."

INTRODUCTION

Everything that comes to us from God comes from his love, and what matters is our response to that love, not the details or circumstances. Gertrude, we are told, always considered whatever God sent to be the best, and so it is. He knows what he is about. It is not wrong, for example, to desire good health in order to be able to serve God better, "but it is more perfect by far to commit oneself entirely to the divine will, trusting that God ordains for each one whatever is best for him and his salvation." Gertrude puts this beautifully at 3:51. She is offered the two hands of the Lord, the right representing health, the left sickness. She chooses neither, but only his heart and his will. We cannot know why he sends us what he does, but the reason may be as simple as this: "The Lord prepares for his elect a hard way in this life, lest pleasures along the way might make them forgetful of those pleasures which are in their true fatherland." It is obvious that conforming one's will to God's makes it easier, so to say, for his graces to flow into our soul. Gertrude expresses it by saying that those who are fully conformed to him draw grace from his very heart while those less conformed draw from the extremities of his body.

What were Gertrude's physical sufferings? She mentions headache, fever, and a liver complaint; we cannot really know and we cannot do better than take her at her word—which, incidentally, is in agreement with that of many other mystical writers of all periods. The effect upon the human body of a close relationship with God can be shattering, especially when it takes the form of mystical "favors" and "experiences." That is suggested by one of the few pieces of verse in the book: the Lord says to her:

> *Amor meus continuus*
> *tibi languor assiduus;*
> *Amor tuus suavissimus*
> *mihi sapor gratissimus.*

That is nearly untranslatable, but might be rendered:

> To you a ceaseless languishing
> is my abiding love;
> To me a most welcome savor
> is your most gentle love (in 3:45, omitted in the present edition).

That sums up the difference between God's love and ours, and makes clear that we have not really the strength to bear his love. More prosaically, she comments to him at 3:44: "If anyone knew what I now feel, they would say that I should abstain from such fervor in order to regain my bodily health." She says categorically, when trying to describe the great vision "face to face," "I truly believe that unless the vision were mitigated by divine power, a soul on whom this favor were conferred, even for an instant, would by no means be permitted to remain in the body," and, speaking of the other great vision, that of the Sunday of "*Esto mihi*"—the only occasion on which her mystical experiences seem seriously to have disrupted her normal life—"It seems more than miraculous that, after such hours of ecstasy, I could still live as a mortal among mortals."

Mystical Experiences

Gertrude is a good example of one who received "felt" or "sensible" mystical favors and consolations from God. They are quite definite and certainly experienced rather than merely known through faith. Such experiences are not necessary to the mystical life and certainly not to the contemplative life, and are not essential concomitants of close union with God or of great sanctity. They are a result, in some people, of the touch of God, but they may be produced in other ways, some quite unconnected with God; close union with him is perfectly compatible with a complete absence of any such felt favors. They are, as Gertrude instinctively realized, often given in a particularly clearly perceived way to a soul who is called to guide others. Perceiving God's action in her own soul, she will be better able to recognize it in the souls of others who perhaps do not experience any felt favors. That seems to have been Gertrude's case. Her biographer understands this too; perhaps she was one of the souls helped by Gertrude in this way. She says in the prologue to Book 1:

It is clear from what follows that she was constantly favored with the divine presence. Whenever the expressions "he appeared" or "the Lord was at her side" are used (although she frequently had him truly beside her as her special prerogative) he showed himself to her in a more imaginative form, for some particular reason and for a set time, according to his purpose to suit the capacity of those for whom the showing was intended. The same is to be understood (as will be seen from what follows) of the variety of the manifestations, because in visiting one soul God the Lover of all is seeking in many different ways the salvation of all.

Gertrude evidently did value her experiences and derived great pleasure and joy from them as she often says; she did seem to gauge her closeness to God by her feelings of closeness, his presence in her soul by her feelings of his presence. She gives no indication that she had ever known real aridity in prayer or even, after her conversion, been less than aware of God's presence except for short and easily explicable periods. Perhaps the nearest she gets to it is the reference to the troubles and depression which immediately preceded her conversion. There is also an episode recounted in 3:10, in which she felt dissatisfied at the less than sublime favors she was receiving. "She would have liked to have been rapt entirely out of herself and, passing utterly into her Beloved, who is called a consuming fire, to have been melted, as it were, by the burning ardor of charity, to have been united intimately and inseparably with him." She could not "achieve this" (!) and so proceeded to pray in another way, but she was eventually granted what she had desired. Her biographer states, "The Lord never failed to gladden her prayers with the blissful consolation of his presence."

That sounds very enviable, yet Gertrude was fully aware of its comparative unimportance. The chapter entitled "Her Growing Intimacy with God" (1:17) is very enlightening on this question. The Lord points out that if one is close enough to kiss a person, one cannot see that person; in other words, greater intimacy with God can actually be accompanied by a lessening of the felt favors. Gertrude understood that "when grace is withdrawn, merits accumulate, provided that during that time one does not relax one's efforts in spite of the greater difficulty."

It is in this chapter that we find an indication that her revelations also changed in nature as she grew closer to God: she no longer received specific answers to questions but had to trust that God was inspiring her words. That is logical, because as souls grow closer to God, more in conformity with him—which is the point of mystical prayer and of all true prayer—their thoughts and responses are more likely to be according to his will without him having to inspire them with specific words. When it was revealed to someone what heights of union with God Gertrude was to reach, it was no longer expressed in terms of mystical experiences but in this apparently more prosaic but in fact far more sublime way: "She will attain to such perfect union with God that she will no longer see with her eyes except as God deigns to see with them; her mouth will not speak except as God wants her to speak, and so on with all her senses." Gertrude needed her experiences at first, as she confesses, to arouse her and to rekindle her fervor when it flagged, but she knew that no emotion or felt graces are of any value unless one is trying to imitate Christ, and she was as detached from these graces as from all else. She knew, too, that the ordinary ways to God are always central; among these the privileged place is held by the sacraments and especially holy communion, which is the sacrament of union par excellence, whether or not one "feels" the union it effects.

It is heartening to note that her prayer—her part of it, not the Lord's—seems to have been very much like everyone else's. She could be tepid and distracted, she could spend an entire Friday without giving a thought to the passion, and when she prayed she did what all her sisters did: she mediated discursively on the psalms, she said devotional prayers which appealed to her, she meditated "on her soul and on God," and she took pleasure in making a little decorated alcove for her crucifix. We do not, indeed, get the impression that Gertrude was externally unusual except in her wholeheartedness and her wisdom; her mystical experiences do not seem (with the one exception) to have intruded in her life and may perhaps have been quite unknown to most of her sisters.

The Later History of Gertrude's Work

Gertrude was famous in her lifetime; people flocked to her for her spiritual counsel. Strangely enough, her fame does not appear to have survived her death. While Mechthild of Hackeborn's *Book of Special Grace* circulated very widely in manuscript and was translated into several languages including English, Gertrude's works seem to have vanished almost without trace. Only five manuscripts of the *Legatus* have survived (it is impossible, of course, to know how many perished during the Reformation), the earliest being one of 1412 now at Munich. It is complete and includes the marginal citations mentioned in the prologue. It was with the invention of printing and with the first

Latin edition of her work, published by the Carthusians of Cologne, that Gertrude leapt to fame, while Mechthild's popularity seems to have dwindled. Edition followed edition: Latin (Cologne, 1536); Italian (Venice, 1560); German (Leipzig, 1505, Cologne, 1579). In seventeenth-century France her trust in and burning love for the Lord were potent antidotes to Jansenism, and editions, both in French and in Latin, multiplied. It has been suggested that Margaret Mary Alacoque heard the French edition of 1671 read aloud in the refectory of her convent at Paray-le-Monial.

The list of those who have been influenced by Gertrude is enormous. One could begin with Louis Blosius, the sixteenth-century author of the *Institutio Spiritualis*. Philip Neri used her prayers and recommended them to others; and Francis de Sales too. In Spain, Fr. Diego, confessor to King Philip II, read the revelations of Gertrude aloud to the king as he lay dying in the Escorial. Her works were popular with the Discalced Carmelites—surely her stress on total, joyful abandonment to God must have appealed to them. Fr. Francisco Ribera, as confessor to Teresa of Avila, recommended her to take Gertrude as spiritual mistress and guide. At the request of King Philip IV of Spain Gertrude was declared patron saint of the West Indies; her feast is celebrated with special splendor in Peru, and a town named after her has been built in New Mexico. More recent admirers have included Dom Prosper Guéranger, the restorer of Benedictine monasticism in France, whose Congregation of Solesmes has been responsible for most of the work done on Gertrude in the last century; Fr. Faber of the London Oratory; and Dom John Chapman. She is twice mentioned in the encyclical of Pope Pius XII on the Sacred Heart, *Haurietis Aquas*.

Every age has recognized in Gertrude something of value for itself, and one would expect that our own would be no exception. It is difficult, if not impossible, to see one's own age objectively, but perhaps one can discern certain needs of our time to which her writings answer. Ours is an age beset with fears, an age which is conscious of many national, international, and even global threats. We find it hard to trust anyone or anything, and in so many parts of the world the sense of God has all but disappeared. The many threats to spiritual and physical safety undergone by the monastery of Helfta never lessened Gertrude's trust and her serenity; nor did her consciousness of her sinfulness. We must not imagine that Gertrude felt no distress or fear, as it is clear that she did. Yet she demonstrates the possibility, and the liberating effect, of that act of trust in an all-powerful and all-loving

God. It is not in relying on ourselves or in seeing things working out according to our will that we find safety or even peace; we desire liberation so much, and rightly so. This woman who preaches and exemplifies to perfection true liberty of heart can show us the way—show us how our powerlessness is a source not of fear but of joy.

Not least of Gertrude's messages to us is her effective disproving of our idea that an abstract dogma or a firm definition is something dry, deadening, limiting. What could be more abstract or more precise than the Catholic doctrine of the Blessed Trinity, three Persons in one God? And what more warm, personal and living than the response which it draws from Gertrude, and the relationship which she has with this God?

Love is, as we have said, Gertrude's message, and a message we sorely need. One could say that the purpose of the *Legatus*—God's purpose and Gertrude's—is to restore us to that love. Her picture of her beloved Lord, the second Person of the Trinity, is, though translated into her own idiom, entirely consonant with the picture given by the gospel. Her desire would be to send her readers back to that divine source, there to meet Jesus for themselves and discover what they had not previously been able to believe: the infinite love of God who supplies for and far outweighs all human defects.

GERTRUDE of HELFTA
THE HERALD OF DIVINE LOVE

Prologue[1]

The Holy Spirit, the Paraclete, distributor of all good things, who breathes where he will, how he will, and when he will (Jn. 3:8), keeps the secrets of his inspiration hidden, but sometimes ordains that they be brought to light, when it is for the good of many. And so it was with this servant of God. Although divine love never ceased to flow into her soul, it was only at intervals that she was ordered to make this known. Thus this book of hers was written at different times, the first part having been written down eight years after grace was received; the other part was not finished until about twenty years afterward.[2] Each time a part of the writing was produced, the Lord signified his gracious acceptance of it.

Now when she had written the first part and was commending it to the Lord with humble devotion, she received this response from God, in his loving mercy: "No one has the power of taking away from me the memorial of the abundance of my divine sweetness."[3] She understood by these words that the Lord wanted to give this title to the book: *The Memorial of the Abundance of Divine Sweetness.* And the Lord added: "If anyone with devout intention desires to read this book for the good of his soul, I will draw him to myself, so that it will be as if he were reading it in my hands, and I will take part in his reading. And as usually happens when two are reading one page, each feels the breath of the other, so I will breathe in the desires of his soul, and these will move me to have mercy on him. Moreover, I will breathe forth over him the breath of my divinity, and he will be renewed by my Spirit within him." And the Lord continued: "Anyone who with intentions like these transcribes what is written in this book will find at each stroke of the pen arrows of love from the sweetness of my divine heart being aimed at him, which will move his soul to rejoice in the delights of divine sweetness."

One night, while the second part was being written, to the great delight of God's will, she was making complaint to the Lord. He soothed her with his usual kindness and said, among other things: "I have given thee to be the light of the Gentiles, that thou mayst be my salvation even to the farthest part of the earth" (Is. 49:6). As she knew that he was speaking of the book, which was scarcely begun, she said wonderingly: "And how, O my God, could anyone be granted the light of knowledge through this little book, since I do not want any more to be written, and I will not allow the little that is already written to be shown to anyone?" To which the Lord answered: "When I chose Jeremiah to be my prophet (Jer. 1:5), he thought he was incapable of speaking with knowledge or discretion, yet by the words of his mouth I reproved peoples and kings. In the same way, my intention to clarify certain things through you by the light of knowledge and truth shall not be frustrated, for no one can hinder what has been predestined from eternity. For those whom I have predestined I shall call, and those whom I have called, I shall justify,[4] in the way which pleases me."

Another time, as she was striving in prayer to persuade the Lord to give her permission to prevent this book being written (since at that time obedience to her superiors did not compel her to write as pressingly as it had previously done), the Lord in his kindness replied to her: "Don't you know that whatever my will commands is to be placed above every obedience? Therefore, as you know that it is my will, which may not be resisted, that this book is to be written, what is the trouble? It is I who inspire what is written, and I will faithfully help you and look after that which is mine." Then she entirely conformed her will to his good pleasure and said to the Lord: "What title, most beloved Lord, would you like this little book to have?" To which the Lord replied: "This book is to be called *The Herald of Divine Love*, because it will give some foretaste of my overflowing love." Filled with wonder, she said: "Since those who are sent as ambassadors or heralds enjoy great authority, what authority will you give to this little book with such a title?" The Lord replied, "By virtue of my divinity, those who read this book for my glory with upright faith, humble devotion, and devout gratitude, seeking edification, will obtain remission of their venial sins, the grace of spiritual consolation, and, what is more, they will be made more receptive to grace."

Afterward, when she perceived that the Lord wanted the two

parts of this work to be joined together in one, with devout prayers she asked him how both parts, which had been given different titles, were to be combined. The Lord replied: "Just as, sometimes, for the sake of their child, both parents are regarded with greater affection, I have ordained that this book should be composed of two parts, and that the words of the title should derive from both, that is *The Herald of the Memorial of the Abundance of Divine Love*, so that it may proclaim my divine love, to perpetuate the memory of that love to my chosen ones."

It is clear from what follows that she was constantly favored with the divine presence. Whenever the expressions "he appeared" or "the Lord was at her side" are used (although she frequently had him truly beside her as her special prerogative), he showed himself to her in a more imaginative form, for some particular reason and for a set time, according to his purpose to suit the capacity of those for whom the showing was intended. The same is to be understood (as will be seen from what follows) of the variety of the manifestations, because in visiting one soul, God the Lover of all is seeking in many different ways the salvation of all.

And although the loving Lord continued to flood her soul with his grace every day, feast day and weekday alike, sometimes through the means of sensible corporeal similitudes, sometimes through the purer intellectual visions, he wanted images of bodily likenesses, appealing to the human understanding, to be described in this little book. And so that it might be within the reach of every reader, it is divided into five.[5]

The first book contains the commendation of the person who received these favors and bears witness to them. The second book contains what she herself wrote with her own hand in thanksgiving, under the impulse of the Spirit of God: it treats of the kind of grace she received. In the third book are described some of the benefits given or revealed to her. In the fourth, the visitations with which the divine love consoled her on certain feast-days. In the fifth are related the revelations that the Lord graciously deigned to show her concerning the merits of departed souls, and also some of the consolations which the Lord deigned to grant her in her last moments.

But, as Hugh says, "Every truth that is not attested by the authority of the Scriptures is suspect to me."[6] And further on, "A revelation, however plausible it may seem, would be unacceptable without the testimony of Moses and Elias, that is to say, of the Scriptures."[7] Therefore I have noted in the margin the texts which, in my simplicity and inexperience, I have been able to call to mind at the moment, in the hope that someone cleverer and more experienced than I am will be able to produce more accurate and more appropriate witness.[8]

Here ends the Prologue.

NOTES

All scripture references in Latin are to the Vulgate and in English to the Douay version of the Bible, unless otherwise stated. PL stands throughout for Migne, *Patrologia Latina*.

1. This Prologue contains revelations which are not found in the book but which are truly from Gertrude's lips. The Prologue is to be found in all the MSS now extant.
2. The "first part" mentioned is actually Book II of the present work, and was the only part of the work to be written by Gertrude with her own hand. The other parts, that is, Books III, IV and V, may have been dictated by her, and Book I was composed after her death. For a fuller discussion of the books and the years in which they were completed, see the Introduction.
3. Ps. 144:7, *Memoriam abundantiae suavitatis tuae eructabunt* ("They shall publish the memory of the abundance of thy sweetness"). "The memorial of thine abundant kindness shall be showed" (Book of Common Prayer). Cf. St. Bernard, *De Diligendo Deo* 3,10 (PL 182. 980A). This text was a favorite with, among others, William of St. Thierry; he cites it three times in his *Epistola ad fratres de Monte Dei* (PL 184.326C; 347B; 350C) and in his other works, for example the *Enigma Fidei* (PL 180.406B). Citing "the wonderful verse of the Psalm: *Memoriam abundantiae suavitatis tuae eructabunt*," Jean Leclerq says: "*Memoriam*: it is a question of remembering God, a 'remembering' which Cassian says (*Conlat.* X,10, CSEL XIII) should be continual; *ad perpetuam Dei memoriam*, of that 'remembering', delightful, sweet and joyful—*abundantiae suavitatis*—overflowing into the witness that is borne in his regard, in that *eructatio* which is the Biblical symbol of enthusiasm and love" (*La Preghiera nella Bibbia* [Rome, 1964], p.968).
4. Cf. Rom. 8:30. This is a frequently cited passage in the *Legatus*. Cf., for example, Bk. I, ch. 1.
5. The word *libros* is missing from the Munich Codex of 1412, and

therefore from the edition of *Sources Chrétiennes*, followed by the present translator.

6. "Hugh": The reference is to Richard (not Hugh) of St. Victor, *Beniamin Minor*, ch. 81 (PL 196.57C): "*suspecta est mihi omnis veritas quam non confirmat scripturarum auctoritas.*"

7. Ibid. 57D. "*Nec rata poterit esse quantumlibet verisimilis revelatio sine attestatione Moysi et Helyae (id est) sine scripturarum auctoritate.*" The text of the Prologue has *quamlibet* for *quantumlibet* and *Moysis* for *Moysi* but is otherwise the same as in PL.

8. These marginal references are clearly visible in several MSS, including the Munich Codex of 1412. They are copious and interesting, but it has not generally been considered practical to include them in editions of the *Legatus* since they present considerable textual problems. Some examples are given in the Introduction to the *Sources Chrétiennes* edition of 1968 (pp. 83–91). It would be impossible, indeed, to list exhaustively Gertrude's references to scripture. In common with all religious writers of the period, her work is built around a framework of scriptural and liturgical reminiscence. Cipriano Vagaggini comments: "The *Legatus* and the *Exercises* are, even in their composition and literary expression, entirely imbued with the liturgy by reason of their being strewn throughout with passages liturgical in their reminiscences. This is so much the case that, especially in some parts of the *Exercises*, the work takes on the appearance of a cento made up from the liturgy and from Scripture, and the latter itself often enough coming to it by way of the liturgy" (*Theological Dimensions of the Liturgy* [Collegeville, 1976], p. 742). The readers of the writings of St. Gertrude will discover for themselves their own personal set of references.

Book I

Chapter 1. The Commendation of Her Person

Oh, the depths of the riches of the wisdom and of the knowledge of God! How incomprehensible are his judgments, and how unsearchable are his ways! (Rom. 11:33) How admirable, how mysterious, and how varied are the ways by which God calls those whom he has predestined! After he has called them, he justifies his elect (cf. Rom. 8:30) by the free gift of his grace; indeed, it is in his justice that he grants them grace, as if he found them worthy of sharing all his riches and delights, as appears in this his chosen one.

Like a white lily, he freely planted her in the perfumed garden of the church, that is to say, among the assembly of the just. As a little girl of four years old he withdrew her from the turmoil of the world to introduce her into the bridal chamber of holy religion.[1] To the innocent candor of this soul was added brilliance and freshness, as of all kinds of spring flowers, so that not only did she please the eye of all who beheld her, but she won their hearts also. Even at this tender age, she already possessed the wisdom of a mature person. She was so amiable, clever, and eloquent, and so docile that she was admired by all who heard her. As soon as she was admitted to the school, she showed such quickness and intelligence that she soon far surpassed in learning and knowledge all the children of her own age and all her other companions as well. Gladly and eagerly she gave herself to the study of the liberal arts. And so the years of her childhood and youth were passed with a pure and innocent heart, and she was preserved by the Father of mercies (2 Cor. 1:3,4) from the many vain trivialities which often lead young people astray (cf. Wisd. 4:11–14) For this, may praise and thanks be given him for ever!

He had set her apart from her mother's womb (cf. Gal. 1:15) and she hardly had been weaned when he placed her in the care of a monastic Order. And now it pleased him to call her, by his grace, from exterior occupations to interior ones, from the practice of bodily exercises to the pursuit of spiritual ones. He did this by means of an unmistakable revelation, as will be seen later.[2] Then she realized that she was far from God, in a land of unlikeness.[3] Through her excessive attachment to secular studies up to that time she had neglected to adapt the high point of her mind to the light of spiritual understanding.[4] By attaching herself with such avid enjoyment to the pursuit of human wisdom, she was depriving herself of the sweet taste of true wisdom. Then exterior things began to lose their attraction for her, as was but right, for the Lord had at that point led her to a place of joy and gladness (cf. Joel 1:16), to that mountain of Sion (Ps. 47:5) which is the contemplation of himself. There he stripped her of the old man and the old ways, and clothed her in the new man who is created after the image of God in justice and holiness of truth (Eph. 4:22–24).

Hence her love of learning now became desire for knowledge of God.[5] Never tired of pondering over the pages of all the books of Holy Scripture that she was able to obtain or acquire, she filled the coffers of her heart to the brim with the sweetest and most useful sentences of Holy Scripture. And so she was always ready with godly and edifying words to help those who came to consult her and to refute errors with the testimony of Holy Scripture in such a way that no one could demolish her arguments. In those days she could never tire of the sweet pleasure she found in the contemplation of God and in the study of Scripture, which was for her honey in the mouth (Ps. 118:3; Rev. 10:9, etc.), music in the ear, and spiritual jubilation in the heart. As the dove collects grains of corn, she compiled several books full of the sayings of the saints. These she wrote down in order to elucidate certain obscure passages and to explain them to those less gifted in intelligence, and for the use of all who desired to read them. She composed several prayers "sweeter than honey and the honeycomb" (Prov. 16:14) and many other spiritual exercises,[6] written in such an admirable style that all scholars unanimously approved of it and took delight in the way in which it harmonized with the honeyed eloquence of Sacred Scripture to the extent that the theologians and the devout alike found them to their taste. There can be no doubt, therefore, that her writings are to be attributed to the gift of spiritual grace. From what has just been said, matter could be found for praise of her purely human qualities; but as the Scriptures say in the Book of Wisdom: "Favor is deceitful and beauty is vain; the woman that feareth the Lord, she shall be praised" (Prov. 31:30). So let us add here the merits which really deserve praise.

A very pillar of religion, she was a most steadfast defender of justice and truth. Of her it could truly be said what in the Book of Wisdom (Sir. 50:1) is said of Simon the High Priest: that in her life she propped up the house, that is, the house of religion, and in her day she fortified the temple of spiritual devotion, because by her teaching and example she encouraged many people to strive for greater devotion. It could be said that in her day (Sir. 50:3) the wells of water flowed out, for, in truth, no one in our time has given out streams of the doctrine of salvation more plenteously than she. She spoke so sweetly and with such penetrating intelligence, using such eloquent language; her words were so persuasive, effective, and gracious that many who heard her, feeling the marvelous way in which their hearts were moved and their wills changed, bore witness that it was in truth the Spirit of God who spoke in her; for it was the living efficacious word, more penetrating than any two-edged sword, reaching the very division between soul and spirit (Heb. 4:12) which dwelt in her and worked all this. Some, through her words, were brought to repent and were saved; others were enlightened both in the knowledge of God and in their own defects. To many she brought help by the consolation of grace. In others, she lighted the flame of a more ardent love of God. Many people from outside the convent walls, having heard her speak once only, declared that they had received great consolation from her words. Although she possessed in abundance these and similar gifts, such as usually please the world, one must not suppose that what is about to be related in this book was simply the result of her natural qualities, or the liveliness of her intelligence, or what it pleased her to imagine, or indeed, that it was composed as a result of her industry in words or the fluency of her eloquence. Far from it! It must be firmly and unhesitatingly believed that all this proceeded from the fount of Divine Wisdom and was a gift of infused grace from the Spirit who breathes where he wills (Jn. 3:8), to whom he wills, and how he wills, according to the person, the time, and the place.

But, as invisible and spiritual things cannot be understood by the human intellect except in visible and corporeal images,[7] it is necessary to clothe them in human and bodily forms. This is what Master Hugh demonstrates in the sixteenth chapter of his discourse on "The Inner Man":

> In order to refer to things familiar to this lower world and to come down to the level of human weakness, Holy Scripture describes things by means of visible forms, and thus impresses on our imagination spiritual ideas by means of beautiful images which excite our desires. Thus they speak now of a land flowing with milk and honey, now of flowers and of perfumes, now of the songs of men and of the chorus of birds, and in this way the joys and harmonies of heaven are designated. Read the Apocalypse of St. John and you will find Jerusalem ornamented with gold and silver and pearls and other kinds of gems. Now we know that there is nothing of this sort in heaven where, however, nothing is lacking. But if none of these things is to be found there materially, all are there spiritually.[8]

Chapter 2. The Testimony of Grace

May praise and thanks be given to the Lord God, who freely bestows his good and true gifts, by all things that are within the circuit of heaven, the circumference of the earth, and the depths of the abyss! (cf. Sir. 24:8). And may they sing the praise eternal, immense, immutable, proceeding from uncreated love which finds in itself full satisfaction![9] May he be praised for the overflowing abundance of his love, poured out over the valley of human frailty, and among others, especially over her to whom he was attracted by nothing so much as by his own gifts.

As Scripture says that "in the mouth of two or three witnesses shall every word stand" (Deut. 19:15; Matt. 18:16; 2 Cor. 13:1), and as there are many witnesses, there is no doubt that the Lord chose her as a special instrument to show forth the secrets of his love.

The first and principal witness is God himself, who often verified her predictions and openly declared what he had made known to her in secret. He permitted many to feel the effectiveness of her prayers, and indeed granted prayers through her merits, even freeing from temptation those who made supplication with devout and humble hearts. We shall cite a few cases among many.

On a certain occasion, at the time of the death of Rudolph, king of the Romans, she was praying with the others for the election of his successor. On the day and, it is believed, at the hour of his election, which took place in another district, she notified the mother abbess of our monastery that it had been made. She added that this new king would be slain by the hand of his successor, which proved in the event to be true.[10]

Another time, an evil man was threatening to molest our abbey. The peril was imminent and seemed inevitable,[11] when she, after having prayed, told the mother abbess of our monastery that, thanks to God, all danger had been averted. The abbey's agent in legal affairs came soon after to tell us that the wicked man had been condemned by a judicial decree, just as she had learned secretly by divine revelation. The abbess and the other persons who had learned of this benefit gave thanks to God with great joy.

A person who had long been troubled by temptations was warned in sleep to commend herself to Gertrude's prayers. When she had devoutly followed this advice she had, through Gertrude's merits and intercession, the joy of being instantly delivered.

This is also worthy of mention: a person was intending to go to communion, when, during Mass, she was assailed by a multitude of thoughts in connection with an occasion of sin which had presented itself some days before. The temptation became so strong that she thought she must give in to it; she began to be afflicted to such an extent that she thought she would not be able to go to communion in this state. Led, as may be supposed, by some divine inspiration, unnoticed, she snatched up a miserable rag which she had seen God's chosen one cast off from her wornout footwear. After having confidently placed it on her heart, she asked the Lord that through the love by which he had purified the heart of his well-beloved from all human affections, had chosen her as a dwelling-place for himself alone, and had filled her with heavenly gifts, he might, through the merits of that same beloved one, deign in his mercy to free her from her temptation. Wonderful to relate and truly worthy of all respect, no sooner had she put the little piece of stuff on her heart, with the devotion which I have described, then all carnal and human temptations were removed and she was never troubled again by anything of the kind.

This does not seem too much to believe, because the Lord himself has said in his gospel: "He that believeth in me, the works that I do he also shall do; and greater than these shall he do" (Jn. 14:12). As the Lord deigned to heal the woman with the flux of blood but who touched the hem of his garment (Matt. 9:20), so through the merits of his chosen one he could equally well, of his bounty, deliver from the danger of temptation a soul for whom he had died. And let these words concerning the first witness suffice to establish what has been said, although it would be easy to add many others.

Chapter 3. The Second Testimony

The second reliable testimony is that of many prudent people. Although different from each other, they are unanimous in affirming that in all they ever understood about her through divine revelation, when they asked God to amend her faults or to increase her perfection, she was always presented as being specially chosen and privileged to receive extraordinary graces. For instance, well-grounded as she was in the solid foundation of humility, she always thought herself most unworthy of all God's gifts. She sometimes therefore sought from others, whom she held to be more highly favored than herself, the Lord's testimony concerning certain gifts of grace which she had received. On investigation their opinion was confirmed by the divine mercy: they affirmed that it had pleased the Lord to exalt her, not only by the graces of which she had spoken to them, but by favors still more sublime.

Attracted, as it were, by the sweet odor of her reputation, a person who had had much experience of divine revelations came to our monastery from afar.[12] As she knew no one among us, she prayed the Lord to put her in touch with someone who would be able to help her to make progress in her spiritual life. The Lord gave her this reply: "Know that she who first comes to sit beside you is the most truly faithful and elect of all!" After these words, as though by a marvelous chance, it happened that Gertrude was the first to sit beside her. In her humility she wished to remain hidden, as though withdrawing herself. The visitor, thinking herself deceived, complained of this to the Lord, groaning in great dejection. The Lord assured her that this really was his most faithful one. The visitor afterward had a talk with Dame Mechthild, our chantress of blessed memory,[13] and was charmed with her discourse, full of the authentic sweetness of the Holy Spirit. She asked the Lord how it was that he exalted the first above all others and seemed to pass over the second. The Lord replied: "I shall do great things in that one, but those that I do in this one are greater, and in her I shall do greater ones still" (cf. Jn. 14:12).

While another person was praying for her and was admiring the ineffably tender affection the Lord had for her, she said to the Lord: "And what, O God of Love, do you expect of her that you make so much of her and so tenderly incline your heart toward her?" The Lord replied: "It is my own love, freely given, which impels me; that love, by a special gift, perfects and conserves in her soul five virtues in which I take particular delight: true purity, through the continued influence of my grace; true humility, through the abundance of my gifts, because the more I do great things in her[14] the more she abases herself in the depths of her humility, through knowledge of her own frailty; true goodness, which incites her to desire, for my glory, the salvation of the whole world; true fidelity, through which she cease-lessly and wholeheartedly gives of the good things she has received, for my praise and for the salvation of the whole world; lastly, true charity, which causes her to love me fervently with all her heart, all her soul, all her strength, and her neighbor as herself (cf. Lk. 10:27) for my sake."

After having said this, the Lord showed this person a splendid jewel which adorned his breast. In shape it was triangular, like a trefoil, and it was of marvelous workmanship. The Lord continued: "I shall always wear this jewel in honor of my spouse. The three angles will be clearly understood by the court of heaven: by the first, they will understand that she is 'my close one,' for no one on earth is closer to me[15] through the purity of her intentions and her goodwill; by the second it will be evident to them that I am so well disposed to no other soul, nor do I look on any other soul with more delight; by the third the fact will shine forth that no one on earth is more faithful to me than she, because she always gives me praise and honor for all my gifts to her, and this is a reflection of her love." To this the Lord added: "You will not find me abiding anywhere in the world with greater love than in the sacrament of the altar, and consequently in the heart and soul of this my lover, on whom I have bestowed in a wonderful way all the delights[16] of my divine heart."

Another day a man to whose prayers she had devoutly recom-mended herself was praying for her and received this answer: "I am entirely hers, and I give myself with delight to her loving embraces. The love of my divinity unites her inseparably with me, as the heat of the fire unites gold and silver to make an alloy." The person asked: "What, then, most loving Lord, do you do with her?" He replied: "Her heart pulsates continuously with the heartbeats of my love, and in this I take ineffable delight. But the full force of my heartbeats I am keeping within myself until the hour of her death; at that moment she will feel from them three great effects: the first will be the glory to which the Father will call her; the second, the joy with which I shall receive her; the third, the love in which the Holy Spirit will unite us."[17]

When the same person was praying for her again, he received this answer: "She is my dove without gall or bitterness, because she whole-heartedly detests all sin like gall. She is the lily I love to hold in my hands, because my supreme happiness is to take pleasure in a chaste and pure soul. She is like my fragrant rose, because she is patient and gives me thanks in adversity. She is the blossoming flower on which I delight to gaze, because I see in her soul the desire to acquire virtue and to achieve perfection. She is a melodious sound echoing sweetly in my diadem, for from it hang all the sufferings she endures, like little golden bells ringing in the ears of the inhabitants of heaven" (cf. Exod. 28,29).

Once she was reading before the community the lesson prescribed to be read before the fast of Lent, and she placed particular stress on the passage which tells us how the Lord is to be loved with one's whole heart, one's whole soul, and with all one's strength.[18] One of her hearers, moved to compunction by the tone of her voice as she pronounced the words, said to the Lord: "Ah, Lord God, how this soul must love you, when she teaches us to love with such words!" The Lord replied to her: "From her childhood I carried her and brought her up in my arms, keeping her for myself unspotted from the world (cf. Jas. 1:27) until the day when she spontaneously united herself to me with her whole will; then I gave myself to her with all the strength of my divine power, giving myself up in my turn to her embraces. The ardor of the love in her heart causes me inwardly to melt (cf. Song 5:6; Ps. 21:15), and as fat melts at the fire, so the sweetness of my divine heart, melted by the warmth of her love, falls drop by drop continually into her soul." The Lord continued: "My soul takes such pleasure in her soul that when others offend me, I find in her heart a sweet repose, while allowing her to endure some suffering of mind or body. She bears her afflictions so patiently and humbly, in union with my passion, receiving them so gratefully that, appeased by her love, I pardon innumerable sinners."

One day, while a person was praying to God at her request for the amendment of her defects, he was answered in this way: "That which my chosen one counts as defects are rather occasions of great progress for the perfection of her soul, for her human frailty would hardly be able to preserve the graces which I work in her from the wind of vainglory, if they were not hidden under these apparent defects. Just as a field covered with dung becomes more fertile, so she, through knowledge of her own wretchedness, will derive from them the fruits of more exquisite graces." And the Lord added: "For each of her defects I have enriched her with a gift which entirely redeems it in my eyes. But in time I shall change them completely into virtues, and then her soul will shine with a dazzling light."

That is sufficient here for the second witness; other points will be added in appropriate places.

Chapter 4. The Third Testimony

A third and even more convincing testimony is that of her own life. In word and in deed she plainly showed that she truly sought not her own glory but God's. Not only did she seek his glory, but she sought it out with all the ardor of her soul, so that for its sake she was ready to make light not only of her own honor, but of her life and, in a sense, of her soul also. The words of the Lord in the gospel of St. John could be applied to her: he that seeketh the glory of him that sent him, he is true and there is no injustice in him (cf. Jn. 7:18).

O truly happy soul, whose life manifestly shows her to be approved by such a great witness as the truth of the gospel! Of her it could be said, in the words of the Book of Wisdom: The just, bold as a lion, shall be without dread (Prov. 28:1). The love of the praise of God was, in fact, such a constant motive with her in upholding justice and truth that, making light of everything else, she bore adversity gladly, so long as the glory of God could be increased.

She labored tirelessly at collecting and writing down everything that might be of use to others, purely to procure the glory of God, without expecting any thanks, desiring only the salvation of souls. She imparted her writings to those most likely to profit by them and, if she heard that in certain quarters books of Holy Scripture were lacking, she endeavored to obtain them, that she might gain all for Christ (cf. Phil. 3:8). She thought nothing of curtailing her sleep, delaying her

meals, or omitting any of her personal comforts, for this was to her a
joy rather than a trouble. Besides all this, it often happened that she
had to break off her sweet contemplation in order to help someone who
was being tried by temptation, to console the afflicted, or to perform
some other charitable office. As iron when it is plunged into the fire
becomes itself fire,[19] this soul, all on fire with divine charity, became
herself charity, desiring nothing but that all might be saved.

Although to the best of our knowledge no one else on earth at that
time was having such frequent converse with the Lord's majesty, her
humility grew but deeper. She used to say that the graces which she
(unworthy and ungrateful) received from the Lord in his excessive
bounty were, because of her own vileness, as if hidden under dung as
long as she kept them to herself, but when she revealed them to others,
these treasures became like gems set in gold. For she thought every
person to be more worthy than herself; and believed that everyone
else, on account of the purity and holiness of their lives, gave more
glory to God by a single thought than she could do by giving her whole
self, body and soul, because of the unworthiness of her life and all her
negligences. That was the only reason why she sometimes disclosed
the gifts God gave her. She thought herself to be so entirely unworthy
of all God's gifts that she could not believe that they were meant for
her alone, but thought, rather, that they were for the salvation of
others.

Chapter 5. Of the Nature and Description of the Spiritual Heaven

According to what has already been said, that two or three witnesses are enough to establish the truth of any assertion, it would not
do to refuse to admit the truth when it is stated by so many true and
reliable witnesses. Anyone who still remains incredulous should blush
with shame if, because he has never deserved to receive anything of the
kind himself, he refuses to accept the evidence and, careless of the
goodness and generosity of God, fails to rejoice in all that he has done
for his chosen one and to be glad of it.

There is no doubt that she was one of his elect, one of those
blessed ones of whom St. Bernard has written in his sermons on the
Song, saying: "I think that a soul in a state of grace is not only heavenly
on account of its origin, it is even not unworthy itself to be called

heaven on account of its imitation of heaven: it is heaven in its manner of life.[20] It is of souls like these that it is written in the Book of Wisdom: 'The soul of the just is the throne of wisdom' (Prov. 12:23 [LXX]). And again: 'Heaven is my throne' (Is. 66:1). As he knows that God is a spirit, therefore he has no hesitation in ascribing to him a spiritual throne. I am confirmed in this belief by the true promise: 'To him (that is, to the holy man) we shall come and shall make our dwelling with him' (Jn. 14:23). The prophet was making the same point when he said: 'But thou dwellest in a holy place, the praise of Israel' (Ps. 21:4). And the Apostle declares that Christ dwells by faith in our hearts (cf. Eph. 3:17). But I aspire from afar[21] to the state of those truly blessed ones of whom it is said: 'I will dwell in them and walk among them.'[22] Oh, how great is the breadth of that soul and how glorious are the merits of her who has within her the power of the divinity, and who is found worthy of receiving him and able to contain him, in whom there is room enough for the fulfillment of the work of his Majesty! She grew into the holy temple of the Lord; she grew, I say, in the measure of charity, which is the dimension of the soul. Therefore, in the heaven of this holy soul she has her intellect as a sun, faith as a moon, and virtues as stars. Certainly the sun of this soul is the sun of justice[23] or the fervor of burning charity, and the moon is continence. Nor is it surprising that the Lord Jesus willingly dwells in this heaven. This soul was not like others; he did not merely speak so as to create it (cf. Ps. 148:5), but he fought to win it, and he laid down his life to redeem it. After his labors, as he saw his desire fulfilled, he said: 'This is my rest for ever and ever: here will I dwell, for I have chosen it' " (Ps. 131:14). Thus far Bernard.

And now, to show to the best of my feeble ability that she is of the number of those blessed ones of whom St. Bernard says that God has chosen them for his dwelling in preference to the physical heavens, for his glory, I shall relate what a spiritual friendship of many years has enabled me to know. St. Bernard says frequently that the spiritual heaven, that is, the holy soul which is become a worthy dwelling for the Lord, should be adorned not by the sun, the moon, and the stars, but by the beauty of all the virtues. Now I shall show briefly and as best I can what those virtues are which shone in her with special brilliance, that there may be no doubt that the Lord of might and power had his dwelling within her, because of the beauty which radiated from her, shone around, and so wonderfully adorned even her outward appearance.

Chapter 6. The Constancy of Her Justice

Justice, that is to say, the zeal of burning charity, which St. Bernard in the passage just cited calls the sun of the soul, shone in her with such brightness that if occasion had called upon her to fight in its defense, she would have faced the armed battalions of a thousand armies drawn up in battle array (cf. Song 6:3–9). There was no friend, however dear, whom she would have consented to defend against the most deadly of foes, not even by a single word, if it meant straying from the paths of justice. She would have preferred to see her own mother harmed (if right reason demanded it) rather than consent to any injustice, even toward the most troublesome of enemies.

If she had occasion to give good advice to anyone, she would conceal all the reluctance which her modesty made her feel (although this virtue shone in her more brightly than any other), and would renounce all inordinate fear of human opinion. Full of confidence in him whose armor of faith she wore (cf. Rom. 8:12) and to whom she would have liked to subject the whole universe, with the pen of her tongue dipped, as it were, in her heart's blood, she formed in her zeal such gracious words of love and wisdom that the hardest hearts were softened by her words and the most perverse of her hearers, if they had but a spark of piety, conceived the will, or at least the desire, to amend their lives. If she saw that a soul was moved to compunction by her advice, she surrounded it with such affectionate compassion and such tender love that her heart seemed to melt in her efforts to console it. And she procured this consolation less by her words than by the outpouring of her desires and her fervent prayers to God. For in her conversation with others she was always careful never to draw the heart of any creature into such a friendship with herself as might be the cause of estrangement from God, even the slightest. She rejected like poison any friendship that was not founded, as far as she could judge, in God, and it was not without great suffering of heart that she could hear even one word of friendship from anyone who betrayed too natural an affection. Indeed, she would always refuse even any necessary service that such a person might offer her; she would much sooner choose to be without all human aid than consent to occupy inordinately the heart of any human creature.

Chapter 7. Her Zeal for the Salvation of Souls

Her words and her deeds provide the clearest evidence of her great zeal for souls and her love of religion. When she saw some defect in the soul of another, she longed for the person to correct it; if she did not see any improvement, she was inconsolable until she was able to bring this about, at least in some measure, by her prayers to God, her exhortations, or the help of another person. If, as is but human, someone, by way of consolation, happened to say that she should not trouble about a person who would not correct himself, because he would atone for it by paying the due penalty, she felt as much pain as though a sword had pierced her heart and said she would rather choose death than have consolation in the face of a person's fault when he would feel the force of it only after his death and would have to pay the penalty of eternal damnation.

When she found in Holy Scripture certain passages which she thought would be of use, if they seemed to her to be too difficult for persons of lesser intelligence, she would translate them into simpler language so that they might be of greater profit to their readers. She passed her life from morning to night with the sacred texts, either abridging long passages or explaining difficult ones, to the glory of God which she so much desired and for the salvation of others. The beauty of this work is well described by Bede: "What occupation more sublime or more pleasing to God could there be than to take one's daily study to convert others to the grace of their Creator and to add to the total number of the faithful souls ever increasing the joys of heaven?"[24] And by Bernard: "The characteristic of true and chaste contemplation is that the soul, aflame with divine fire, conceives such a vehement desire to attract other souls to God to love him equally, that it gladly leaves the leisure of contemplation for the active work of preaching. It returns again to contemplation with an ardor that is all the greater for being able to take into consideration the fruits of its labors."[25] And if, according to Gregory, there is no sacrifice which gives so much praise to God as zeal for the salvation of souls,[26] it is not surprising that the Lord Jesus should have deigned to lay himself voluntarily upon this living altar, whence the pleasing odor of such a precious offering mounts ceaselessly toward him.

Once the Lord Jesus, fairest of all the children of men,[27] appeared to her. He was standing and bearing on his princely shoulders the weight of a house of a very great size which seemed about to fall in ruins. The Lord said to her: "See the effort I am making to support this house of my holy religion, which I love so much.[28] All over the world this house is threatened with ruin because so very few people are to be found willing to work faithfully or to suffer in its defense and for its expansion. Look at me then, beloved, and have compassion on my weariness." And the Lord went on to say: "All those who promote religion by word or deed are like columns supporting my burden and they help me to bear it in proportion to their powers." Profoundly moved by these words, she was filled with compassion for God, her beloved Lord, and she resolved to work still harder for the advancement of religion. In observing the *Rule*, she even went beyond her strength in order to give a good example.

After she had spent some time in the faithful exercise of these labors, the kind Lord, in his goodness, could no longer bear to see the efforts of his beloved, but wanted instead to call her to the sweet repose of contemplation, though she had not been deprived of it during her labors. He let her know through some of his friends that she should leave off her active occupations in order to have leisure thenceforth to devote herself entirely to her Well-beloved in her soul. She accepted the invitation with gladness and gave herself up with avidity to the leisure of contemplation,[29] eagerly intent on seeking in the inmost interior of her soul him who, in his turn, communicated himself to her by efficacious effusion of his grace.

Here I should like to add some words of a devout servant of God who, as if by the inspiration of God, wrote to Gertrude: "O devoted spouse of Christ, enter into the joy of the Lord (cf. Matt. 25:21)! The divine heart feels for your soul a very tender affection, an ineffable love, because of the devotion with which you have employed your strength unsparingly in the defense of truth. For his pleasure and yours he wants to see you reposing in the peaceful shade of his consolation (cf. Song 2:3). As the well-rooted tree that is planted by the water side (Ps. 1:3) brings forth abundant fruit, you yourself, cooperating with God's grace in every thought, word, and deed, offer the sweetest fruits to your Beloved. The scorching wind of persecution can never dry up your soul, because it is frequently watered by the plentiful grace of God. In seeking God's glory and not your own is all that you do, you are offering to your Beloved the hundredfold of all that you would like to do yourself and to see accomplished in others. And in addition, the Lord Jesus will make up to his Father all the deficiences which you deplore in yourself or in other people. And he is disposed to reward you one day as though your acts had never been anything but perfect. The heavenly hosts rejoice at this sight, exulting marvelously in your happiness, and in their thanksgiving they praise the Lord on your behalf."

Chapter 8. Her Compassionate Charity

Along with this ardent zeal for justice, she also possessed the gift of tender and compassionate charity. If she saw that anyone was in distress for a good reason, or if she heard that someone, even at a distance, was in trouble, she at once tried to help them in any way she could, by word of mouth or in writing. Like a sick man with a high fever who hopes for relief from his sickness day after day, so hour after hour she besought the Lord to console those whose afflictions were known to her. Her tenderhearted compassion was aroused not only by human sufferings, but by those of every creature. When she saw little birds or other animals suffering from hunger or thirst or cold, she was moved to pity for the works of her Lord. At once she offered their woes to the Lord, devoutly and eagerly, to his eternal praise, in union with that dignity by which every creature is supremely perfected and ennobled in him, imploring the Lord to be merciful to his creatures and to deign to relieve them in their want.

Chapter 9. Her Admirable Chastity

Chastity, which St. Bernard calls the moon of the spiritual heavens, shone in her with the clearest radiance. She declared that in her whole life she had never looked at the face of a man with sufficient curiosity to distinguish his features. All those who knew her could say the same. When she conversed with some holy man of God, however intimate the conversation and however long it lasted, she left him without once raising her eyes to his face. This admirably decorous behavior showed itself not only in the custody of the eyes, but was observed by her in all her movements and in every circumstance, whether she was speaking or listening. It was a pleasantry among the other nuns to say that the purity of her heart was such that it could have been placed on the altar with the reliquaries. This is not to be wondered at, for I have known no one who found, as she did, all her pleasure in Holy Scripture and consequently in God himself, which is the best way of preserving chastity. That is why Gregory says: "To one who has tasted spiritual things, everything carnal is insipid."[30] And Jerome says: "Love the Scriptures, and you will cease to love the vices of the flesh."[31] Had there been no other proof, the fact that she was so intent on reading the Scriptures would in itself have been sufficient and evident indication of the shining virtue of her chastity.

When, as sometimes happened in reading the Scriptures aloud, she came across some passage which afforded a reminder of something carnal, in her maidenly modesty she would omit it without appearing to do so. And when it was impossible for her to do this, she concealed it as well as she could by reading rapidly, as though she did not altogether understand it. But the rosy color of her cheeks betrayed the discomfort she was feeling, in her gracious modesty, and which she was unable to hide. If people less intelligent than herself persisted in questioning her about such passages, she would decline to reply, modestly feigning not to understand, as though she thought it would be less painful for her to be pierced with a sword than to hear such words. If, however, this kind of talk was necessary for the salvation of souls, without hesitation and almost as though it were not abhorrent, she did what she saw was expedient.

One day she spoke to an old friend of great prudence and experience about the familiar companionship with which the Lord favored her. He said afterward that, having considered the purity of her heart, he knew no one more a stranger to the motions of the flesh than she was. Her other virtues are not under consideration here since he was considering only this one gift of God, but he said that it was no wonder that God had chosen her as the one to whom he would reveal his secrets, for in the gospels it is said: "Blessed are the pure in heart, for they shall see God" (Matt. 5:8). Augustine says: "It is not with the outward eye, but with the heart that God is seen." And: "If the light is seen only by an eye in good condition, God is seen only by a pure heart, not with a conscience disturbed by sins, but one which is God's holy temple."[32]

In order to prove once more the perfection of her chastity, I should like to cite yet another reliable witness. A person who prayed to the Lord, asking to be entrusted with a message to his chosen one, that is, to her of whom we are speaking in this book, received the answer: "Say to her from me: 'Beautiful and lovely.'" As this person did not understand, she repeated her question a second and a third time, and always received the same answer. Astonished, she said: "Please tell me, most loving Lord, what these words mean!" "Tell my beloved that she pleases me because she is beautiful within, because the splendor of my purity and my immutable divinity shine in her soul with an incomparable luster. Again, she pleases me with the special charm of her virtues, because the joyous springtime of my deified humanity flourishes with incorruptible vigor in everything she does."

Chapter 10. The Gift of Trust Which Shone So Wonderfully in Her

How brightly the gift of trust (I call it a gift rather than a virtue) shone in her can be demonstrated by excellent evidence. Her soul was always in such a state of serene confidence that neither tribulations, nor loss, nor hindrances of any kind (cf. Rom. 8:35–39), nor even her own faults, could cloud or shake this firm confidence in the infinite loving mercy of God. If it happened that God deprived her of the consolation to which she was accustomed, she was undismayed, because to enjoy grace or to be deprived of the enjoyment of grace was all the same to her; except that sometimes, in times of trial, this hope even increased her strength, for she was convinced that everything, exterior or interior, would work together for good (Rom. 8:28). As one waits hopefully for the messenger who brings long-desired news, so she awaited gladly a richer flood of divine consolation, for which she knew she had been made more apt by the preceding adversity. The sight of her own faults could not depress or discourage her for long, because at once she was borne up again and sustained by divine grace, ready to receive whatever gifts God was to restore to her. If she saw herself as dark as a dead cinder, she strove to raise herself to the Lord, by at once cooperating with God's grace. So she began to breathe again and was ready to receive the likeness of God in herself once more.[33] Like a man who steps from the shadows into the sunlight and finds himself suddenly inundated with light, she felt herself to be illuminated by the splendor of the divine presence and to be adorned with every ornament, clothed in the embroidered golden robe, as befits the queen who is to appear before the eternal, immortal King (Ps. 44:9, 14–15; 1 Tim. 1:17), made ready and chosen for divine union and companionship.

She made it a habit to throw herself often at the feet of the Lord

Jesus in order to be cleansed of the stains without which no mortal life can be led, except during those times when she received, as has been said, an abundant influx of the divine mercy. Then she willingly abandoned herself to God's good pleasure, as an instrument designed to show, in and through herself, the operations of his love to such an extent that she did not hesitate to play the part of an equal with God, the Lord God of the universe.

Again, with regard to holy communion, this trustfulness of which we have already spoken gave her so much grace that she could never read anything in Scripture, or listen to anything that was said about the danger of communicating unworthily,[34] and indeed she always communicated gladly and confidently, trusting in God's mercy. So little did she esteem her own labors, holding them to be worthless, that if she forgot to recite the prayers and other devotions by which people usually prepare to receive communion, she did not abstain from communicating, considering that all human efforts compared with the excellence of that free gift are like a tiny drop of water in comparison with the immensity of the ocean. And although she could see no way of preparing worthily, after having put her trust in the unchanging goodness of God, in preference to all other preparations, she strove to receive this sacrament with a pure heart and devout piety. She attributed to her trust in God all the spiritual graces she received, and held them to be all the more gratuitous in proportion as she realized that this very gift of trust was accorded her by the Dispenser of all graces, without any merit on her part.

It was this trust in God which caused her to say frequently that she wanted to die, but in perfect conformity with the will of God; thus to live or to die was at all times a matter of indifference to her. By dying she hoped for eternal beatitude, and by living she hoped for the greater glory of God (cf. Rom. 14:8).

One day while she was walking along a road, she slipped and fell on a fairly steep slope. At first she felt a wonderful kind of elation, and in spirit she said to the Lord: "How good it would be for me, my beloved Lord, if this fall might be the occasion of my coming to you at once!" And as we were all amazed and asked her if she were not afraid to die without the sacraments of the church, she replied: "I desire with all my heart to be fortified by the sacraments of salvation, but I consider that the will of my Lord and what he has ordained are the best and most saving preparation. Therefore I will go to him gladly in whatever way he wants, whether my death be sudden or long foreseen, knowing that his mercy will not fail, for without it I know that I cannot be saved, whether death is long foreseen or sudden."

All the events of her life found her serene and happy, rejoicing because she always had her soul steadfastly turned toward God; of her these words could truly be said: "He who trusts in God is as bold as a lion."[35]

Our Lord deigned to give the following testimonial to the virtue of his chosen one: One day, when a certain person was surprised that she had received no answer after praying to God, the Lord finally gave her this reply: "I have kept you waiting for the answer you desire because you do not trust the way in which my goodness operates quite freely in you. My beloved, on the contrary, is so firmly rooted and grounded in faith that she always abandons herself to my goodness. That is why I shall never refuse her anything that she wants of me."

Chapter 11. The Virtue of Humility, and Her Several Other Virtues, Discussed Together

Among the many resplendent virtues, shining like so many stars, with which the Lord had wonderfully adorned this soul wherein he intended to dwell, humility was the virtue which shone most brightly. This virtue is the treasury of every grace and the custodian of all virtue. Now Gertrude was led by her very humility to consider herself so unworthy of God's gifts that she could not be induced to believe that they were given her for her own advantage. She saw herself as a channel through which, by some mysterious disposition of God, his grace flowed to his elect, since she herself was so unworthy and received all God's gifts, small or great (so she thought), in the most inadequate and unfruitful fashion, save only that she took the trouble to distribute them to others in speech or writing. This she did with so much fidelity as regards God, and with such great humility as regards herself, that she often thought to herself: "Even if after all this I have to suffer the torments of hell as I deserve, I rejoice all the same that the Lord is able to gather in others the fruits of his gifts."

It seemed to her that any other person, no matter how wretched, would have been more fruitful soil for the reception of these gifts than herself. And yet she was ready and willing at all times to receive any of

God's gifts in order to use them for the good of others, as though they were less her own affair than that of those who received them through her.

She judged herself by the light of truth, and so she considered herself as the least of those of whom the prophet spoke: "All nations are before him as though they had no being at all" (Is. 40:17); and, further on, he says "like a little dust" and so on. Just as a little dust hidden under a pen or some similar small object is kept from the sun's beams by this slight shadow, she strove to hide herself from the light which the sublime gifts of God might throw on her. She gave all the glory to him who is able to inspire those whom he calls, whose help accompanies those whom he justifies;[36] and she kept for herself only that guilt due, as it seemed to her, because of unworthiness and ingratitude for free gifts like these. However, her desire for God's glory was so great that she could hardly refrain from revealing his goodness to her; and with this intention she said to herself in her heart: "It is not right to defraud God of the greater profit that others might bring him through the benefits he has accorded me, most depraved and wretched as I am."

One day when she was out walking, she said to the Lord in great dejection: "I deem it the greatest of your miracles, Lord, that the earth does not refuse to bear such an unworthy sinner as myself!" The Lord, who exalts the humble (Lk. 1:52), deigned in his kindness to be touched by these words, and replied: "The earth bears you gladly, while the heavens in all their immensity, in a mighty surge of exaltation, dance for joy, awaiting the hour when they shall have the honor of receiving you."

Oh, what sweetness there is in the truly wonderful condescension of God who raises a soul to heights proportioned to the humility into which it has been cast by the consideration of its own vileness!

Gertrude made so little of vainglory that if some thought of the kind came into her head while she was praying or doing some good work, she did not even fight it, but thought to herself: "If someone sees you doing this work and is led to imitate you, then your Lord will gain from it the fruit of praise." Whatever work she did, she regarded herself as being of no more value in the church of God than some scarecrow on a farm, worthy only to be tied to a tree to frighten away the birds and preserve the crops.

In her invaluable writings she has left ample evidence of the fervor and sweetness of her spiritual devotion, and, moreover, he who sees into our hearts (Ps. 7:10, al.) has deigned to give us this testimony. One day a very devout man felt a great sense of fervor, and in his prayer he understood that the Lord was speaking to him: "The sweet consolation which you now enjoy frequently fills the soul of my chosen one, whom I have chosen as my dwelling."

The wonderful way in which she rejoiced in the Lord (Phil. 4:4) is clearly shown by her attitude to transitory pleasures, which she viewed with positive distaste. As Gregory says: "To one who has tasted spiritual things, everything carnal is insipid."[37] And St. Bernard says: "To God's lovers, everything is a burden, if it frustrates their one desire."[38]

One day, wearied by the consideration of the vanity of earthly pleasures, she said to the Lord: "I can find no pleasure in anything on earth save in yourself alone, my sweetest Lord!" (Ps. 72:25). To which the Lord in his turn replied: "And in the same way, I find nothing in heaven or on earth which could please me without you, because I associate you in love with all that pleases me, and so I always find in you all that gives me pleasure. And the greater these pleasures are for me, the greater will be the profit for you."

That she was assiduous in prayers and vigils is clear from the fact that she never neglected to observe any of the canonical hours unless she lay sick in bed with some infirmity or was engaged in some charitable work for the glory of God or the salvation of others. And because the Lord never failed to gladden her prayers with the blissful consolation of his presence, she prolonged her spiritual exercises long after her strength would have been exhausted by any other occupation. She observed so lovingly all the statutes of her Order concerning assistance at Choir, fasting and manual work, that she never omitted any of them without feeling grievous dissatisfaction. St. Bernard says: "Oh, if you have once been inebriated by the taste of charity, soon every labor and sorrow is made mirthful."[39]

The freedom of her spirit was so great that she could not tolerate for an instant anything that went against her conscience.[40] The Lord himself bore witness to this, because when someone asked him in devout prayer what it was that pleased him most in his chosen one, he replied: "Her freedom of heart." This person, most astonished and, so to speak, considering this an inadequate answer, said: "I should have thought, Lord, that by your grace she would have attained to a higher knowledge of your mysteries and a greater fervor of love." To which the Lord answered: "Yes, indeed, it is as you think. And this is the result of the grace of the freedom of her heart, which is so great a good that it leads directly to the highest perfection. I have always found her ready to receive my gifts, for she permits nothing to remain in her heart which might impede my action."

As a consequence of this great freedom, she could not bear to keep for her own use anything which was not indispensable, and if she accepted presents, she at once distributed them to others, taking care to give first to those who had most need, regardless of whether they were most loving or most hostile toward her.

If she had something to do or to say, she did it at once, lest it should hinder her in the service of God or in the work of contemplation. One day Dame Mechthild, our chantress, saw the Lord seated on a high throne.[41] She of whom we write was walking up and down, coming and going before him, frequently turning to look at the face of the Lord and eagerly attending with the most ardent desire to the aspirations of his divine heart. As Mechthild looked on in wonder, she received this response: "You see what the life of my chosen one is like. She is always in my presence, as though walking ceaselessly up and down. She ardently desires and seeks at every moment how to please my heart. As soon as she has found out what I want, she at once sets about busily to do my will, with all her heart; and when she has done what I wanted her to do, back she comes again to find out what is my further pleasure, and goes off to do it; in this way she gives her whole life faithfully to me in praise and honor." Then Mechthild said: "O my Lord, if her life is like that, how can it be that she sometimes judges with severity the excesses and defects of others?" To this the Lord replied kindly: "Certainly it is because she allows no spot to stain her own heart, and so she cannot tolerate with equanimity the defects of others."

In her dress and in the things that were for her own use, she contented herself with what was necessary rather than with what was stylish or particularly pleasing. These things pleased her only to the extent to which they helped her to serve God—like the book she read most often, the tablet on which she used to write, the books which others most enjoyed reading, or which they said were most edifying to them. These things and others like them were dearest to her, because it seemed to her that they gave greatest glory to the Lord. It was not for herself that she made use of things created by the Lord, but in order that the Lord might be eternally praised. And so in a wonderful way she always rejoiced when making use of anything, because it was as though she were offering it on the altar of the Lord, to his honor and glory, or distributing alms. Whether she slept or whether she ate, or whatever other useful thing she received, she rejoiced that she was giving all of it to the Lord. She saw herself in him and him in her, according to his teaching: "If you do it unto the least of these my brethren, you do it unto me" (cf. Matt. 25:40). Deeming herself in her unworthiness to be the least and most wretched of all creatures, it seemed to her that in giving anything to herself she was giving it precisely to the least of God's creatures.

The Lord showed her how acceptable this intention of hers was to him in the following way. One day she was tired and suffering from a headache. She tried to relieve it, to the glory of God, by sucking some aromatic substance. The good Lord leaned down toward her lovingly and gently, and it seemed as though he himself were revived by the aromatic scent. Then he arose, breathing a sweet sigh, and with an exultant expression on his face, and in the presence of all the saints, he said with pride: "Behold this new gift which I have received from my spouse!"

Her happiness was all the greater when she could give something to others, and then she was as happy as a miser who was received a hundred marks instead of a single little coin.

She lived so closely united with the Lord that when any food or clothing or any such-like thing were offered her to choose from, she would stretch out her hand with her eyes shut, meaning to take in this way whatever God wanted her to have. She accepted whatever she received in this way with as much gratitude as though the Lord had given it to her with his own hand, and whether it were the best or the worst she was as pleased as if it had been incomparably perfect. She did all things with this intention and derived great satisfaction from it, so much so that she always reflected with compassion on the sad state of pagans and Jews who were not able in such a way to make their choices in union with God.

That the virtue of discretion shone brightly in her is best illustrated by her unequalled knowledge of the meaning and words of Holy Scripture. The numerous people who came to seek her counsel were astonished that she could give so many prudent replies in a single hour on so many different topics; and yet, in all that concerned her own conduct, with humble discretion she sought the opinion of others, even those far inferior to herself, and listened to them with deference. The result was that she would rarely do what she herself would have liked, and always gladly followed the opinion of others.

It would be superfluous to add with what splendor there shone in her all the other virtues, such as obedience, abstinence, voluntary poverty, prudence, fortitude, temperance, brotherly love, constancy, gratitude, altruism in rejoicing in the good fortune of others, contempt of the world, and all the rest; for the virtue of discretion, mother of all virtues, was in possession of her soul.[42]

Above all, she possessed the virtue already mentioned, namely trust, foundation of all other virtues. Nothing of what they desire is refused to those who have this trust, especially in the matter of spiritual goods, and she was in a wonderful way entirely enveloped in it. And the noble virtue of humility, which diligently keeps guard over all the others was, as has been said, deeply rooted in her. What is more than all besides, charity toward God and toward others, charity, of all queenly virtues the queen, was firmly enthroned over both her interior and exterior actions, as will most clearly be seen in the whole text of this book. For the sake of brevity, therefore, I shall not, as I could do, speak of each virtue in particular, although many of the things which could be said are even more interesting than those which are mentioned here and are of a kind to delight rather than tire the mind of the devout reader. Enough has been said to prove that this chosen soul really was one of the heavens set with stars in which the King of kings deigns to establish his throne.[43]

Chapter 12. More Evident Proof of the Spiritual Heaven

In another place the Scripture, in celebrating the glory of the spiritual heavens, speaks thus of the apostles: "These are the heavens where you dwell, O Christ; your thunder is in their words, your lightening flashes in their miracles, through them you spread the dew of your grace!"[44] I will show as far as I can how this soul resembled the apostles in these three ways.

Her words had an inherent force, which was so effective that it was rare that they went unheeded, and she always succeeded easily in obtaining from anyone whatever she desired. The verse of the Proverbs could aptly be applied to her: "The words of the wise are as goads, and as nails deeply fastened in" (Eccles. 12:11).

Human weakness is such that it recoils sometimes from the truth of words spoken by a soul on fire with burning zeal. One day she reproved one of her companions with some rather harsh words. Another sister, moved by charity, tried to obtain from God the favor of moderating such ardent zeal. She was given this instruction by the Lord: "When I was on earth, I too was moved by ardent affections; I could not bear the slightest injustice; and in this she is like me." The sister rejoined: "Lord, while you were on earth you spoke harshly only to sinners, while she sometimes wounds even people who are held to be virtuous." To which the Lord replied: "The Jews in those days were considered to be holy people, and it was they who were the first to be scandalized by me" (Matt. 11:6).

The Lord deigned, nonetheless, to let his grace descend through the words of his chosen one. Many testified to having been more profoundly moved by a single word of hers than by a long sermon by any of the best preachers. This is attested by the tears of sincere contrition shed by those who came to speak with her. Sometimes they came with rebellious hearts, seemingly indomitable, but after hearing only a few words from her they were so moved by compunction that they promised to yield in everything and to do whatever was their duty.

Many felt the effects of grace not only in her counsels but also through her prayers. After having recommended themselves to her many people found they were delivered from great and apparently interminable troubles so that, filled with wonder, they frequently asked her friends to give thanks to God and to herself. We must not omit to mention that some people relate that they were warned in dreams to confide their trials to her. Having done this, they were certain of finding relief.

It seems to me that these marvels are not far short of miracles, for the alleviation of mental suffering is of no less value than the relief of bodily pain. But to prove that the power of the Lord truly worked in her, I shall add some striking evidence which shows it in the clearest light.

Chapter 13. Some Miracles

In the month of March the cold was so intense that the lives of humans as well as of animals were threatened. She heard the people say that this year there would be no harvest, because according to the phases of the moon the cold weather was going to last a long time. One day at Mass when she was going to communion she was devoutly praying to the Lord for this intention and for many other graces as well. When she had finished her prayer, she received this reply from the Lord: "Be certain that all the intentions for which you have prayed will be granted." To which she responded: "Lord, if I am certain of being heard, and if it is therefore right to thank you, show me a proof by mitigating the rigor of this cold weather." That said, she thought no more about it, but when Mass was over and she was coming out of Choir, she found the path quite flooded by the melting of the frozen ice and snow. Those who saw this change, contrary to the laws of nature, were astonished. As they did not know that God's chosen one had obtained the thaw by her prayers, they repeated that, alas, it would not last, as it was contrary to the ordinary course of nature. However, the thaw was followed by fine spring weather which continued for the whole season.

Another time, in the harvest season, it was raining continuously and everyone was praying for fear of losing the harvest. She, joining with the others, offered such efficacious and insistent prayers to placate the Lord that she obtained from him a formal promise that, for her sake, he would moderate the intemperate weather. This took place the same day. Although the sky had been covered with clouds, the sun came out and the splendor of its rays shone over the whole earth.

However, that evening, after supper, the community had gone out to do some work in the courtyard. The sun was still shining splendidly, but rain clouds were to be seen gathering in the sky. I heard her say to the Lord, with a deep and heartfelt sigh: "O Lord, God of the universe, I do not want to compel you to obey my unworthy will, but rather, if it is for my sake that, in your infinite goodness, you are keeping back the rain, and if it is contrary to what would be in accordance with your strict justice, I ask you to release it instantly, that your adorable will may be done." Wonderful to relate, as soon as she had finished speaking, the weather broke and there was a violent thunderstorm with heavy raindrops. Stupefied, she said to the Lord, "O most merciful God, if it pleases your goodness, keep back the rain until we have finished this work which we are doing in obedience to our instructions." At this petition the kind Lord held back the thunderstorm until the community had finished the work they had been told to do. As soon as it was finished and while they were still outside, rain began to fall and there was a violent storm with flashes of lightning and peals of thunder, so that those who still remained in the courtyard were completely drenched.

On many occasions she received divine assistance in a way that was almost miraculous, seemingly without praying, even with a word spoken in jest. When she was sitting on a heap of hay, and her pen or her needle or some other small object dropped from her hand and could not be found among all the hay, she said to the Lord, within the hearing of everyone: "Lord, however much I might look, I should never find it! Grant that I may find it!" Without looking in any direction, she stretched forth her hand and took it from among the hay as easily as though she had seen it lying on the bare ground. Acting like this in every circumstance, in big things and in small, she always called on the Beloved of her soul to come to her aid, always finding in him a most faithful and gracious helper.

Yet another time she was praying to the Lord about the winds which were drying up everything, and she received this response: "Sometimes I need a reason for hearing the prayers of my chosen ones, but between you and me no reason is necessary; through my grace, your will is united with mine and you cannot will anything except as I will. I shall tell you, then, that I want this bad weather in order that some rebellious people may be forced to pray to me, at least for this intention. And so I shall not grant your prayer, but instead I shall give you some spiritual gift in exchange." Hearing this, she gladly agreed, and thenceforth she always rejoiced on such occasions if her prayers could be heard in no other way than that which was pleasing to God. St. Gregory says that the proof of sanctity is not in performing miracles, but in loving others as oneself,[45] and of this we have already spoken at sufficient length. Enough has also been said to show how the Lord had truly chosen her as his habitation. For there is no lack of striking miracles to silence the mouths of those who speak evil things against God's gracious condescension, and to ensure that the confidence of the humble may be increased, since they may hope to derive some profit for themselves, of God's gift, from the benefits he has granted to each of his elect.

Chapter 14. Special Privileges Granted Her by God

I must add here some other characteristic anecdotes of the same kind. I had as much trouble unearthing them as if they had been buried beneath a great stone. I have included also some eyewitness accounts which I have from people of the greatest reliability.

Several people came to consult her in their doubts and difficulties, especially to ask her whether, for one reason or another, they should abstain from going to holy communion. After having given some wise counsel to each, she exhorted them to go to the Lord's sacrament, trusting in God's mercy and grace, and sometimes she almost compelled them. Once, however, as usually happens sooner or later to every sincere soul, she began to fear that her advice was more presumptuous than was right. She turned to God, trusting in his customary mercy and love, and disclosed her fears. This was the consoling response: "Be not afraid, but be consoled, take comfort, and be secure, because I am the Lord God your Lover, who made you for myself out of pure love, and chose you as a dwelling-place wherein to find my pleasure. Without doubt, I give a true answer to those who ask of me through you, humbly and devoutly. You may take this as a certain promise: I shall never permit anyone whom I consider unworthy to partake of the life-giving sacrament of my body and blood to question you about it. If, therefore, I send some weary and afflicted soul to you to be comforted, say to whomever it may be to come with confidence to receive me. Because of the love and the grace I give you, I shall not exclude them from my fatherly care, but I shall extend to them my most affectionate embrace and I shall not deny them my sweet kiss of peace."

Afterward, when she was praying for someone, she was afraid that this person hoped to obtain through her intercession more than she could have obtained for herself. The Lord very kindly replied: "Whatever people aspire to obtain through your intervention, they will certainly receive. Moreover, I shall most certainly give them everything which you have promised in my name; even if they are prevented by human frailty from feeling the effects of it, I shall work in their soul to bring about the perfection you had promised them."

After some weeks had passed, remembering these words of the Lord and unable to forget her own unworthiness, she asked the Lord how he could perform such wonders by means of a creature so base. The Lord replied: "Does not the whole church possess what I promised only to Peter, when I said: 'And whatsoever thou shalt bind upon earth, it shall be bound also in heaven'? (Matt. 16:19). The church believes that this same power still resides in all her ministers. Why do you not believe that, prompted by love, I can and will perform whatever I have personally promised to do?" He touched her tongue, saying: "Behold, I have given my words in thy mouth (Jer. 1:9). And in truth I confirm all the words which, inspired by my Spirit, you shall speak for me. And whatsoever you promise on earth, relying on my goodness, I shall ratify in heaven." To this she objected: "Lord, I should be unhappy if someone suffered damnation because the Spirit obliged me to tell him that his sin could not go unpunished, or something of the kind." The Lord replied: "If you say such a thing for justice's sake or through zeal for souls, I shall surround that person with my merciful love and induce him to feel compunction, so that he will not merit my vengeance." Then she asked the Lord: "Lord, if you really speak with my mouth, as you have just told me in your loving kindness that you do, how is it that sometimes the words which I speak with so much desire for your glory and for the salvation of souls have so little effect?" To which the Lord answered: "Do not be surprised that your words are at times spoken in vain, since I myself during my earthly life often preached with all the fervor of my divine Spirit, and yet with certain people my words had no effect. Everything comes to pass in time by my divine ordinance."

One day, while she was reproving a certain person for some fault, she took refuge with the Lord, devoutly praying that he would deign to enlighten her understanding with the light of his wisdom so that she would not say anything that was not pleasing to his divine will. And the Lord said to her: "Fear not, daughter, but have confidence. I have given you this special privilege that if anyone comes humbly and sincerely to ask you about anything, you will discern the case in the light of my divine truth and judge as I do, according to the nature of the case and the person. Those whose case I judge with severity, you will deal with more severely, and, again, if I treat it more lightly, you will reprove them more gently."

Then, in a spirit of humility, acknowledging her own unworthiness, she said to the Lord: "O Ruler of heaven and earth, withdraw from me (cf. Lk. 5:8) and restrain your too abundant condescension, since, as I am but dust and ashes (cf. Gen. 18:27), I am altogether unworthy of such gifts." The Lord responded sweetly and gently: "Why does it seem such a great thing if I allow you to pass judgment on those who are in enmity with me, when I have often given you experience of the secrets of my friendship?" And he added: "No one who comes with a heavy heart in simplicity and sincerity to seek consolation from your words shall be defrauded of his desire, for I, your God, dwelling in you in the boundless mercy of my love, desire through you to do good to many. And the joy your heart feels is truly drawn from the overflowing abundance of my divine heart" (cf. Is. 12:3; Ps. 35:9).

Another day she was praying for some people who had been recommended to her and she received this answer from the Lord: "In former times, anyone who could touch the corner of the altar could rejoice in having found sanctuary (3 Kings 1:31, 2:28); since in my gracious condescension I have deigned to choose you for a dwelling, anyone who commits himself with confidence to your prayers will be saved by my grace."

For this we have the testimony of Dame M. the chantress, of sweet memory. When she was praying one day for the soul of whom we write, she was shown to her in her heart in the likeness of a very solid bridge, supported on one side by the humanity of Jesus Christ and on the other by his divinity, as though by a wall. She heard the Lord say: "None of those who try to come to me by this bridge can fall or go astray." That is to say, none of those who hear her words and obey her injunctions will ever be lost.

Chapter 15. How the Lord Compelled Her to Publish These Favors

After this the Lord gave her to understand that it was his will that the story of these graces should be put down in writing for others to read. She asked herself wonderingly what good there could be in this; for in her heart she had firmly decided that she would never permit any of it to be known during her lifetime, and it seemed to her that if it were published after her death it would only cause trouble by disturbing the minds of the faithful, who would realize that they could now derive no profit from it. The Lord answered her thoughts thus: "And what good do you think it does to read that when I was visiting blessed Catherine[46] in prison I say to her: 'Be of good cheer, daughter, for I am with you!' Or when I called my special apostle John and said: 'Come to me, my beloved!' Or the many other things which one reads of these and of others? Is it not that devotion is increased in this way, serving as a reminder of my love for human beings?" And the Lord added: "When they hear about these graces that you have received, others may be brought to desire them for themselves, and by thinking about them, they may try somewhat to amend their lives."

81

On another occasion she was wondering why the Lord had been insisting for so long within her spirit that she should publish what is written in this book,[47] for she was not unaware of the fact that some people have such small hearts that gifts such as hers would often be despised and could become a pretext for calumny rather than for edification. The Lord instructed her in this way: "I have poured out my grace in your heart because I require great profit from it. That is why I want those who have received gifts similar to yours and who are careless enough to underestimate their value and make light of them to read about you; then they can recognize their own gifts and grow in gratitude and so increase in grace themselves. As for those with hearts so evil that they should want to calumniate my gifts, may their sins be on their own heads, while you remain blameless; as the Prophet said by my inspiration: 'I will lay a stumbling block before them' " (cf. Ez. 3:20). These words made her understand that sometimes God makes his saints do things which are a source of scandal to others. The elect should not fail to do these things in the hope of making peace with perverse people, because true peace consists in overcoming evil with good (Rom. 12:21). That is, while we should not omit anything that may give glory to God, we should placate perverse people with kindness, for in this way do we gain our neighbor (Matt. 18:15). If this does not succeed, we will not lose our reward. Hugh says: "As the faithful can always find a reason for doubting, if they wish, so unbelievers can find a reason for believing; it is with justice that the faithful are rewarded for their faith, and unbelievers punished for their incredulity."[48]

Chapter 16. In Revelations to Others, the Lord Gives Clear Proof of the Truth of Hers

When she reflected on her wretched and worthless state, she thought she was quite unworthy of such great gifts as those with which she knew God was constantly enriching her. She went to Dame Mechthild of happy memory, who was held in great esteem and honor for her grace of revelations. She humbly begged her to ask the Lord about the gifts mentioned above, not because she was in any doubt or wanted to be reassured, but because she wanted to arouse in herself a greater sense of gratitude and to be confirmed in faith, lest afterward she should be led to doubt by her sense of her extreme unworthiness. Dame Mechthild, as she had been asked, took counsel with the Lord in prayer.

She saw the Lord Jesus as a Spouse, full of grace and vigor, fairer than a thousand angels. He was clad in green garments that seemed to be lined with gold. And she for whom she had prayed was being tenderly enfolded by his right arm, so that her left side, where the heart is, was held close to the opening of the wound of love; she for her part was seen to be enfolding him in the embrace of her left arm. Full of wonderment, blessed Mechthild desired to know what the meaning of this vision might be. The Lord said to her: "Know that the green color of my garments lined with gold signifies that my divine works are ever green and flourishing with love." And he continued: "Everything in this soul is green and flourishing. And this close proximity of her heart to the wound in my side means that I have so joined her heart to mine that she is able to receive, directly and at all times, the flow of my divinity." Again she asked: "My Lord, is it true that you have given your chosen one such gifts that she can with certainty solve, according to the truth of your judgment, the problems of those who desire her help for any reason, and that those who seek the way of salvation through her will find it? She has disclosed to me the words in which you deigned to make this promise to her, humbly coming to me for instruction." To which the Lord replied with great kindness: "Certainly I have given her these special privileges, so that everyone can hope to obtain without any doubt all that he desires through her intervention. I shall never reckon as unworthy those whom she judges to be worthy of communion. I shall, indeed, regard with particular affection those whom she urges to go to communion; also, she will judge the faults of those who come to consult her as grave or slight according to my divine discernment. And as there are three who bear witness in heaven, the Father, the Word, and the Holy Spirit (1 Jn. 5:7), she should always base her decisions on a three-fold assurance: First, when she has to speak to other people, she should be aware of the interior inspirations of the Spirit. Second, she should consider whether the persons to whom she speaks are sorry for their fault, or want to be sorry for it. Third, she should consider whether they show good will. If these three signs are present, she should reply without hesitation in the way she thinks best, and I will ratify whatever she promises in the name of my merciful love." And the Lord added: "Each time she wants to speak with others, she should draw into her soul a deep breath of inspiration from my divine heart. Whatever she says will then be spoken with certainty; neither she nor those who hear her can be deceived, because the secret intentions of my divine heart will be revealed in her words." He continued: "May she keep the faithful testimony of your words, and if, with the passage of time, and among many different occupations, she should think she feels my grace growing cold in her soul, as sometimes happens, she must not lose her trust, because I shall undoubtedly preserve the gift of these privileges in her as long as she lives."

Dame Mechthild asked the Lord whether her conduct were not perhaps rather reprehensible, because she always hastened to do whatever came into her head; and how it was that it was all the same to her and no trouble to her conscience whether she prayed, read, wrote, gave instruction, corrected, or consoled others (cf. Rom. 14:8). The Lord replied: "I have deigned to join my heart so courteously and so inseparably with her soul that she is become one spirit with me (cf. 1 Cor. 6:17) and her will is always in perfect harmony with my own in all things and above all things, just as the members of the body are in harmony among themselves and with the will. When a man thinks in his mind and says to his hand: Do this, at once the hand moves to perform the action. Again he says: Look at that, and at once the eyes are open without delay. Thus, through my grace, she is always intent on asking me what I want her to do. For I have chosen to dwell in her in such a way that her will, and the works which stem from this good will, are so firmly fixed in my heart that she is, as it were, the right hand with which I work. Her understanding is like my own eye with which she perceives what pleases me; the movement of her spirit is like my own tongue, since, inspired by the Spirit, she says what I intend to be said. And her discretion is like my nostrils . . .[49] for I incline the ears of my mercy toward those for whom she is moved to compassion. And her attention is like feet for me, because she is always bent on going where it is fitting for me to follow. Therefore it is necessary for her to be always hurrying, according to the promptings of my Spirit, so that as soon as she has finished one thing, she may be ready to begin another, at my bidding.[50] And if in doing this she has to neglect something, her conscience is never troubled, because by doing my will she makes up for it in some other way."

Another person, very experienced in spiritual things, while praying to God, devoutly thanking him for the grace conferred on this soul, also received a revelation concerning what has been written of her privileges and gifts and her union with God. It may be stated with certainty that this came from God, whose witness is worthy of all belief. The ears of the understanding of both these people received, as it were by stealth, the breath of his whisper, like the murmur of a breeze (cf. Job 4:12; 3 Kings 19:12–13). Both of them knew as little of each other's revelations as the Romans know what is being done at the same moment by the inhabitants of Jerusalem. But in telling her revelations, this second person declared also that the gifts that Gertrude had received up to that time were but little compared to those which the Lord was disposed to pour into her soul. And she added: "She will attain such perfect union with God that she will no longer see with her eyes except as God deigns to see with them; her mouth will not speak except as God wants her to speak; and so on with all her senses. At what time and in what way God will bring this to pass is known to him alone and to those who are fortunate enough to experience it, nor are the gifts of God hidden from those whose sensitivity is sufficient to recognize them."

Another time, Gertrude besought Dame Mechthild to petition the Lord for her, especially for the virtues of gentleness and patience, of which she thought she had much need. Praying as she had been asked, Mechthild received this answer from the Lord: "The gentleness which pleases me in her takes its name from 'dwelling with' or 'indwelling.'[51] And because I dwell in her soul, she should be like a young bride who enjoys the presence of her spouse all the time; and if she must go out, she takes him by the hand and makes him follow her. And so each time that she finds it necessary to leave the repose of interior enjoyment[52] to gain profit by instructing others, she must first make the sign of the cross of salvation on her breast and call upon my name, just that one word, and then, in my grace, she can confidently say whatever occurs to her. The patience which pleases me in her takes its name from 'peace' and 'science' or 'knowledge'; and such is her diligence in acquiring the virtue of patience that even in adversity she does not lose the peace of her heart, but always patiently strives to remember why it is that she suffers. Of course it is out of love that she does it, as a sign of true fidelity."

Another person, a man to whom she was entirely unknown except that she had recommended herself to his prayers, was praying for her and received this answer: "I have chosen to dwell in her because it delights me to see that everything that people love in her is my own work. Those who know nothing of interior, that is, spiritual, things, love in her at least my exterior gifts, such as intelligence, eloquence, and so on. Therefore I have exiled her from all her relatives, so that there should be no one who would love her for the sake of the ties of blood, and that I may be the only reason why all her friends love her."[53]

Another man, at her request, asked the Lord why it was that, although she had lived so long in the presence of God, she seemed to be living in such a negligent way, without, however, committing any serious sin, such as would cause the Lord to be offended with her. This person received the following answer: "If I never seem to be offended with her, it is because she always finds everything that I do really just and esteems it to be the best, and is never disturbed by anything that I do. Even if she has any afflictions to bear, she always tempers her trouble with the thought that my divine providence orders all things. As Bernard says: "He whom God pleases cannot but be pleasing to God."[54] And so I always show myself pleased with her."

After she had heard how the Lord in his mercy had replied to him, she felt herself inspired with feelings of great gratitude, and gave thanks to the Lord, saying these words among others: "How can it be, my dearest Lover, that in your love you deign to conceal from yourself all the evil there is in me, since, after all, the sublime perfection of your works, my Lord, cannot displease me—something that proceeds not from my virtue but from your perfect sanctity?" To which the Lord said in reply: "When the characters in a book seem too small to be read easily, one uses a magnifying glass to make the writing appear larger; it is not the book which has wrought the change, but the lens. Even so, in the abundance of my love, I make up for whatever defect I may find in you."

Chapter 17. Her Growing Intimacy with God

As it happened to her sometimes to be deprived of the Lord's visit without feeling any particular distress, one day she took the opportunity of asking the Lord how this could be. The Lord replied: "Too great a proximity sometimes prevents friends from seeing each other clearly. For instance, if they are very near to one another, as sometimes happens in embracing and kissing, it is not possible for them to have the pleasure of seeing each other clearly at the same time." And with these words she understood that when grace is withdrawn, merits accumulate, provided that during that time one does not relax one's efforts in spite of the greater difficulty.

And while she was asking herself why the Lord now visited her with different graces than he had formerly, the Lord gave her to understand: "Formerly I used to instruct you with responses which you could use to show my good pleasure to others. Now I let you feel in your spirit my inspiration in your prayers, because it would be very difficult to translate them into words. I have collected as in a treasury the riches of my grace, so that everyone may find in you what he wants. You will be like a bride who knows all the secrets of her spouse, and who, after having lived a long time with him, knows how to interpret his wishes. All the same, it would not do to reveal to others the secrets of the spouse, as this grace of mutual intimacy belongs to her alone."

She was to experience the truth of this reality, recognizing when she prayed for some intention which had been recommended to her that it was no longer possible for her to wish to obtain an answer from the Lord such as she used to have in former times. It was enough for her then to feel the grace of praying for some intention; it was another proof of divine inspiration, just as formerly the divine response had been. It was the same when others asked her for counsel or consolation. At once she felt that the grace of replying to them had been accorded to her, and this grace was accompanied by so much confident certainty that she would have been ready to suffer death in order to assert the truth of her words, even though she had previously known nothing about the matter on which she had been consulted, either in writing or by word of mouth, and had not been able to reflect upon it. But if she received no direct revelation about the intention of her prayer, she rejoiced to think that divine wisdom is so inscrutable and so inseparably united with love that the best thing is to abandon everything to him. And this thought held more charm for her than she could have found had she been able to penetrate the hidden secrets of God.

NOTES

1. Gertrude entered the cloister in 1261, in her fifth year.
2. See Bk. II, ch. 1.
3. In a land of unlikeness (*in regione dissimilitudinis*): Cf. St. Augustine, *Confessions* VII, 10. But for an exposition of the doctrine of St. Bernard on *regio dissimilitudinis*, see E. Gilson, *The Mystical Theology of St. Bernard*, trans. A.H.C. Downes (Kalamazoo, 1990), ch. 2:

> The precise meaning is as follows: Man is made to the image and likeness of God in his free-will, and he will never lose it; he was made to the likeness of God in respect of certain

virtues, enabling his to choose well (Divine Wisdom), and to do the good thing chosen (Divine Power); now these he has lost. It is therefore by virtue of his free-will that he is chiefly made to the image of God, since this is the sole analogy that he can never lose without thereby ceasing to exist (p. 225, n. 45).

4. *Acies mentis*, or "high point of the mind" is a technical term for the soul's highest power found in Augustine, e.g. *Confessions* VII, 1; and Bernard of Clairvaux, *Sermons on the Song of Songs*, 62,3.

5. *Unde ex hinc de grammatica facta theologa:* As it seems impossible to translate this phrase literally without giving a misleading impression as to its meaning, the present translator has attempted to give the correct meaning by use of a paraphrase, which in turn requires some explanation. The course of medieval studies was arranged thus: (1) the *Trivium*, consisting of (a) grammar, that is to say, the theoretical study of language and literature; (b) rhetoric, or the technique of oratory; and (c) dialectic, or the art of reasoning; and (2) the *Quadrivium*, which consisted of arithmetic, geometry, astronomy, and music. J. Leclercq affirms that "in monastic schools, the Trivium and the Quadrivium were taught and not sacred doctrine" (*The Love of Learning and the Desire for God*, trans. Catherine Misrahi [New York, 1961]). The first discipline of the *Trivium*, grammar, often sufficed to designate the whole of the first cycle; and *Grammaticus* became synonymous with an educated man, a scholar or a man of letters, literate. Gertrude soon became proficient in the studies taught at Helfta. However, too little is known about the education of Benedictine nuns in Germany in the thirteenth century, even in a convent with such a high cultural and spiritual level as Helfta, for any assumptions to be made as to the precise nature of these studies. The author of Book I here means no more, perhaps, than that Gertrude passed from one stage of spiritual knowledge to another, as a student (in the most general meaning of the term) passed from the *Trivium* to the disciplines of the *Quadrivium*. It is worth noting also that *theologia* (and so the derivative *theologus*) in the medieval, pre-Scholastic sense had not the meaning that it has today. Rather than referring to knowledge of God acquired through academic study, it suggests knowledge gained in prayer and contemplation; indeed, St. Bede, in his commentary on St. Luke (II,11) says "*Una . . . et sola est theologia, id est contemplatio Dei*" ("There is only one theology, and that is the contemplation of God").

6. *Exercitia spiritualia:* The *Spiritual Exercises* of St. Gertrude (the

title is probably not original), seven in number—the number seven as a sign of perfection is used no doubt with a mystical intention—comprise a little treatise on spiritual perfection, beginning with the renewal of the baptismal vows and ending with a meditation on death. They are included by Lanspergius in his Latin edition of the works of St. Gertrude, published at Cologne in 1536. They are not to be found in any manuscript, but from the style and internal evidence, scholars are unanimous in attributing them to Gertrude. See the Introduction.

7. Cf. Rom. 1:20: "For the invisible things of him, from the creation of the world, are clearly seen, being understood by the things that are made." St. Bernard says "Let us seek the understanding of the invisible things of God by those things that are made" (*Sermons on Diverse Topics*, IX,2) and the theme is a recurring one in many of Gertrude's favorite authors, for example, Richard and Hugh of St. Victor.

8. No work of Hugh (or Richard) of St. Victor with this title has survived. It is more than likely that the phrase *de interiori homine* is intended simply to refer to the subject of the work and not to its title. It is therefore uncertain to which work Gertrude's biographer is referring. I have not found this passage among the works of either of the Victorines.

9. Cf. the concluding doxology of Bk. II, ch. 23, and the note *ad loc.*

10. Rudolph, the first Habsburg king of the Germans, died in 1291. He was first succeeded by Adolph of Nassau, elected by the Diet of Frankfurt in May 1292. Adolph, who had been elected for political motives rather than for his character or capacities, was an unpopular ruler and was deposed at Mainz in 1298 through the influence of Rudolph's son, Albert of Austria, who was then elected to succeed him. In the Battle of Gölheim which followed, Adolph was killed, probably by Albert himself.

11. There is another reference to this incident in Book III, chapter 48. The Solesmes edition of 1875, in the note *ad loc.*, suggests that the reference is to King Adolph, who, leading his army against that of Albert of Austria in 1294, occupied the region of Eisleben.

12. It has been suggested (for example, by L. Paquelin in his 1875 edition of the *Legatus*) that the person here referred to is Mechthild of Magdeburg. There seems no real reason to suppose this, but it is not impossible. The dates of her entry into the monastery of Helfta and of her death are disputed. In his edition of the *Legatus* P. Doyère comments: "This [the identification of this person with Mechthild of Magdeburg] is is not very likely, since the Beguine finally entered

Helfta in 1270. At that date Gertrude was only fourteen years old, and her mystical life properly so called did not begin until eleven years later. Thus it looks likely that the incident reported here took place after the death of the Beguine in 1282" (p. 134).

13. Dame Mechthild of Hackeborn (St. Mechthild), the sister of Abbess Gertrude of Hackeborn. Her revelations, known as the *Book of Special Grace* may well have been written down, at least in part, by St. Gertrude herself. See the Introduction.

14. The context—the humility of Gertrude—suggests that an echo of the Magnificat of the Virgin Mary (Lk. 1:49) is intended here.

15. "My close one": The Latin word is *proxima*. *Proximus* really means "neighbor," and in the Vulgate is used to translate the Greek *plēsion* and the Hebrew *ʿamith*. It is surprising to find the Lord using such a word of Gertrude, his beloved. Perhaps a reference to the previous paragraph is intended, and therefore a suggestion that the Lord loved her as himself? It is worth noting, however, that the word translated in the Song of Songs as *amica* ("friend" or "beloved") is in fact the Greek *plēsion*, Hebrew *ʿamith*; therefore more correctly to be translated as *proxima*.

16. "Delights": The Latin word is *delectamentum*. To St. Gertrude there is an intimate connection between the eucharist and the Sacred Heart; her biographer echoes that here. In referring to the delights of the Sacred Heart immediately after speaking of the eucharist, she no doubt intends an echo of Wisdom 16:20: "Thou didst feed thy people with the food of angels, and gavest them bread from heaven, prepared without labor: having in it all that is delicious (*omne delectamentum*) and the sweetness of every taste." The immediate reference is to the manna in the desert, but the passage has always been seen, like the manna itself, as being fulfilled by the eucharist.

17. A similar idea is found elsewhere in the *Legatus*, for example, in Book III, chapters 51 and 52; and also in the *Book of Special Grace* of Mechthild of Hackeborn, for example, in Book I, chapter 5, and Book V, chapter 32.

18. The reference may again be to Luke 10:27 or to its source, Deuteronomy 6:5, or possibly to the *Rule* of St. Benedict, chapter 4.

19. Cf. Bernard, *On Loving God*, 28: "*Et quomodo ferrum ignitum et candens igni simillimum fit, pristina propriaque exutum forma . . .*" ("As a kindled and glowing iron becomes most like the fire, having put off its original and natural form . . .").

20. Cf. Bernard, *Sermons on the Song of Songs* (henceforth *Song*) 27,8–

10. The whole of this paragraph is an abridged and adapted version of Bernard's text. The texts do not always correspond verbatim; it is in fact a sort of mosaic of words. Perhaps Gertrude's biographer is quoting from memory.

21. "I aspire from afar": The Latin is *suspiro*. The text of Bernard has "*suspicio*" ("admire" or "look up to").

22. 2 Cor. 6:16. The Vulgate is "*Quoniam inhabitabo in illis, et inambulabo inter eos.*" Our text reads "*Et habitabo in eis, et deambulabo in illis.*" Bernard has "*inhabitabo.*"

23. Mal. 4:2. Generally the "sun of justice" is taken to refer to Christ. Perhaps the intention here is to stress Gertrude's likeness to Christ and the fact that all her virtues had their origin in him.

24. Bede, *Homily for the Vigil of St. John the Baptist.*

25. Bernard, *Song* 57, 9.

26. St. Gregory the Great, *Homilies on Ezekiel* 12,30.

27. Ps. 44:3. This verse is used as a Gradual on the Feast of the Transfiguration of the Lord, August 6, and also during the season of Christmas, very dear to St. Gertrude.

28. Compare the story of the dream of Pope Innocent III, who, after meeting St. Francis of Assisi for the first time in 1210, dreamt that he saw him propping up the Lateran basilica which seemed about to fall in ruins.

29. "The leisure of contemplation" (*otium contemplationis*) is a standard phrase for monastic contemplative prayer. See Jean Leclercq, *Otia Monastica. Études sur la vocabulaire de la contemplation au moyen âge* (Rome, 1963).

30. St. Gregory the Great, *Moralia in Job* 36.

31. St. Jerome, *Letter* 125,11.

32. St. Augustine, *Letter* 147.

33. See note 3 above.

34. The Latin has "*nec in scriptura, nec ab hominibus.*" It would be tempting to understand *scriptura* as meaning simply "in writing," contrasted with the spoken word *ab hominibus*. But since that usage is not paralleled elsewhere in the *Legatus* (though the word is used loosely of the liturgy in chapter 12 of this book), the reference is presumably to 1 Cor. 11: 27–30.

35. The author seems to be quoting, from memory and inaccurately, Proverb 28, 1: "The just, bold as a lion, shall be without dread."

36. This is certainly an intentional reminiscence of the prayer, used, for example, after the litany of the saints: "*Actiones nostras, quaesumus,*

Domine, aspirando praeveni et adiuvando prosequere" ("Inspire the beginning of our actions, Lord, we pray, and accompany them with your help").

37. Cf. note 30 above: St. Gregory the Great, *Moralia in Job* 36.

38. The reference is probably to St. Bernard's Letter 111.3.

39. Quotation not identified.

40. The phrase *libertas spiritus* (cf. 2 Cor. 3:17) was, of course, a crucial one in late medieval mysticism. Gertrude gives it a fully orthodox usage.

41. Cf. Is. 6:1: "I saw the Lord sitting upon a throne high and elevated." The author probably has in mind the use of this text as the Long Responsory of First Vespers of All Saints.

42. St. Benedict calls discretion "the mother of all virtues" in chapter 64 of his *Rule*.

43. The phrase recalls the second antiphon of the feast of the Assumption: "*Maria Virgo assumpta est ad aethereum thalamum in quo Regem regum stellato sedet solio*" ("The Virgin Mary has been taken up into the heavenly bridal chamber, where the King of kings is sitting on a starry throne").

44. From the Sequence *Coeli enarrant* to be found in old German missals for the feast of the Dispersion of the Apostles. The word *Scripture* (*Scriptura*) is here used in an unusually wide sense to mean liturgy.

45. The author may be referring to *Dialogues* 1,12, in which St. Gregory comments "The value of a life is to be judged not by the performing of miracles, but in the virtue of one's actions."

46. St. Catherine of Alexandria, virgin and martyr, patroness of Christian philosophers; her feast-day is November 25. Nothing certain is known about this legendary figure, famous in the Middle Ages. Adam of St. Victor wrote a poem in her honor, and she is frequently depicted in art.

47. "This book": The reference is to the revelations contained in Books II, III, IV, and V of the *Legatus*, which were already extant in writing before the first book (Book I), concerning the life of our saint, was written.

48. Hugh of St. Victor, *Noah's Ark* 4,3.

49. The text is certainly corrupt at this point. The scribe, by homotelechy, has omitted a phrase between "my nostrils" and "for I incline. . . ." The phrase omitted must have explained the comparison of Gertrude's discretion with the Lord's nostrils and introduced the

comparison of her compassion with his ears. The omission is of ancient origin; all the extant MSS have the faulty reading. Lanspergius, in his edition of 1536, replaced "nostrils" (*naribus*) by "ears" (*auribus*) to make the text at least intelligible, but this is unlikely to be correct. The virtue of discretion was traditionally compared to the organ of smell, which distinguishes good and bad odors. See, for example, St. Gregory the Great, *On the Song of Songs* 7,4: "*In naso odoris discretio habetur*" ("The nose's sense of smell is to be taken to refer to discretion"). This whole passage is very reminiscent of Psalm 113:5–7. The parts of the body referred to are the same, though in a slightly different order. The power of the true God, working through his creature, is thereby stressed.

50. Cf. St. Bernard, *Song* 58,1.

51. This etymology is not, of course, correct. The Latin word here translated as "gentleness" (*mansuetudo*) derives not from "indwelling" or "dwelling-with" (*commanendo*) but from *manussuesco*, contracted to *mansuesco*, literally "to accustom to the hand" and so "tame." However, it is an interesting etymology in connection with the word *hypomone*, used by St. Paul for "endurance," for example at 2 Thessalonians 3:5. It is clearly associated with the word *mone*, used by St. John to signify God's dwelling in the heart of the person who loves him and keeps his word, for example at John 14:23. For a more detailed discussion, see *The Way*, vol. 1, no. 1, p. 48.

52. "The repose (*accubitus*) of interior enjoyment": The enjoyment of the repose or leisure of contemplation. St. Bernard (*Song* 53,1) called it *sancta quies* ("holy repose"). William of St. Thierry often discusses the *accubitus* in his *Exposition on the Song of Songs*.

53. This is taken to be an allusion to Gertrude's mysterious origin. Brought to the convent of Helfta as a child of four, nothing is known of her parentage.

54. St. Bernard, *Song* 24,8. "*Qui non placet Deo, non potest illi placere Deus. Nam qui placet Deus, displicere Deo non potest*" ("Whoever is not pleasing to God, cannot find God pleasing; for whoever finds God pleasing cannot be displeasing to God"). This is almost certainly Gertrude's source, but Bernard is in his turn citing Augustine, *Homily 2 on Psalm* 32,1: "*Ille placet Deo, cui placet Deus*" ("The man to whom God is pleasing, is pleasing to God").

Book II.
The Memorial of
the Abundance of
Divine Sweetness[1]

Prologue

In the ninth year after receiving these favors (reckoning from February to April),[2] on Maundy Thursday, she was waiting with the community while the body of the Lord was being carried to a sick person. Moved by a most violent impulse of the Holy Spirit, she seized the tablets which hung at her side and, in overflowing gratitude, she wrote the things which she had experienced in her heart in intimate converse with the Beloved, in her own hand and in his praise, in the following words:

Chapter 1. The Way in Which the Lord First Visited Her: As the "Dayspring from on High"

May the depths of uncreated wisdom call to the depths (cf. Ps. 41:8) of infinite power, worthy of all admiration, to extol that marvelous goodness which, through your overflowing mercy, has flowed down into the valley of my misery!

I was in my twenty-sixth year. The day of my salvation was the

Monday preceding the feast of the Purification of your most chaste Mother, which fell that year on the 27th of January.[3] The desirable hour was after Compline, as dusk was falling.

My God, you who are all truth, clearer than all light, yet hidden deeper in our heart than any secret,[4] when you resolved to disperse the darkness of my night, you began gently and tenderly by first calming my mind, which had been troubled for more than a month past. This trouble, it seems to me, served your purpose. You were striving to destroy the tower[5] of vanity and worldiness which I had set up in my pride, although, alas, I was—in vain—bearing the name and wearing the habit of a religious. This was the way in which you sought to show me your salvation (Ps. 49:23).

At the stated hour, then, I was standing in the middle of the dormitory. An older nun was approaching and, having bowed my head with the reverence prescribed by our rule,[6] I looked up and saw before me a youth of about sixteen years of age, handsome and gracious. Young as I then was, the beauty of his form was all that I could have desired, entirely pleasing to the outward eye. Courteously and in a gentle voice (cf. Gen. 50:21) he said to me: "Soon will come your salvation; why are you so sad? Is it because you have no one to confide in that you are sorrowful?"[7]

While he was speaking, although I knew that I was really in the place where I have said, it seemed to me that I was in the Choir, in the corner where I usually say my tepid prayers; and it was there that I heard these words: "I will save you. I will deliver you. Do not fear." With this, I saw his hand, tender and fine, holding mine, as though to plight a troth, and he added: "With my enemies you have licked the dust (cf. Ps. 71:9) and sucked honey among thorns. Come back to me now, and I will inebriate you with the torrent of my divine pleasure (Ps. 35:9)."

As he was saying this, I looked and saw, between him and me, that is to say, on his right and on my left, a hedge of such length that I could not see the end of it, either ahead or behind. The top of this hedge was bristling with such large thorns that there seemed no way to get back to the youth. As I hesitated, burning with desire and almost fainting, suddenly he seized me and, lifting me up with the greatest ease, placed me beside him. But on the hand with which he had just given me his promise I recognized those bright jewels, his wounds, which have canceled all our debts (Col. 2:14).

I praise, adore, bless, and thank you to the best of my ability for your wise mercy and your merciful wisdom! For you, my Creator and my Redeemer, have sought to curb my stiff-necked obstinacy[8] under your sweet yoke with the remedy best suited to my infirmity. From that hour, in a new spirit of joyful serenity, I began to follow the way of the sweet odor of your perfumes (Song 1:3), and I found your yoke sweet and your burden light (Matt. 11:30) which a short time before I had thought to be unbearable.

Chapter 2. The Heart's Enlightenment

Hail, my Salvation and Light of my soul! (Ps. 26:1). May thanks be given you by all things that are under the cope of heaven, within the circumference of the earth (Es. 13:10) and the depths of the sea, for the exceptional grace by which you have led me to know and consider the interior of my heart which until then I had heeded as little, if I may put it thus, as the interior of my feet. But at that time I became deeply aware of so much in my heart that might offend the perfection of your purity, and all the rest in such disorder and confusion that it was no fitting dwelling for you who wished to make your abode in it (cf. Jn. 14:23).

Nevertheless, my most loving Jesus, neither this condition nor any wretchedness of mine prevented you from favoring me very often with your visible presence on the days when I approached the life-giving food of your body and blood; although it was like seeing you in the dim light of dawn. With this loving courtesy you drew my soul toward you, to the touch of a more intimate union, a more discerning contemplation, a freer enjoyment of your gifts.

I was intent on preparing myself for this task on the feast of the Annunciation of the Lord to holy Mary, the day of your espousals with human nature in the Virgin's womb,[9] you who, before we call upon you, say "Lo, I am here."[10] You anticipated the feast; you surprised me, all unworthy, with the sweetest blessing[11] on the vigil of the feast, during the Chapter which, because of the Sunday, was being held after Matins.[12] No words of mine, O Dayspring from on high, can express the affectionate way in which you visited me, in the warmth and sweetness of your love (cf. Lk. 1:78). Give me, therefore, Giver of gifts,[13] the grace to offer in gratitude a joyful sacrifice[14] on the altar of my heart; so that I may obtain the grace I ardently desire for myself and for all your elect to experience frequently the union which is sweetness, the sweetness which is union with you, the grace which before that hour was completely unknown to me. When I consider how my life was spent before that day and what it has been since, I must confess in very truth that this was a grace given freely and in no way deserved. But from that time you gave me a knowledge of yourself so luminous that I have found myself more touched by the tender love of your friendship that I could have been by the severe punishments which were my due. However, I do not remember having enjoyed these favors except on the days when you summoned me to the banquet of your royal table. But whether this was a dispensation of the providence of your divine wisdom, or whether it was the result of my persistent heedlessness, I am not quite sure.

Chapter 3. The Pleasant Indwelling of the Lord

So you were with me in all my actions, stirring my spirit within me. One day between Easter and Ascension I went into the garden before Prime, and, sitting down beside the pond, I began to consider what a pleasant place it was. I was charmed by the clear water and flowing streams, the fresh green of the surrounding trees, the birds flying so freely about, especially the doves. But most of all, I loved the quiet, hidden peace of this secluded retreat.[15] I asked myself what more was needed to complete my happiness in a place that seemed to me so perfect, and I reflected that it was the presence of a friend, intimate, affectionate, wise, and companionable, to share my solitude.

And then you, my God, source of ineffable delights, who, as I believe, did but inspire the beginning of this meditation to lead it back to yourself, made me understand that, if I were to pour back like water the stream of graces received from you in that continual gratitude I owe you; if, like a tree, growing in the exercise of virtue, I were to cover myself with the leaves and blossoms of good works (cf. Ps. 1:3; Jer. 17:8); if, like the doves (Ps. 54:7) I were to spurn earth and soar heavenward; and if, with my senses set free from passions and worldly distractions, I were to occupy myself with you alone; then my heart would afford you a dwelling most suitably appointed from which no joys would be lacking.

I pondered these thoughts all day in my mind, and at evening, as I was kneeling in prayer before going to rest, suddenly there came into my head this passage from the gospel: "If anyone loves me, he will keep my word. And my Father will love him; and we will come to him and make our abode with him" (Jn. 14:23). And inwardly my heart of clay felt your coming and your presence.

Oh, how I wish, a thousand times I wish that all the sea, turned into blood[16] would pass over my head, so that this sink of utter vileness in which your inconceivable Majesty has deigned to choose to dwell might be overwhelmed by the purifying flood! Or again that my heart might be torn this instant from my body and thrown in pieces among burning coals! Purged of dross (Is. 1:25) it would be, I will not say a worthy, but a less unworthy dwelling for you!

From that time, my God, when you showed yourself to me, sometimes you looked serene, sometimes severe. This was according to whether I mended my ways or was careless. But to tell the truth, had the whole of my life been passed in perfect rectitude instead of attaining to such perfection only for a moment or two, I could never have been worthy of a single one of your looks, even that severe one which I had to endure after committing a multitude of faults and, alas, grave sins. For in your infinite tenderness, you often seemed to me to be rather sad than angry on account of my faults. I have seen you put up with my shortcomings with an equanimity which was a greater sign of your patience than that which you showed to the traitor Judas during your life here on earth.

However much my mind wandered away or sought pleasure in temporal things for hours or days at a time—yes, alas, and even weeks—when I came to myself again, I always found you there. And I cannot pretend that you have ever withdrawn your presence from me from that day until now—that is, for nine years—for the twinkling of an eye, except once for eleven days before the feast of St. John the Baptist.[17] I think this was because you wanted to show me your displeasure at a certain worldly conversation. This severity lasted from the Thursday till the Monday the vigil of the feast, during the Mass *Ne timeas Zacharia*.[18] In your sweet humility, and in the wonderful goodness of your love, you saw that I had to such an extent taken leave of my senses as to fail to notice the loss of such a treasure. For I do not remember feeling any sorrow, nor any desire to find it again. I cannot understand what madness had taken hold of my mind; or perhaps you wanted me to experience for myself the saying of Bernard: "When we fly, you pursue us; if we turn our back on you, you are there in front of us; you entreat us, we spurn you; but neither confusion nor contempt can dissuade you. Ceaselessly, you are trying to lead us toward that joy which eye has not seen, nor ear heard, nor human heart conceived (1 Cor. 2:9)."[19] From the beginning I was unworthy; afterward I was still more unworthy (just as a second fall is worse than the first), and yet you were good enough to restore to me the saving joy of your presence (Ps. 50:14), which has been with me continually up to the present time. For this, may there be rendered to you that praise and thanksgiving which sweetly proceeds from uncreated love, in a way no creature can comprehend, to flow back again into yourself![20]

In order to preserve gifts so sublime, I offer you your own most excellent prayer (Matt. 26:39, 42, 44). I offer you the prayer to which the extreme anguish of your agony gave such urgency, as the sweat of blood bore witness, and the simplicity and purity of your life on earth made so fervent, the ardent love of your divinity so efficacious. May my union with you be perfected through the virtue of this most perfect prayer, and may you draw me into the intimacy of your heart. So that when it happens that I have to give myself to useful exterior works for the sake of utility, I may derive from them the particular merits which they bring; and, having done them in the most perfect way, for your glory, I may at once return to you, my universal Good, in the interior of my soul like water which, when no longer restrained by obstacles, falls with full force into the abyss![21]

May you ever find me as attentive to yourself as you show yourself to me. Then I shall attain to that perfection to which your justice allows your mercy to raise a soul weighed down with the weight of the flesh,[22] which always resists your love. May I breathe my last breath in the protection of your close embrace, with your all-powerful kiss! May my soul find herself without delay there where you are, whom no place circumscribes,[23] indivisible, living, and exulting in the full flowering of eternity, with the Father and the Holy Spirit, true God, everlasting, world without end!

Chapter 4. The Stigmata of the Most Holy Wounds of Christ

At the time when I first began to receive these favors—I think it was during the first or the second year, in the winter—I found in a book a short prayer in these words:

"Lord Jesus Christ, Son of the living God, grant that I may, with all my heart, all my desire, and with a thirsting soul, aspire toward you; and in you, most sweet and pleasant, take my rest. With my whole spirit and all that is within me, may I sigh always for you in whom alone true blessedness is to be found. Inscribe with your precious blood, most merciful Lord, your wounds on my heart, that I may read in them both your sufferings and your love. May the memory of your wounds ever remain in the hidden places of my heart, to stir up within me your compassionate sorrow, so that the flame of your love may be enkindled in me. Grant also that all creatures may become vile to me, and that you may become the only sweetness of my heart."

I was so pleased with this little prayer that I repeated it often with great fervor; and you, who never refuse to grant the requests of the humble, were to grant me the effects of the prayer.

Soon afterward, during the same winter, after Vespers, at supper in the refectory, I found myself sitting next to a person to whom I had in some measure revealed my secret in such matters. Let me say here in parenthesis, for the benefit of anyone who may read these words, that I have very often found an increased fervor in devotion as a result of such confidences. Whether I was guided in this, Lord God, by your Holy Spirit or by the sentiments of human affection, I do not clearly perceive. However that may be, I have heard from someone experienced in such matters that it is useful to open one's soul to some confidant on whose friendship one can rely, to be respected because of age. As I have said, I do not know what made me do this, and I abandon myself to your unfailing providence, in whose Spirit, sweeter than honey, all the power of the heavens is established (Ps. 32:6). If my conduct were really guided by human sentiment, it would be all the more fitting that I should plunge myself into an abyss of gratitude. Your gracious condescension, my God, is so much the greater in that you have deigned to unite the dust of my nothingness with the gold of your inestimable greatness, so that these gems of your grace might be mine.

At the time I mentioned, while I was devoutly meditating on these things, I felt, in my extreme unworthiness, that I had received supernaturally the favors for which I had been asking in the words of the prayer I spoke of. I knew in my spirit that I had received the stigmata of your adorable and venerable wounds interiorly in my heart, just as though they had been made on the natural places of the body. By these wounds you not only healed my soul, but you gave me to drink of the inebriating cup of love's nectar. Even so, unworthy as I am, I found that the depths of your love were not exhausted. Did I not receive of the overflowing of your generous love another remarkable gift? On any one day that I recited five verses of the psalm "Bless the Lord, O my soul" (psalm 102) while venerating in spirit the marks of your love impressed on my heart, I cannot claim that I was ever denied some special grace.

At the first verse, "Bless the Lord, O my soul," I was granted to lay down upon the wounds of your sacred feet the scouring rust of sin[24] and all attachments to the worthless pleasures of the world. Then, at the second verse, "Bless the Lord, O my soul, and never forget all that he has done for you," I was to wash away all the stains of fleshly and ephemeral pleasure in the fountain of your cleansing love, whence blood and water flowed for me.[25] At the third verse, "Who forgiveth all thy iniquities," like the dove who builds her nest in the cleft of the rocks, I was to find rest for my soul (Song 2:14; Ps. 83:4–5) in the wound of your left hand. Then, at the fourth verse, "Who redeemeth thy life from destruction," approaching your right hand, I was to draw confidently from the treasures which it held all that I lacked for the perfection of every virtue. Thus honorably adorned,[26] through the fifth verse, "Who satisfieth thy desire with good things," I was purged from the infamy of sin. My deficiencies were made good by your sweetest and most longed-for presence. Now indeed I, who was of myself unworthy, was made worthy enough to rejoice in your chaste embrace.

In this way you granted the petition of my prayer, the grace to read in these wounds your suffering and your love. It was, alas, for a short time only. I do not claim that you withdrew these favors from me, but my complaint is that I lost them myself through my own ingratitude and negligence. In your infinite mercy and love, you seemed not to notice this. Up to the present time you have preserved your first and greatest gift, the impression of your wounds, although most unworthy as I am, I did nothing to deserve it.

May glory, honor, and power with joyful praise be given to you in all eternity!

Chapter 5. The Wound of Love

Seven years later, before Advent, as you, the Author of all good things had ordained, I made a certain person undertake to say for me each day during her prayers before the crucifix these words: "By your wounded heart, most loving Lord, pierce her heart with the arrow of your love, so that it may become unable to hold anything earthly, but may be held fast solely by the power of your divinity."

I am sure that these prayers were answered on the Sunday when *Gaudete in Domino* ("Rejoice in the Lord") is sung at Mass.[27] In the exuberance of your lavish generosity you mercifully permitted me to approach the communion of your most sacred body and blood, and you inspired me with a vehement desire which caused me to exclaim in these words: "Lord, I confess that I am not worthy (Matt. 8:8) through any merits of my own to receive the least of your gifts, but according to the merits and desires of all here present, I implore you of your goodness to transfix my heart with the arrow of your love!"[28] I soon knew that my words had reached your divine heart, as much by the interior signs of infused grace as by certain signs which now appeared on the picture of your crucifixion.

After I had received the life-giving sacrament, on returning to my place, it seemed to me as if, on the right side of the Crucified painted in the book, that is to say, on the wound in the side,[29] a ray of sunlight with a sharp point like an arrow came forth and spread itself out for a moment and then drew back. Then it spread out again. It continued like this for a while and affected me gently but deeply. But even so my desire was not fully satisfied until the Wednesday when, after Mass, the faithful venerate the mystery of your adorable Incarnation and Annunciation.[30] I too tried to apply myself to this devotion, but less worthily. Suddenly you appeared, inflicting a wound in my heart, and saying: "May all the affections of your heart be concentrated here: all pleasure, hope, joy, sorrow, fear, and the rest; may they all be fixed in my love."

At once it occurred to me that I had heard it said that wounds have to be bathed, anointed, and bandaged. You had not then taught me how to do this, but afterward you showed me through another person.[31] She was more accustomed, I believe, to listen more frequently and consistently, for the sake of your glory, to the soft murmur of your love (Job 4:12) than was I, alas. She now advised me to meditate devoutly on the love of your heart as you hung on the cross, so that from the fountains of charity[32] flowing from the fervor of such inexpressible love I might draw the waters of devotion that wash away all offenses; and from the fluid of tenderness exuded by the sweetness of such inestimable love, I might derive the ointment of gratitude,[33] balm against all adversity; and in efficacious charity perfected by the strength of such incomprehensible love, I might derive the bandage of holiness, so that all my thoughts, words, and deeds, in the strength of your love, might be turned toward you and thus cleave indissolubly to you.

What the malice and wickedness of my own perversity have done to corrupt this devotion can be made good by the fullness of the power of the love which dwells (Col. 1:19) in him who sits on your right hand (Col. 3:1), who has become bone of my bone and flesh of my flesh (Gen. 2:23). Now it is through him that you have granted us, in the Holy Spirit, the capacity for noble sentiments of compassion, humility, and reverence. And through him I offer you my laments for the very many infidelities and sins which I have committed in thought, word, and deed, offending against the divine nobility of your goodness, but especially for being so unfaithful, careless, and irreverent in the use of your gifts. If you had given me, in my unworthiness, no more than a thread of flax as a memento,[34] I should have respected it and treated it more reverently.

You, my God, know all my secret thoughts (Dan. 3:42); you know that I am compelled by a force which is external to me, and indeed is against my will, to commit these things to writing. I consider that I have profited but little from your gifts, and so I cannot believe that they were meant for me alone, because in your eternal wisdom you cannot be misled. That is why, Giver of gifts, you who have so freely loaded me with gifts unmerited, I ask you to grant that at least one loving heart reading these pages may be moved to compassion, seeing that through zeal for souls you have permitted such a royal gem to be embedded in the slime of my heart. May such a one be led to praise and exalt your mercy, with hymns of heart and lips, such as: *Te Deum Patrem . . . Ex quo omnia . . . Te jure laudant . . . Tibi decus . . . Benedictio et claritas.*[35] And so you will somehow make good all my deficiencies.

Here she ceased writing until October.[36]

PART II

Chapter 6. The More Noteworthy Visit of the Lord on the Feast of the Nativity

Oh, how inaccessible, how admirable, is the height of your infinite power! How deep is the abyss of your inscrutable wisdom! How wide, how immense, is the breadth of your most desirable charity![37] How mightily the torrents of your honey-sweet divinity overwhelm my nothingness, miserable little worm that I am, crawling about on the parched sands of my negligence and defects! While still on my earthly pilgrimage, I want to recapture what I can of the prelude to the delectable bliss and sweetest delights of that state in which a soul united with God becomes one spirit with him.[38] It has been given to me, poor little speck of dust that I am, to dare to lap up (Matt. 15:27) some of the drops of this infinite beatitude, overflowing so abundantly in the way I am about to relate.

It was in the holy night, when the dew of divinity came down, shedding sweetness over all the earth, and the heavens were melting, made sweet like honey.[39] My soul, like a dampened fleece on the threshing-floor of the community (Judg. 6:37–8) was meditating on this mystery. Through the exercise of this devotion, I was trying to give my poor services in assisting at the divine birth when, like a star shedding its ray, the Virgin brought forth her son,[40] true God and true man.[41] In an instant I knew what it was that I was being offered and what it was that I received, as it were, into the heart of my soul: a tender newborn babe. In him was hidden the supreme gift of perfection, truly the very best of gifts. And while I held him within my soul, suddenly I saw myself entirely transformed into the color of the heavenly babe—if it is possible to describe as color that which cannot be compared with any visible form. Then I received in my soul intelligence of those sweetest and most ineffable words: "God shall be all in all" (cf. 1 Cor. 15:28). I rejoiced that I was not denied the welcome presence and delightful caresses of my Spouse. With insatiable avidity, therefore, I drank in, like deep draughts from a cup of nectar,[42] divinely inspired words such as these: "As I am the figure of the substance of the Father (Heb. 1:3) through my divine nature, in the same way, you shall be the figure of my substance through my human nature, receiving in your deified soul the brightness of my divinity, as the air receives the sun's rays and, penetrated to the very marrow by this unifying light, you will become capable of an ever closer union with me."[43]

O most excellent balm of divinity, whose growth and flowering is in eternity, spreading out in boundless rivers of charity[44] to fill the whole earth at the end of time! Oh, what invincible power is shown by the right hand of the Most High, that such a fragile vessel of clay as mine,[45] cast into ignominy through her own defects, should hold and keep a liquid so precious![46] Oh, what unmistakable proof this is of the overflowing love of God! While I was still straying so far off in the devious paths of sin, he never abandoned me, and he has made known to me, according to the measure of my small capacity, the sweetness of this blessed union with him!

Chapter 7. A More Excellent Union of Her Soul with God

On the most holy feast of the Purification, after a serious illness, I was obliged to stay in bed. Toward daybreak, I was filled with sadness. I complained within myself of being deprived, through bodily infirmity, of that divine visitation which had so often consoled me on this feast day. She who is our mediatrix, the mother of him who is the mediator between God and humankind (1 Tim. 2:5) comforted me with these words: "Just as you do not remember ever having suffered any greater bodily pain, know that you have never received from my son a nobler gift than the one which this bodily weakness has given your soul the strength to receive worthily." These words consoled me, and just before the procession was due to start, after I had received the food of life and as I was meditating on God and myself, I saw my soul, like wax melting in the heat of the fire (Ps. 21:14), being placed close to the Lord's most sacred breast, as though to take the imprint of a seal (Song 8:6; Wisd. 9:10). Suddenly, as I looked, it seemed to be spread around and even to be drawn into the interior of that treasury wherein all the fullness of the Godhead corporeally dwells (Col. 2:9). Thus it was sealed with the imprint of the resplendent and ever tranquil Trinity.

O devastating coal (Ps. 119:4), my God, burning inextinguishably with living heat, heat which it has within it and gives out and impresses with such strength on the damp and slippery morass of my soul, first drying up in it the tide of earthly pleasures, and afterward softening the hardness of my self-will, which with time had become so extremely obdurate. O truly consuming fire; you who exert your power against our vices in order then to let the soul feel your gentle anointing![47] From you alone and not otherwise can we receive the power to be reformed (Acts 3:12,18) to the image and likeness of our original state.[48] O fiery furnace of ever-increasing heat,[49] in which is seen the joyous vision of true peace,[50] whose action transforms dross into gold (Is. 1:25), fire-tried and precious, as soon as the soul, weary of illusions, aspires at last with all the ardor of which she is capable to be attached to you alone, her very Truth!

Chapter 8. A More Intimate Friendship

After this, on the Sunday of *Esto mihi*[51] during Mass, you roused my mind and increased my longing for those more magnificent gifts which you intended to grant me, by two phrases in particular, which made a deep impression on my soul: the verse of the first Responsory: "I will bless thee . . . ,"[52] and the verse of the ninth Responsory: "All the land which thou seest I will give to thee and to thy seed for ever."[53] With this, you placed your adorable hand on your most blessed breast, giving me to understand that that was the promised land of your infinite generosity.

O holy land, blessed and sanctifying, overflowing with blessings (Gen. 2:5,15), harvest field of delights, the smallest grain from which could amply satify the desire of all the elect and could give them all that human heart could conceive, all that is desirable, pleasant, delightful, joyous, and sweet!

While I was meditating attentively, if not as attentively as I ought yet as attentively as I could, on that which was worthy of all attention, behold, there appeared the goodness and kindness of God our Savior (Titus 3:4,5). This was not through any good works which I have been able to do, unworthy as I am, but in accordance with his own ineffable merciful design, by adoptive regeneration, fortifying me (in my extreme baseness and unworthiness) and making me capable of this wonderful, this tremendous grace, worthy of honor and adoration,[54] more than heavenly and beyond all price, the grace of intimate union with you!

But to what merits of mine, my God, and to what judgments of yours, is due so great a gift? It must be that love, unmindful of its own honor but prompt to honor,[55] love, I say, imperious love, which does not wait for judgment and dispenses with all reason, has, as it were, my most sweet Lord—if I may dare to speak thus—inebriated you even to madness, in that you should join yourself with one so unlike you. But it would be more fitting to say that, in the goodness and sweetness that is inherent in your nature, moved by your exquisite charity, which causes you not only to love but to be yourself Love (1 Jn. 4:16), you have directed the natural flow of this love toward the salvation of the human race. This love it is which has persuaded you to call the least of human creatures, the one lacking every endowment of fortune or grace, despicable in her life and conduct, to call her from afar, from her low estate to raise her to a share in your royal—rather, divine—grandeur, so that the confidence of all souls here below might be increased and strengthened. It is my hope and desire for all Christians, out of reverence for God, that no one may be found who makes worse use of God's gifts, or who gives greater scandal to their neighbors, than I do.

The invisible things of God are manifested to the intelligence by the exterior things of creation,[56] as I have said already. The Lord appeared to me, and I saw that that part of his sacred breast to which he had taken my soul on the day of the Purification and held it like wax being carefully melted at the fire was now moist with perspiration and breaking out violently in beads of sweat, as though the wax of which I had formerly had sight were melting in the intense heat of the hidden fire which was burning there.[57] And yet this divine treasury (Eph. 3:8), with marvelous and ineffable power, absorbed these drops in an indescribable way. Who could doubt the mighty power of the boundless love stored up therein, disclosing a mystery so great and so unfathomable?

O eternal solstice,[58] happy fields where joy securely dwells, containing all manner of delights, paradise of bliss that never cloys, where flows a stream of inestimable pleasure! Blossoms and spring flowers of every kind and hue gladden the sight; one is moved softly by sweet harmonies, sweetly influenced, rather, by the melodies of spiritual songs and music; revived by the aromatic odors of life-enhancing perfumes; intoxicated by sweet savors interiorly tasted; one is wonderfully changed by gentle and secret embraces![59]

Oh, thrice happy, four times blessed and (if it may be said) a hundred times holy he who, with innocent hands, a pure heart, and unpolluted lips, led by your grace, has deserved to approach this paradise! Oh, what will he not see, hear, smell, taste, feel![60] But even if my tongue were to stammer out something from thence, I who have been admitted, favored by divine goodness, if only by way of my own vices and negligences, as though all covered with a thick crust,[61] I should never really be able to grasp any of it. Although the knowledge of angels and human beings were to be worthily combined, even that would not suffice to form one single word that might accurately express even a shadow of such sovereign excellence.

Chapter 9. The Inseparable Union of Her Soul with God

Not long after, toward the middle of Lent, I lay once more very sick in bed. One morning all were about their various occupations, and

107

I was left lying there alone. The Lord, who abandons no one who is deprived of human comfort, was at my side, fulfilling the prophetic words of the Psalmist: "I am with him in tribulation" (Ps. 90:15). He showed me, issuing from his left side as though from the innermost depths of his blessed heart, a stream of flowing water as pure as crystal and as solid (cf. Rev. 22:1). It proceeded to cover his adorable breast like a jewel. I saw that it was transparent, colored in hues of gold and rose, alternating in various ways. With this, the Lord gave me to understand these words: "The sickness from which you are now suffering has so sanctified your soul that whenever for my sake you condescend to others in thought, word, or deed, you will never be far from me, as is shown you in this stream. And just as the gold and rose colors gleam through the purity of the crystal and are enhanced by it, so will your intentions be pleasing, seen through the cooperation of the gold of my divinity and the perfecting power of the patience of the rose of my humanity."

Oh, the dignity of this minutest speck of dust that has been lifted up out of the mud and taken as a setting for the noblest gem of heaven! Oh, the excellence of this tiny flower which has been drawn up out of the mire by the sun's rays, so that it might shine with the sun's light! Oh, the beatitude of that blissful and blessed soul whom the Lord's Majesty esteems so highly! For although he exercises his omnipotence in the act of creation, yet the soul which he has made (although it is beautiful in his image and likeness) is as far distant from him as is the creator from the creature. And therefore a thousand times blessed the soul to whom it is given to persevere in such a state as that to which I, alas, I am afraid, have never for a moment attained. But I desire that God in his mercy will give me some grace, through the merits of those whom he has preserved for so long, I believe, in such a state.

O gift of gifts! (Phil. 2:9). To be satiated so fully in that storeroom of divine spices! To be inebriated with the overflowing wine of charity in that wine cellar of pleasures (Song 1:3, 2:4, 5:1, et al.), to be so overcome, rather, as not to be able to stir a step from these confines outside which this precious liquid (it is to be surmised) would lose its fragrant warmth and potency! Furthermore, when charity induces one to go out, to carry with one, as it were, the scent of wine on one's breath, so as to be able to share with others the rich sweetness of divine wealth.

I am entirely confident, Lord God, that you can do everything, and that you can bestow this gift on all your elect. I do not doubt for a moment that you wanted to give it to me in your loving kindness. How, in your inscrutable wisdom, you were able to bestow it on my unworthy self, I am unable to discover. All the more, rather, I glorify and magnify the wisdom and goodness of your infinite power. I praise and adore the infinite power and goodness of your wisdom. I bless and give you thanks for your infinite power and wisdom and goodness, Lord, because I have always received of your generosity all the graces that could be accorded to me, always immeasurably surpassing that which I could deserve.

Chapter 10. The Divine Infusion of Grace

I thought it so unseemly to write down all these things that I could not bring myself to listen to the voice of conscience and kept on putting it off until the feast of the Exaltation of the Holy Cross. That day, during Mass, as I was intending to apply my mind to other thoughts, the Lord recalled me to my senses with these words: "Know for certain that you will never leave the prison of your flesh until you have paid the last farthing (Matt. 5:26) that you are keeping back."

As I was reflecting that I had repaid all God's gifts, if not indeed by writing, then by word of mouth, for the benefit of others, the Lord reproached me with the words I had heard read at Matins that night: "If the Lord's teaching had been only for the sake of those then living, there would have been spoken words only and no Scripture; but now truly the Scriptures are destined for the salvation of many."[62] And the Lord added: "I desire to have in your writings incontrovertible proof of my divine love, as I propose through them to do good to many souls in these modern times."[63]

Then, with a heavy heart, I began to consider within myself how difficult, not to say impossible, it would be for me to find the right expressions and words for all the things that were said to me, so as to make them intelligible on a human level, without danger of scandal. The Lord, as a remedy for such faintheartedness, seemed to send down a shower of drenching rain over my soul. Like a young and tender plant, I felt myself now beaten down to the ground by the violence of the downpour. In my human misery I could take in nothing of what was said, except for some particularly weighty words which I should never have been able to find for myself. This only made me more downcast, and I asked myself what would come of it. But in your loving kindness, my God, and with your customary fondness, you lightened the burden and revived my soul with these words: "As you do not think you have been able to derive any profit from this down-pour, I am going to hold you close to my divine heart, so that by repeated inspiration[64] my influence may act gradually upon you, pleasantly and sweetly, just as much as you can bear." O Lord my God, I acknowledge the truth of this promise in its perfect fulfillment![65]

During four days, each morning at the most favorable hour, you inspired me with a part of what I have already written. You imparted this instruction so excellently and so sweetly that, without any effort, I wrote of things which I did not know before, as though it were a lesson long since learned by heart. And you acted with such moderation that after I had written the daily task it was impossible for me, even with the exertion of every effort, to find any more of those words which next day presented themselves with such fluency and abundance, and without difficulty of any kind. Acting in this way you restrained my impetuosity, as we learn from Scripture that no one should be so attached to the active life as to neglect the contemplative.[66] Thus, in your incessant zeal for the salvation of my soul, you allowed me to enjoy at times the delightful embraces of Rachel, without depriving me, however, of the glorious fecundity of Lia.[67]

May you in your loving wisdom deign to assist me in combining to your satisfaction the active with the contemplative life.

Chapter 11. The Devil's Tempting

In how many ways and how often have you let me feel the saving health of your presence! And with what blessings of sweetness have you come to meet me (Ps. 20:4) in my nothingness, especially during the first three years, and more especially at those times when I was permitted to partake of your precious body and blood! As I shall never be able to make any return, no, not one for a thousand (Job 9:3), I shall leave that to the eternal gratitude, immense and incommunicable, by which you, O resplendent and ever tranquil Trinity, from yourself, through yourself, and in yourself, make reparation for every debt, and in this also I associate myself, infinitesimal speck of dust though I am. I offer you in this way, through him who stands before you, having my nature,[68] all the thanksgiving that you have made available through him in the Holy Spirit, for all your benefits,[69] and especially for the one by which you have enlightened my ignorance, showing me how I was corrupting the purity of your gifts.

Once when I was assisting at a Mass during which I was to go to communion, you let me feel your presence; and with wonderful humility, you instructed me with this similitude: I saw that you were thirsty and asking me to give you to drink.[70] As I was lamenting my inability to help you, because, in spite of all my efforts, I was unable to wring from my heart a single tear, I saw that you were offering me a golden cup.[71] As soon as I had taken it, my heart melted with tenderness and a flood of loving tears gushed forth. Meanwhile, a contemptible figure had appeared on my left, stealthily placing in my hand something bitter and poisonous, trying without being seen but with all his might to make me throw it into the cup to pollute it.[72] At that instant there arose in me such a vehement temptation to vainglory that it was easy to see in it a device of our old adversary,[73] jealous of your gifts to us.

But thanks to your faithfulness, Lord, thanks to your protection, truly one Divinity, one and threefold Truth, threefold and one Godhead,[74] you do not allow us to be tempted beyond our powers (1 Cor. 10:13). Although you sometimes give the enemy the power to tempt us, in order to exercise us in spiritual progress, if you see that we continue to strive confidently, trusting in your help, you make the strife your own; in your boundless generosity you keep the battle for yourself, and attribute the victory to us, if only we cleave to you of our own free will; and among all your gifts this one in particular is always preserved for us by your grace, to increase our merits. Not only do you never allow our enemy to take our free will from us, but you never have the slightest wish to take it from us yourself.[75]

On another occasion and by another similitude, you taught me that by giving in easily to the adversary we allow him to grow in audacity, for the perfect beauty of your justice requires your merciful power to be hidden sometimes during the dangers we incur through our own negligence. The more promptly we resist evil, the more profitable, fruitful, and successful is our resistence.

Chapter 12. Bearing with Human Defects

In the same way I thank you for yet another similitude, no less useful and acceptable. You made me understand with what loving patience you bear with our faults so that in amending them we may be blessed.

One evening I had given way to anger, and the next day, before dawn, I was taking the first opportunity to pray when you showed yourself to me in the form and guise of a pilgrim; as far as I could judge, you seemed to be destitute and helpless. Filled with remorse, with a guilty conscience, I bewailed my lapse of the previous day. I began to consider how unseemly it was to disturb you, Author of perfect purity and peace, with the turmoil of our wicked passions, and I thought it would be better—rather, I considered that I would actually prefer—to have you absent rather than present (but at such a time only) when I neglected to repel the enemy who was inciting me to do things so contrary to your nature.

This was your reply: "What consolation would there be for a sick person who, leaning on others, has just succeeded in going out to enjoy the sunshine when he is suddenly overtaken by a storm, had he not the hope of seeing clear sky again? In the same way, overcome by my love for you I have chosen to remain with you during the storm brought on by your sins and to await the clear sky of your amendment in the shelter of your humiliation."

Since my tongue is ineffective to express how, in this showing, you granted me still more abundantly the abiding gift of your grace, may the affection of my heart do so, and from the depths of my humility—to which I was brought by your loving condescension—may I learn to direct my gratitude effectively through the affective movement of my heart toward your love.

Chapter 13. The Custody of the Affections

Once again I give you thanks for your merciful love, kindest Lord, for having found another way of arousing me from my inertia. Although it was at first through the intervention of another person, you yourself completed what you had begun with no less mercy than goodness. This person showed me how, according to the gospel (Lk. 2:8–16), when you were born on earth, it was the shepherds who found you first, and added these words, sent to me from you: that if I really wanted to find you, I must watch over my feelings like the shepherds watching over their flocks.[76] This advice did not please me very much and I deemed it most inappropriate in my case, knowing that you treated my soul quite differently, not as if I served you as a hireling shepherd serves his lord.

I pondered these thoughts all day long, turning them over in my mind in great dejection. After Compline, when I withdrew to my place for prayer, you soothed my sorrow with the following similitude: If a bride who sometimes feeds her husband's falcons is not in the very least deprived of his embraces on that account, neither should I be deprived of the sweetness of your grace if, for your sake, I were to apply myself diligently to watching over my feelings and affections. To do this you gave me, in the form of a green rod, the spirit of fear, so that, without leaving your arms for a single instant, I might avoid those pathless wastes in which human affections are wont to stray. You added that, as often as some impulse made its way into my mind, attracting my inclinations and affections—either to the right, like hope or joy, or to the left (cf. Josh. 1:7; Prov. 4:27, al.), like fear, sorrow or anger—I should at once fend it off with the rod of your fear, and, mastering my senses, I should lead it to the center of my heart, there to immolate it, like a tender young lamb, simmering on the fire of my heart, so that it might be a dish fit to serve at your table (cf. Gen. 27:8).

Truly, daily impelled by malice, through the levity and confusion of my words and deeds, I relax my vigilance and, as soon as an occasion presents itself, that which at first I wanted to give you I seem almost to snatch away from between your very teeth to give to your enemy! But even then you looked at me with so much sweetness and goodness, as though you never could have suspected me of the least guile and as though you took it for a mark of affection. And thus from that time you have led my soul to experience such sweet emotions of love that I do not think that, had I been intimidated by threats, I could have been as much influenced to amend and to be on my guard as I was by so much affection.

Chapter 14. The Uses of Compassion

Once, on the Sunday before Lent, when Mass was just about to start—it was the Mass of *Esto mihi*[77]—you gave me to understand that you were being tortured and persecuted in various ways and that this Introit was a direct appeal to me, and was a request for a home in my heart in which to rest. And during the next three days, each time I entered into my interior, I seemed to find you resting, like a poor weak invalid, reclining on my breast. And during those three days I could find no more fitting way of caring for you than by prayer, silence, and other mortifications, for your honor and for the conversion of worldly people.

Chapter 15. The Recompense of Grace

In your love for me you enlightened my understanding once more. Several times you revealed to me how a soul dwelling in a frail human body is darkened and is like a person standing in the middle of a small room, enveloped on all sides as if by a cloud emanating from walls, ceiling, and floor, such as that given off by a boiling pot.[78] Again, when the body is afflicted and touched by suffering, it is as though the soul were bathed in air and sunlight, which comes to it through the suffering member, and this imparts to it a marvelous clarity. The more intense the pain, or the more general the suffering, the more the soul is purified and clarified. This is especially true of afflictions and trials of the heart. When these are borne with humility, patience, and other virtues, they lend a wonderful luster to the soul, the nearer, the more effectively, and the closer they touch it. But it is works of charity above all that cause it to shine with a pure brilliance.

Thanks be to you, lover of humankind, for attracting me so often to the virtue of patience. But alas, a thousand times alas, how seldom have I consented to practice this virtue, or rather, I have never practiced it as I ought. You know, O Lord, how my spirit grieves, confused and downcast, and how my heart desires and longs (Ps. 37:10) that you may be compensated in some other way for my defects.

Again, while I was assisting at a Mass at which I was going to communion, you were gratifying me with such lavish indulgence that I tried in my turn to find out how to respond, at least a little, to this gracious condescension. Wisest of teachers, you suggested to me the words of the Apostle: "For I wished to be anathema from Christ for my brethren" (cf. Rom. 9:3). You had already taught me that the soul resides in the heart, but now you showed me that it dwells in the brain as well. I may say that I have since found proof of this in the Scriptures, although I did not know it before. And you said it was a great thing when a soul renounced for your sake the sweetness which the heart enjoys, watching over the senses of the body and performing charitable works for the good of others.

Chapter 16. The Gracious Showings on the Feast of the Birth of Our Lord and on the Feast of the Purification of the Blessed Virgin Mary

On the day of your most holy nativity, I took you out of your crib, a tender Babe, wrapped in swaddling clothes. I pressed you to my heart where I gathered up into a bundle of myrrh lying between my breasts (Song 1:12,13) all the bitterness of your childish needs and, like a grape of divine sweetness, it was squeezed and offered to quench the thirst of the most intimate longings of my soul. And as I was thinking that I could never have a greater gift, you, who often add a subsequent and even nobler gift to the preceding one, in the overflowing of your saving grace deigned to give me a different kind of gift, as I shall relate.

The following year, in fact, on the same feast-day, during the Mass *Dominus dixit*,[79] I received you from the womb of your virginal mother as a most tender and delicate little newborn Babe, and held you for a moment, clasped to my breast. In doing this, it seemed to me that there was mingled with my feeling some of the compassion I had felt in praying, before the feast, for a certain afflicted soul. But I must confess, alas, that I cared for this gift with less than due fervor and devotion. But whether this was owing to your justice or to my negligence, I do not know. All the same, I believe that your justice tempered with your mercy was disposing everything in order that I might see my own unworthiness more clearly, and therefore I fear that it happened through my negligence in allowing myself to be distracted by idle thoughts. But whatever the cause, do you, Lord my God, answer for me (Is. 38:14).

However, making some effort to recollect myself, so as to warm you gently with my loving caresses, I seemed to be making little progress until I started to pray for sinners, for souls in purgatory, and for other afflicted souls. I soon felt the effects of my prayer, particularly one evening when I proposed to pray for all souls. While, up to that time, I had always preferred to begin by praying for my parents, with the Collect: "Almighty eternal God, who commanded us to honor our father and mother . . .",[80] now, instead, I began by praying for your special friends with the Collect: "Almighty eternal God, who art never invoked without hope of mercy . . ."; and I saw that in this I pleased you better.[81]

Moreover, I could see that you were sweetly affected when I began to chant in Choir, exerting all my powers to sing and fixing my attention on you at each note, like a singer who has not yet learned the melody and follows it carefully in the book. How often have I been careless in these things and in others which I knew were to be done in your praise! I confess to you, kindest Father, uniting myself with the bitter passion of your most innocent son, Jesus Christ, in whom you said you were well pleased: "This is my beloved Son, in whom I am well pleased" (Matt. 3:17; 17:5). It is through him that I shall amend, through him that reparation will be made for all my negligences.

Then, on the day of the most holy Purification, while the procession was taking place in which you, our Savior and Redeemer, chose to be carried to the Temple with the sacrificial victims, while they were chanting the antiphon *Cum inducerent*,[82] your virginal mother asked me to give you back to her, you, the lovely little child of her womb. Her face wore a severe expression, as thought she were not pleased with the way I was looking after you, the pride and joy of her immaculate virginity.[83] And, remembering that it was because of the grace she found with you that she was given for the reconciliation of sinners and to be the hope of the hopeless, I exclaimed in these words: "O Mother of Love, was it not for this that the Source of Mercy was given you as your son, so that through you all the needy might obtain grace, and that you might cover with your copious charity the multitude of our sins and defects (cf. 1 Pet. 4:8)?" At that her face assumed an expression of serene benignity. She seemed to be appeased, showing me that, although I had deserved her apparent sternness because of my wickedness, she was in reality entirely filled with loving kindness, being penetrated to the very marrow with the sweetness of divine charity. Her face soon lighted up at my poor words, which had dispelled all appearance of severity and brought back the serene sweetness which was inherent in her nature. May your Mother, with her unfailing love, be my gracious advocate with you for all my defects!

After that there was no restraining the excess of your sweetness. This became clearer than day when, the following year on this same holy feast, you favored me with a gift not unlike the preceding one, but greater, as though I had earned it by the fervor of my devotion to you. Actually, however, I had not merited this subsequent gift, but a just punishment for having lost the first one. During the reading of the gospel, then, at the words "She brought forth her first-born son" (Lk. 2:7), your immaculate mother with hands undefiled held you out to me, you, the son of her virginal womb, a darling little child who made every effort to embrace me. And as I, so unworthy of holding you, was allowed to take you from her, a tiny child, you clasped my neck with your frail little arms. The sweet-smelling breath of your Spirit exhaled by your sacred mouth was for me as life-giving as it was refreshing to my senses. From henceforth, let my soul bless you for ever, O Lord my God, and all that is within me praise your holy name! (Ps. 102:1)

And as your blessed mother was preparing to wrap you in the swaddling bands of infancy, I asked to be swaddled with you, so as not to be separated, even by a linen cloth,[84] from him whose embraces and kisses are sweeter by far than a cup of honey. And I saw that you had been wrapped in the white linen of innocence and bound with the golden bands of charity; and that if I desired to be wrapped and bound with you, I should have to labor after purity of heart and works of love.

Thanks be to you, Creator of the stars![85] You arrayed the luminaries of the starry skies, and you adorn the earth in spring with flowers of every hue; you have no need of my goods (Ps. 15:2). But afterward, for my instruction, on the feast of the holy Purification, you asked me to clothe you, a dear little infant, before you were carried into the temple. An inspiration from the hidden treasures of your grace showed me how to do this. With all the diligence of which I was capable, I was to try to extol the immaculate innocence of your most pure humanity with such an entire and faithful devotion that if I in my own person might have anything to glory in (cf. 2 Cor. 12:5; Jn. 8:54), I might freely give it up on behalf of your most gracious innocence, so that in your innocence you might be given more praise. Whence, from these intentions of mine, I saw that you, whose infinite power calls those things that are not, as those that are (Rom.

117

4:17), were clad in a white robe in the form of a darling little babe. Pursuing these thoughts with devotion, as I was thinking about your profound humility, it seemed to me that you had put on a green tunic as well, a symbol of your grace which is never dried up but always flourishing and green in the lowly valley of humility. Afterward, while I was reflecting on the incentive which always sets in motion all your actions, you had put on a purple mantle, to show that this truly royal garment is the garment of charity, without which no one may enter the kingdom of heaven (cf. Matt. 22). And then, as I was venerating as well as I could these same virtues in your glorious mother, I saw that she was wearing similar garments. May this blessed Virgin, rose without a thorn,[86] immaculate white lily, in whom there flourishes an abundance of every virtue, enrich our poverty; may she be for us, we pray, a perpetual intercessor.[87]

Chapter 17. Divine Forbearance

One day after washing my hands I was waiting with the community in the cloisters before going into the refectory,[88] when I noticed the brightness of the sun, shining at the height of its noontide strength. Marveling, I said to myself: "If the Lord who created the sun, the Lord of whom it is said that the sun and the moon admire his beauty,[89] and who is himself a consuming fire (Deut. 4:24; Heb. 12:29), is really united with my soul in the way in which he so often reveals himself to me, how is it that I can treat my fellows so coldly, so discourteously and even wickedly?" And suddenly you, whose speech is always sweet (Song 4:3), but was then the sweeter the more my vacillating heart had need of it, led me to infer this saying: "How would my infinite power be extolled if I did not reserve to myself the power, in whatever place I might be, of keeping myself to myself, so that I might make myself felt or seen only in the way that is most fitting according to places, times, and persons? For from the beginning of the creation of heaven and earth, and in the whole work of the Redemption, I have employed wisdom and goodness rather than power and majesty. And the goodness of this wisdom shines forth best in my bearing with imperfect creatures till I draw them, of their own free will, into the way of perfection."

Chapter 18. Fatherly Instruction

On a certain feast-day, as I saw several people who had asked for my prayers approaching holy communion while I, for my part, was prevented by bodily infirmity from partaking of the sacrament—or rather, as I fear, repulsed by God as unworthy of it—I passed over in my mind all your many benefits, Lord God, and I began to fear that the wind of vainglory would dry up the stream of divine grace, and I desired to understand how to guard myself against this in the future. In your fatherly love you told me that I should regard your affection for me like that of a father who takes pleasure in hearing his large family of children complimented by retainers and friends for their elegance and grace. This father has a small child also, who has not yet attained to the elegance and perfection of the others, but for whom he feels a compassionate tenderness, pressing him more often to his breast, fondling and caressing him with more endearing words and little gifts than he gives to the others. You added that if I really believed that I was the least and most imperfect of all, then a torrent of your honey-sweet divinity (Ps. 35:9) would always continue to flow into my soul.

I thank you, O most loving God, lover of humankind, through the mutual gratitude of the Persons of the adorable Trinity,[90] for this lesson and for many others through which you, best of teachers, have so often enlightened my ignorance. I unite my regrets with the bitterness of the passion of Jesus Christ, offering his sufferings and his tears for all the grievous negligences which have stifled in me the sweet breath of your Spirit (Wisd. 12:1). And I implore you in union with the efficacious prayer of your beloved Son, in the virtue of the Holy Spirit, to amend my faults and supply for all my sins and defects. Graciously deign to hear me through the same love which restrained your wrath when your most dearly beloved only Son, who gave you such pleasure in your fatherhood, was reputed with the wicked (Is. 53:12).

Chapter 19. Praise of the Divine Graciousness

I give you thanks, most loving God, for your kind mercy and for your merciful kindness and for revealing to me the proof of your most gracious tenderness, confirming my irresolute and vacillating soul, when, according to my custom, I was imploring you with importunate longing to deliver me from the prison of this miserable flesh (Rom.

7:24). This was assuredly not in order to be rid of the miseries of this world, but to free you from the debt of grace which, in your irresistible love of your own divinity, you have contracted for the salvation of my soul. Not that you, Divine Omnipotence and Eternal Wisdom, gave unwillingly, as though compelled by some sort of necessity, but rather that you freely bestowed your love, out of the boundless flood of your loving generosity, upon an unworthy and ungrateful creature. You, the splendor and crown of celestial glory (cf. Wisd. 18:14; 1 Thess. 2: 19,20), seemed to be descending, softly and gently, from the royal throne of your majesty; and through this condescension there flows across the heavens such a flood of sweetness that all the saints, bowing down in gladness, quench their thirst with joy (cf. Is. 12:3) at the torrents of pleasure (Ps. 35:9), waters sweet as nectar, breaking into melodious songs of praise of the divine glory. Meantime, I heard you say: "Consider how harmoniously these desirable praises strike the ears of my majesty, reaching the most intimate recesses of my loving heart, causing it to melt. Cease, then, to desire so importunately to die and to be dissolved (Phil. 1:23), even though you desire it in order not to continue to be, in the flesh, such a person as you are, upon whom I now lavish the free gift of my love; for the more unworthy the one to whom I incline, the greater will be the reverence with which I shall be justly extolled by all creatures."

I was given this consolation just as I was approaching your life-giving sacrament, and, as I had my attention directed toward it, as was but right, to what had been revealed to me you added this thought: That all people should approach the most holy communion of your body and blood in this way and with this intention: that through love of this sacrament they should make so little of the love of the glory which comes from you that they would be willing—if such a thing were possible—to eat utter damnation to themselves (1 Cor. 11:29) provided that thereby the divine goodness might shine out more clearly, in that it did not refuse to communicate itself to one so unworthy. At this, however, I protested, in order to excuse anyone who, thinking himself unworthy, abstains from communion, saying that he does so for fear of committing some irreverence through presumption to this august sacrament. I received your blessed response in these words: "With such dispositions it is not possible for anyone to approach unworthily." For such words, may praise and glory be given you for ever and ever.

Chapter 20. Special Graces

May my heart and soul with all my fleshly being and all the powers and senses of my body and spirit, together with the whole of creation, give praise and thanks to you, sweetest Lord, most faithful Lover of man's salvation,[91] for the loving kindness of your mercy, which could not have succeeded in hiding from your love the fact that over and over again I was not afraid to approach the most excellent banquet of your sacred body and blood without due preparation, had not the ineffable abyss of your generosity toward me, the most worthless and useless of your instruments, deigned to grant me, in addition to all your other gifts, the following. That is, that through your grace, I learned with certainty that if anyone desires to approach your sacrament, but having a timid conscience is kept back by fear, and is led to seek comfort with me, the least of your servants, you will, in your overflowing love, reward this humility of his by judging him worthy of the sacrament. When he then receives it, it will bear fruit for him for his eternal salvation. You added that you would not grant to those whom you in your justice deemed unworthy of frequenting this sacrament the humility to seek counsel with me.

O my supreme Lord and Master, you who inhabit the heavens and look down on our lowliness (Ps. 112: 5,6), what were your merciful designs when you saw me so often approaching your sacrament unworthily and meriting in this your just condemnation?[92] As you wish to make others worthy by the virtue of humility—although the same result might have been obtained better without me—you had mercy on my great poverty and decreed in your goodness to do it through me, that at least in this manner I might share in the merits of those who have obtained the fruits of salvation through my advice.

But, alas, my misery needs more than one remedy, and your pity, kindest Lord, would by no means be satisfied with only one such remedy. Therefore you have given me, utterly unworthy as I am, the assurance that if anyone comes with a contrite and humble heart[93] to consult me about some fault, then you, merciful God, would judge him to be more or less guilty or innocent according to what he heard me pronounce to be the degree of gravity of his fault;[94] and that afterward, through your grace, he would be strengthened and fortified, so that the fault would no longer weigh on him as perilously as before. In this way you relieved my own miserable poverty also—I, who have been so negligent all the days of my life that, alas, I have never known how to overcome the least fault in the right way—by giving me a share in the victory of others. In this, my good God, you have graciously made use of me, the most worthless of your instruments. Through my poor words, I have been the means of giving the grace of victory to other and worthier friends of yours.

Third, the abundant liberality of your grace has enriched the poverty of my merits with the assurance that if, confident in your loving kindness, I were to promise any benefit or the pardon of any fault, in your gracious love, you would respect my words as faithfully as if they had been spoken and solemnly promised by your blessed lips. And this is so true that you added that if these souls should find they had to wait longer than they liked for the answer to their prayers, they should resolutely remind you of the promise that I had made them in your name. And so once again you were providing for my salvation, in the words of the gospel: "For with the same measure that you shall mete withal it shall be measured to you again" (Lk. 6:38). Thus, although I, alas, never stop falling into so many grave sins, at least you would have occasion to judge my sins more leniently.

You added yet a fourth necessary benefit, assuring me among other things that anyone who commended himself humbly and devoutly to my prayers would undoubtedly obtain all the fruit that he might hope to obtain through the prayers of any other person. In this, too, you are mindful of my carelessness, in being so negligent in discharging my duty of praying for the church, whether by prayers of obligation, or those which I freely chose (and through which I could, after all, gain something for myself, as it is written: "And thy prayer shall return into thy bosom" (cf. Ps. 34:13).) Thus you have granted me a share in the fruits of your elect whom you have given benefits through my unworthy intercession; in order in this way to make up for some of my deficiencies.

Even then you did not cease to promote the work of my salvation; but you found yet a fifth way, by giving me this special gift: that no one who came with a right intention and humble trust to consult me about his spiritual welfare should go away without some edification or spiritual consolation. You saw what a suitable way this was of providing for my needs. The talent of eloquence, which you have entrusted to me in your goodness, unworthy as I am, is so often wasted and flows away in useless words; alas, I scatter them on the ground, as it were;

but at least some spiritual profit may accrue to me from someone else's gain.

The sixth of your generous gifts, kindest Lord, is one more necessary to me than any other. You gave me the assurance that anyone who would have the charity to pray faithfully for me, the most worthless of God's creatures, for the amendment of the sins and ignorance of my youth (Ps. 24:7)—indeed, my malice and wickedness—whether by reciting prayers or by doing good works, would receive as a reward of your generous love the assurance that he would not leave this world without being given such grace that his conduct would be so pleasing to you that you would have the joy of a specially close friendship with his soul. In this you show your fatherly love and my dire necessity. You know how much, and in how many ways, I need to amend my innumerable faults and negligences.[95] In your merciful love, you do not want me to perish. On the other hand, in your admirable justice, you could not allow me to be saved with so many imperfections. At least you have provided for me that, by my sharing in the gain of many, the share of each might increase.

In your extravagant generosity, kindest Lord, you added that if anyone knowing of the familiar companionship with which you have treated me, in my nothingness, during my lifetime, should humbly commend himself to my unworthy intercession after my death, you would without doubt deign to hear him as readily as you would ever grant the desire of anyone through the intercession of any other person; if, in reparation for his past negligence, he offer you thanks with humble devotion, especially for five graces:

The first is the love with which, in your merciful kindness, you chose me from all eternity.[96] I can truthfully say that this is of all graces the most freely given. For you could not have been ignorant of how perverse my conduct would be, nor of all the details of my malice and wickedness and the baseness of my ingratitude. You might justly have denied me the honor due to human reason, even among pagans, but in your love which so greatly exceeds our misery[97] you have chosen to confer on me, of all Christians, the dignity of being consecrated a religious.

The second is that you have drawn me to yourself for my salvation. And I am bound to confess that I owe this to the gentleness and goodness of your nature. You have won this rebellious heart (cf. Ez. 2:4) of mine (which in all justice deserves to be bound in iron chains), drawing it to yourself by your sweet caresses, as though you found in me a fit consort for your gentleness, and were quite delighted by your union with me.

The third is that you have so intimately united yourself with me. And this I can but attribute to your overflowing, immense, and boundless generosity. As though the number of the just were not sufficiently great to occupy your great love, you have called me, the least deserving of all, not in order to justify more easily the most suitable, but so that the miracle of your condescension might be reflected with greater brilliance in the least suitable.

Fourth, that you should take pleasure in this union. This I can only ascribe to the folly of your love, if I may dare to speak in this way. As you have yourself asserted, you find your happiness in some incredible way in uniting your infinite wisdom with a being so unlike you and so unfitted for such a union.

Fifth, you are leading me graciously toward a blessed end. I humbly and firmly believe that I shall receive this gift from you, in the sweet kindness of your beneficent love, according to your faithful promise and despite my great unworthiness; and I embrace it with unshakable love and gratitude. It is not through any merit of mine, but solely through the free gift of your mercy, O my all, my supreme, my only true, eternal Good![98]

All these gifts are the effect of such astonishing condescension on your part and are so little in keeping with my misery that no thanksgiving of mine could ever be enough. Here, too, you have graciously deigned to come to my assistance, in my poverty, through the promises you have made to other souls whose thanksgiving may make good my deficiency. May praise and thanks be given to you by everything that is in heaven and earth and under the earth (cf. Phil. 2:10)!

As well as giving me all these gifts, Lord, in your inestimable love you graciously deigned to confirm them all by a pact. One day, as I was turning all these things over in my mind, rejoicing to see that your love so much outstripped my wickedness (cf. Rom. 5:20), I was led to the presumption of reproaching you with not having sealed this pact in the customary way, by clasping hands. With your infinitely compliant sweetness, you promised to satisfy me, saying: "Cease these reproaches and come and receive the confirmation of my pact." And immediately (in my nothingness) I saw you opening with both hands the wound of your deified heart, the Tabernacle of divine faithfulness and infallible truth, and commanding me (perverse, like the Jews asking for a sign

[Matt. 12:38]) to stretch forth my right hand. Then, contracting the aperture of the wound in which my hand was enclosed, you said: "See, I promise to keep intact the gifts which I have given you. And if it happens that at times, in the wise disposition of my providence, I deprive you of their effects, I oblige myself to give you afterward threefold gain, in the name of the Omnipotence, Wisdom, and Goodness of the sovereign Trinity, in which I live and reign, true God, for ever and ever."

After these words of sweetest love, when I withdrew my hand, there appeared on it seven circles of gold, like seven rings, one on each finger and on the ring finger three, in faithful testimony of the seven privileges for the confirmation of which I had asked. In the exuberance of your love you added these words: "Whenever, mindful of your misery and knowing yourself to be unworthy of my gifts, you abandon yourself trustfully to my goodness, by so doing you will be offering me payment of the tribute which is due on the goods which are mine."

Oh, with what ingenuity your fatherly love cares for the needs of your children who have fallen into the greatest degradation![99] After the goods of innocence have been squandered, and as a consequence, the grace of devotion to you, you graciously accept what I cannot conceal, the recognition of my own unworthiness!

Grant that I may recognize this in all your gifts, both interior and exterior, for your glory and for my salvation, and also that in everything I may have perfect confidence in your love, Giver of gifts, from whom all good things proceed,[100] without whom nothing is reliable, nothing good![101]

Chapter 21. Effect of the Divine Vision

As I considered all the beneficence of your loving mercy which you have freely shown toward me, and my own great unworthiness, I decided that it would be wholly unjust to pass over in silence, as if I were not grateful for it, the grace which I received from you one Lent in the wonderful condescension of your great friendship and love.

On the second Sunday in Lent, before Mass, as the procession was about to start and they were singing the Response, "I saw the Lord face to face,"[102] my soul was suddenly illuminated by a flash of indescribable and marvelous brightness. In the light of this divine revelation there appeared to me a Face as though close to my face, as Bernard says: "Unformed but forming everything, it touches not the eye of the body but rejoices the face of the heart, and charms not by any visible color but with the radiance of love."[103] In this sweetest vision in which your eyes, shining like the sun,[104] seemed to be gazing straight into mine, how you, my dearest and sweetest, touched not only my soul but my heart and every limb, is known to you alone and as long as I live I shall be your devoted slave.

Although a rose in spring, when it is fresh, blooming, and fragrant, is more pleasing by far than one found in winter when, long since withered, its sweet scent is evoked in words, yet the latter can to some extent revive the memory of former loveliness.[105] And so I want, if I can, in my nothingness, to find some similitude to describe what I felt in that most blissful vision of you, in praise of your love. Then perhaps some reader, having received a similar or even a greater grace, may be reminded to give thanks. And I myself, by often recalling it, may disperse somewhat the darkness of my negligences through the rays of my gratitude reflected in this mirror.

When you showed me your most longed-for face,[106] full of blessedness, as I have just said, so close to mine (though I am so undeserving), I felt as though an ineffable light from your divine eyes[107] were entering through my eyes, softly penetrating,[108] passing through all my interior being, in a way beyond measure wonderful, working with marvelous power in every limb. At first it was as though my bones were being emptied of all the marrow, then even the bones with the flesh were dissolved so that nothing was felt to exist in all my substance save that divine splendor which, in a manner more delectable than I am able to say, playing within itself, showed my soul the inestimable bliss of utter serenity (cf. Wisd. 7:22, 23–26).

Oh, what more shall I say of this? Shall I say again that it was a most sweet vision? Because to tell the truth, it seems to me that no one, even possessing the eloquence of every tongue, were that person to try all the days of my life, no one could ever have convinced me of the possibility of seeing you in so sublime a way, even in the glory of heaven, had not you, my God, only salvation of my soul (cf. Ps. 34:3), deigned to lead me to experience it for myself.[109]

And yet I add with joy that, if things are with God as they are with humankind, no doubt the power of your gaze[110] surpasses this vision by far, so that I truly believe that, unless the vision were mitigated by divine power, a soul on whom this favor were conferred, even for an instant, would by no means be permitted to remain in the body.

Although I know that in the inscrutable, infinite power of your bound-less love[111] in showing such visions, embraces, kisses, and other mani-festations of love, you always adapt them without the least incongruity to suit places, times, and persons, as I have myself frequently experi-enced; because (and I thank you for it, uniting myself with the mutual love of the ever adorable Trinity) I have often experienced the favor of your infinitely sweet kiss. Seated in profound meditation, lost in con-templation of yourself, during the Office or vigils of the dead, often ten times or more during the course of one psalm, you have placed the sweetest kiss upon my lips, a kiss far surpassing every fragrance or honeyed drink. On many occasions I have noticed your look of tender love and felt in my soul your close embrace. I must say, however, that in spite of the wonderful sweetness of these caresses, in none of them did I feel the same effect as in that all-excelling look of love of which I have just been speaking. For this and for all the other graces known to you alone, may you be offered that dew of sweetness, a sweetness transcending every sense, which is most joyously distilled from Person to Person in the heavenly storeroom of the divinity.

Chapter 22. Thanksgiving for a Certain Great but Secret Gift

May a similar thanksgiving, or a greater, if possible, be given you for an all-excelling gift, known to you alone. Its greatness prevents me from expressing it in words, and yet it will not allow me to pass over it in silence; so that if human frailty should somehow, most unjustly, allow it to fade from my memory—which God forbid—I shall at least be recalled to remembrance and thanksgiving by what I have written here. But in your loving kindness, my God, may you entirely avert such perverse folly from me, your most unworthy creature! May you never permit me voluntarily to withdraw my gratitude, even for the twinkling of an eye, from the free gift of your presence, in which I rejoice exceedingly. I accepted this free gift freely of your boundless liberality and I have preserved it for so many years without any merit of my own. For, although I know that I am the least worthy of all, I acknowledge that I have received in this gift more than anything any-one could merit for himself in this life. I therefore expect of your sweet love that, having bestowed this entirely undeserved gift freely upon me, who am no more than refuse (1 Cor. 4:13), with the same gracious condescension you will keep it for me, for your glory, and make it effective in its action on myself. For this, may you receive infinite praise from all your creatures. Because the more my unworthiness shall appear, the more brightly will shine the glory of your kindest love.

Chapter 23. Thanksgiving

with an exposition of various benefits, which she was accustomed to read, with the prayers which precede and follow, with great devotion and, as far as possible, at set times

May my soul bless you (Ps. 102:1), Lord God my creator! May my soul bless you and, out of the very marrow of my inmost being, let me proclaim the mercies of the overflowing love with which you enfold me, O my sweetest lover!

I thank you as best I can for your great mercy, and I praise and glorify the long-suffering patience which has led you to overlook all the years of my infancy and childhood, my girlhood and youth. Almost up to the end of my twenty-fifth year, in fact,[112] in my blindness and stupidity it seems to me that I would have felt no remorse in following my instincts in all places and in everything—thoughts, words, and deeds—had you not prevented me from doing so, both by giving me an inborn loathing of evil and delight in well-doing, and by the correction and guidance of other people. And so I should have lived, like a pagan among pagans,[113] without ever realizing that you, my God, reward good and punish evil. And yet, from infancy, in my fifth year to be precise, you chose me to be formed among the most faithful of your friends, to live in the household[114] of your holy religion.

Your blessedness, my God, cannot change, neither can it be increased or diminished, and you have no need of our goods (Ps. 15:2). Yet the guilt and negligence of my life could be blamed as being detrimental to the flow of ceaseless praise which ought to ascend to you from myself and from every creature without a single moment's interruption. What I feel, or could feel about this in my heart, profoundly moved to the depths of my being by your gracious condescension, is known to you alone.

Prompted by these feelings, I offer you for the amendment of my sins, most loving Father, the passion and all the sufferings of your dearly beloved Son, from the hour when he was lying in the manger on

the hay, uttering his first childish cries, and afterward in all the needs
of infancy, his childhood's weakness, the trials of his adolescence, and
the sufferings of his youth, until the hour when he bowed his head on
the cross and with a loud cry gave up the ghost. In the same way, to
compensate for all my negligences I offer you the holy life of your
only-begotten Son, perfect in all his thoughts, words, and deeds, from
the hour when he was sent from his heavenly throne and entered by
the ear of a Virgin into our earthly regions[115] until the hour when he
presented to your fatherly eyes the triumphant glory of his victorious
humanity.[116]

And since it is right that the loving hearts of your friends should
sympathize with you in all adversities, I pray, through your only-
begotten Son, in the power of the Holy Spirit, that those who, at my
instigation, or led in some other way, should of their own accord—in
your praise—want to make good my defects, even by a single sigh or
by some other trivial act, during my life or after my death, would have
you receive their offering of the passion and Life of your beloved Son
in reparation and for the amendment of all their sins and negligences. I
pray that this desire of mine may be always before you, unchanged,
until the end of the world, even after you have called me, in your
mercy, to reign with you in heaven.

Again, I give you thanks, plunging myself into the profoundest
abyss of humility. I praise and adore at the same time the supreme
excellence of your mercy together with the sweetest goodness by
which, Father of mercies (2 Cor. 1:3), while I was still leading my life
of perdition you were thinking of me, thoughts of peace and not of
affliction (Jer. 29:11). You were lifting me up by the multitude and
magnitude of your gifts, as though I were better than any other mortal
and my life on earth had been one of angelic innocence.[117]

I began to feel the effects of this benevolence in the Advent preceding my twenty-fifth birthday, which took place on the following Epiphany. My heart began then to be agitated by some sort of trouble which
gave me a great distaste for all the pursuits of my youth. This was the
way you were preparing me to receive you in my heart. My twenty-
sixth year, then, had already begun when, on the Monday before the
feast of the Purification,[118] after Compline, as dusk was falling, in the
night of the trouble I have mentioned, you, the true light (Jn. 1:9)
shining in darkness (Jn. 1:5), put an end also to the day of my girlish
vanity, obscured and darkened by my spiritual ignorance. For in that
hour, with manifest and marvelous condescension, and in a most de-

lightful way, you approached me. With the greatest friendliness you reconciled me with yourself, making your presence known to me and teaching me to know something of your love; leading me to enter into my interior which before that time was quite unknown to me. Then you began to deal with me in a marvelous and secret way. Like a friend in the house of a friend, or rather, like a spouse with his bride, you would always take pleasure with my soul.

In this loving commerce you visited me at different times in diverse ways, but one time especially is impressed on my memory. This was on the vigil of the holy Annunciation, as well as one day before the Ascension, when I felt your presence beginning to grow more loving in the morning and becoming perfect in the evening, after Compline. And you have accorded me this grace, worthy of the reverence and astonishment of all creatures, continually from that day until the present time, so that not even for the twinkling of an eye could I feel or know that you were absent from my heart. For whenever I entered into my interior, you were always there, except once for eleven days.[119] I can find no words to express the incomparable magnificence and the multitude of the good things with which you have endeared yourself to me, and thereby made your saving presence ever more desirable to me. Give me, Giver of gifts, the grace to offer you from now onward, in the spirit of humility, a joyful sacrifice, in gratitude in particular for having prepared in my heart such a delectable dwelling-place, entirely satisfying to you and to me. All that I have read or heard about the temple of Solomon or the palace of Ahasuerus[120] could not be compared, I think, with the delights you have prepared for yourself in my heart, as I know by your grace. These, in spite of my unworthiness, you have given me the grace to share with you on equal terms, like a queen with the king.

Among these favors there are two which I will mention in particular. They are the seal put on my heart (cf. Wisd. 9:10) with those brilliant jewels which are your salvific wounds, and the wound of love with which you so manifestly and efficaciously transfixed my heart. Had you given me no other consolation, interior or exterior, these two gifts alone would have held so much happiness that, were I to live a thousand years, I could never exhaust the fund of consolation, learning, and feelings of gratitude that I should derive from them at each hour.

In addition to all these favors, you have granted me the priceless gift of your familiar friendship, giving me in various ways, to my indescribable delight, the noblest treasure of the divinity, your divine

130

heart, now bestowing it freely, now as a sign of our mutual familiarity, exchanging it with mine. How often have you revealed to me your secret counsels and your pleasures, melting my soul with your loving caresses! Did I not know the abyss of your overflowing goodness, I wonder whether I could understand how you show such tokens as these marks of your lavish affection even on the creature of all others most worthy of them, your blessed Mother who reigns with you in heaven.

Sometimes you have led me to a salutary recognition of my faults, and you were as careful then to spare my blushes, as if—would it be wrong to say so?—it would be like losing half your kingdom were you to provoke my childish shame, even a little. Also, by an ingenious device you showed me in others the faults which were displeasing to you. Rounding on myself, I found that I was even more guilty of the same faults than those other persons whom you had pointed out to me. But you never gave me the least indication that you found in me any trace of these defects.

You enticed my soul with your faithful promises, showing me the benefits you were ready to confer on me at death and after my death, so that, had I never had any other gifts from you, for this hope alone my soul would never cease to desire you with ardor. And still the ocean of your boundless love is not exhausted. For you constantly grant my prayers, whether for sinners, for souls, or for other intentions, answering them with incredible benefits. I have never found a human friend to whom I would dare to tell all I know; the human heart is too small to bear it.

To all these other benefits you have added a crowning one in giving me your dearest mother, the most blessed Virgin Mary, to take care of me, commending me to her affection as often as a bridegroom commends his dearly beloved bride to his own mother.

Still more, you have often sent the noblest princes of your court on special missions to me. These princes were chosen not only from among the choirs of angels and archangels, but from even higher orders also, according as your love, God of all goodness, judged more fitting for me, to lead me in my spiritual exercises in a way which suited their several natures. But if, however, in your plan for my salvation, you partially withdrew at times the taste of delectation from your gifts, I, most ignoble in my base ingratitude, forgot them at once, and treated them as if they were of no value. If, after a time, touched by your grace, I came to myself again and asked you to give me back what I had

131

lost, or any other gift, in that moment you restored it to me perfectly, as though I had entrusted it to you myself, placing it in your bosom with the greatest care for safekeeping.

More than all these favors and in a marvelous way, much to be preferred to all others, several times, particularly on the feast of the holy Nativity, and one Sunday (it was the Sunday of *Esto mihi*) and another Sunday after Pentecost, I was introduced by you—rapt, rather—into so close a union with yourself that it seems more than miraculous that, after such hours of ecstasy, I could still live as a mortal among mortals. What is really amazing, horrible rather, is that I have not amended my faults as it was just and right that I should do.

But none of this could dry up the fount of your mercy, O Jesus, most loving of all lovers, the only one whose love is sincere, free, and lavished on the undeserving.

Now, as time passed, most wretched, unworthy, and ungrateful of creatures that I am, I began to lose the taste for these graces which should make heaven and earth continually dance for joy, rejoicing that you, from your infinite height, should graciously descend to my extreme lowness;[121] you, O Giver, Renewer, and Preserver of all good things,[122] aroused me from my torpor and revived my gratitude. And this you did by revealing the secret of your gifts to several persons whom I knew to be particularly faithful friends of yours. I am perfectly certain that they could have had it from no human source, for I revealed it to no one. And yet I heard it from their lips in words which I recognized secretly in my heart.

With these words and all the others which now crowd into my mind, I want to render that which is your due. With the sweetly melodious harp of your divine heart, through the power of the Holy Spirit, the Paraclete, I sing to you, Lord God, adorable Father, songs of praise and thanksgiving on behalf of all creatures in heaven, on earth, and under the earth (Phil. 2:10); all which are, were, and shall be.[123]

As gold gleams more brightly when it is contrasted with other colors, and the greatest contrast is with black, because that is the color that least resembles gold, so it is with me. For the blackness of my ungrateful life contrasts with the divine splendor of your incomparable benefits to me. Just as you could give me no gifts but the royal ones which appertain to you and are innate to your divine generosity, so I, because of the churlishness of my nature, could receive them only in a wretched, corrupt sort of way, spoiling everything. And this, with your kingly forbearance, you seemed not to notice, for you did not diminish your goodness to me. When you could have been reclining in the heavenly palace of your Father's love, you chose instead a resting place in my poor dwelling, a hovel. And I, a most unworthy, careless, and neglectful hostess, tried so little to please you that I should have cared better out of purely human sentiments for some poor leper who, after having injured and insulted me, had been forced to seek the shelter of my hospitality.

Again, in return for that benefit which you, who clothed the stars, conferred upon me, in your sweet disposition of my inmost being, through the imprint of your most sacred wounds, through the revelations of your secrets, and through showing me your familiar companionship and your loving caresses, in which you gave me the spiritual experience of sweeter delights than I could have found, I believe, in sensuous pleasures were I to travel round the world from East to West—in return for all this, I have been extremely ungrateful and treated you with contumely. Making light of your favors, I sought consolation in exterior things; with exceedingly great irreverence, I preferred onion and garlic to your heavenly manna (cf. Num. 11:5). And I could not even make an act of confidence in your promises, O God of truth,[124] because I lacked trust in you, as though you were a liar who did not keep his word (cf. Ps. 115:11; Rom. 3:4).

Again, in response to the goodness with which you have so kindly listened to my unworthy prayers, alas, how often have I hardened my heart and resisted your will, so much so—with tears be it said—as to pretend not to understand your will, so that I should not have to obey the goad of conscience.

And in response to your goodness in offering me the advocacy of your glorious Mother and all the blessed spirits in my misery, I have often sought the help of earthly friends, frequently placing obstacles in their way by doing so, when I should have relied on you alone. As, with great sweetness, you continued to keep your gifts to me intact, despite my neglect, it was right that thenceforth I should have been more grateful and taken more care to avoid my negligences. And yet, instead, I lived in a tyrannical—even devilish—way. Rendering evil for good, I simply became presumptuous and took no care of my way of life.

Worse than all, my greatest fault is that after such an incredible union with you, known to you alone, I was not afraid to stain my soul once more with defects which you allowed me to keep in order that you might help me to triumph over them, that afterward I might have greater glory in heaven with you. I was not blameless when, in order to stimulate my gratitude, you betrayed my secret to my friends and I omitted to do what you intended, and the happiness I felt was a human sentiment, while I failed to thank you. Most loving one, who knows my heart perfectly, for all these faults and all the other ones which, through them, might enter into my mind, may my sighs and the groanings of my heart (Ps. 37:9) rise to you! Receive the laments which I offer you for the very many infidelities by which I have offended the noble goodness of your divine clemency, with the noble compassion and respect which you have made known to us through your most loving Son in the Holy Spirit, on behalf of all that is in heaven, on earth, and under the earth!

Therefore, as I am quite incapable of producing worthy fruits of true amendment (cf. Lk. 3:8), I entreat you, of your love for me, my sweetest Lover, to inspire those souls whom you know to be faithfully devoted to you, to please and propitiate you with sacrifices so that my poverty, which so much falls short of your great gifts, may be made good by their groans or prayers or good works of all kinds, so that you, Lord God, may be given the praise which is your due!

You see into my heart;[125] you know nothing could have persuaded me to write this but the pure desire of praising your mercy, so that after my death many who read it may be moved with compassion by the great goodness of your mercy. They will consider that, in your solicitude for humanity's salvation, your love has never descended so low as it has done in permitting so many and such great gifts to be held so cheap and to be treated as I have treated them, alas, spoiling everything you gave me.

But I give you thanks as best I can, Lord God, who have created and re-created me, for your merciful clemency and for this assurance you have given me in your inexhaustible love, flowing down from on high. You have told me that anyone, even a sinner, who remembered me with the intention of which I have spoken, for the sake of your glory, either by praying for sinners or by giving thanks for the elect or by doing some good work with devotion, would not end his life in your displeasure or die before you would grant him the special grace of being so pleasing to you that you would enjoy some intimate delight in his heart.

For this grace, may that eternal praise be given you which, flowing forth from uncreated love, flows back continually into yourself![126]

Chapter 24. Epilogue: Commendation of the Writing

See, O most loving Lord, here is the talent (cf. Matt. 25:27ff) of your most gracious intimacy with me, of all creatures the most ignoble and the most unworthy, the talent you entrusted to me; and it is for love of your love and for the increase of your glory that I am disclosing the precious secret in this writing and in those that follow. Because, and of this I am confident, relying on your grace I dare assert it, for no other cause could I have been induced to speak of such things, were it not according to your will with the desire for your glory and zeal for souls. You are the witness, therefore, to my sincere desire to praise you and to thank you for not withdrawing your overflowing love from my unworthiness. And in this I desire your praise that others reading these pages may rejoice in your sweet love and may be led to experience it in themselves.

Just as students attain to logic by way of the alphabet, so, by means of these painted pictures, as it were, they may be led to taste within themselves that hidden manna (Rev. 2:17), which it is not possible to adulterate by any admixture of material images and of which one must have eaten to hunger for it for ever.

Deign, almighty and most generous God of all goodness, to give us a sufficiency of this nourishment along the way of our exile, until we contemplate the glory of the Face of the Lord, no longer veiled, proceeding from glory to glory, transformed by the breath of your most sweet Spirit (2 Cor. 3:18).

And until then, according to your faithful promise and my humble desire, grant to all who read this writing with humility, joy in your gracious condescension; pity for my unworthiness; and sincere desire for their own perfection; so that from the golden thuribles of their loving hearts such sweet-smelling incense may ascend to you (Rev. 8:4) that through it reparation may be copiously made for all my defects of ingratitude and negligence.

NOTES

1. Title of Book II: *The Memorial of the Abundance of Divine Sweetness.* This is the title given by our Lord himself to St. Gertrude's book. See the Prologue and Prologue, note 3. Although the Douay Version of Psalm 144:7 (of which this title is clearly a reminiscence) reads, "They

shall publish the *memory* of the abundance of thy sweetness," it has been thought best to keep the word *memorial* in the title (cf. Book of Common Prayer: "The memorial of thine abundant kindness shall be showed"). Book II is the only one of the five books of the *Legatus* to have been written by Gertrude in her own hand; it is her spiritual memorial, her autobiography.

2. The first revelation of divine grace was granted to St. Gertrude in the year 1281 (see Bk. II, ch. 1, 2 and 23, and Bk. II, note 3). She began to write her memorial, therefore, in 1289.

3. This reference to Monday, January 27, fixes the event in the year 1281.

4. St. Augustine, *Confessions* 9,1.

5. It is not improbable that Gertrude here intends a reference to the story of the Tower of Babel (Gen. 11).

6. See the *Rule* of St. Benedict, ch. 63. This custom is still in use today. During the daytime the bow is accompanied by the word "Benedicite," but after Compline, during the Great Silence, no word is spoken. Perhaps Gertrude intends to make the connection between her small act of obedience to the *Rule* and of reverence toward her senior, and the beginning of the special graces granted her by the Lord.

7. First Responsory at Matins of the second Sunday of Advent: "*Cito veniet salus tua: quare maerore consumeris? numquid consiliarius non est tibi, quia innovavit te dolor? Salvabo te et liberabo te, noli timere.*" Gertrude quotes this verbatim.

8. The expression here is the traditional one used in the Bible to denote the resistance of the Chosen People to divine guidance: a rebellious and stiff-necked generation.

9. Cf. St. Augustine, *Confessions*, Book IV, ch. 12: "*In ipsum primum virginalem uterum ubi ei nupsit humana creatura*" ("When he first came into that pure Virgin's womb where created manhood was espoused to him . . .").

10. Prologue to the *Rule* of St. Benedict, referring to Is. 58:9.

11. Psalm 20:4. Cf. the Prologue to the *Rule* of St. Benedict, and St. Bernard, *Song* 83,6: "*Felix quae meruit praeveniri in tantae benedictione dulcedinis*" ("Happy the soul whose favored lot is to be prevented with the benedictions of a delight so great").

12. This reference is mysterious. Gertrude seems still to be speaking of the year of her "conversion," 1281. In that year the vigil of the Annunciation was not a Sunday but a Monday; even had it been a Sunday there is no generally accepted monastic custom which would

affect the time of the Chapter normally held after Prime. Perhaps she is speaking of a custom peculiar to Helfta of which the details have not come down to us.

13. This appellation is taken from the Sequence of Pentecost *Veni Sancte Spiritus* by Rhabanus Maurus.

14. The psalms contain many such expressions; perhaps there is also an allusion to St. Benedict's comment (*Rule* of St. Benedict, ch. 5; also cf. 2 Cor. 9:7) that "God loves a cheerful giver."

15. Cf. St. Bernard, *Song* 52,5. He comments: "*Erras, si extra invenire te existimas locum quietis, secretum solitudinis, luminis serenum, habitaculum pacis*" ("You are mistaken if you think you will find outside [your own soul] a place of rest, secluded solitude, unclouded light, the dwelling of peace").

16. Exodus 7:17; also compare the hymn *Pange lingua gloriosi proelium certaminis* of Holy Week (formerly Passiontide): "*Terra, pontus, astra, mundus, quo lavantur flumine*" ("And this flood washes the earth, the sea, the stars, the world").

17. "For nine years": Gertrude began to write her memorial on Maundy Thursday, 1289.

18. As is her custom, St. Gertrude names the whole Mass by the opening words of its Introit (cf. ch. 8 "*Esto mihi*"). "*Ne timeas Zacharia*" ("Fear not, Zachary") are the first words of the Introit of the Vigil Mass of St. John the Baptist. It seems more than likely that the event she relates here took place in the year of her conversion; the vigil of St. John the Baptist in that year (23 June 1281) did indeed fall on a Monday.

19. This text is unidentified; it is not to be found among either the authentic or the apocryphal works of St. Bernard. Probably Gertrude found it in some *florilegium* where it was wrongly attributed.

20. Cf. the closing words of Bk. II, ch. 23, and note *ad loc.*

21. This paragraph has been slightly paraphrased to convey the sense. It is possible that the deliberate contrast between particular and universal, the first applied to works of mercy (action) and the second to the soul's union with God (contemplation) betrays the influence of the Victorines. For while action, and even meditation, direct the soul toward some particular object, contemplation, on the other hand, tends toward the universal: the divinity. Hugh of St. Victor expresses the idea thus (*Hom. I in Ecclesiasten*): "*Et quod meditatio semper circa unum aliquid rimandum occupatur, contemplatio ad multa vel etiam ad universa comprehendenda diffunditur*" ("While meditation always tends to enter into some one single object, contemplation extends itself to embrace

many things, or even all"). This same trend is to be found again among the English mystics of the fourteenth century. In contemplation, one embraces the whole of creation, and more especially (as both Julian of Norwich and the author of the *Cloud* note), the whole of the Mystical Body: this is universality. In good works, whether corporal or spiritual works of mercy—or prayers of concrete petition, or vocal or mental prayer with a specific object—one is always particularizing. Gertrude is not necessarily intending to suggest an antithesis between the two ideas; they are complementary.

22. "The weight of the flesh": There is here an echo of Wisdom 9:15 and also perhaps of Gregory the Great, *Moralia* 5,57: "*etsi hanc spiritus ad summa evehit, caro tamen ipso adhuc corruptionis suae pondere deorsum premit*" ("Even if the spirit raises it [the soul] to the heights, the flesh, by the very weight of its corruptible nature, bears it down again").

23. "Whom no place circumscribes": The Latin is *illocalis*, literally "placeless" or "unlocated." William of St. Thierry uses the corresponding abstract noun *illocalitas*. The translation used here is suggested by St. Augustine, *Confessions* 5,2: "*Ubique sis quem nullus circumscribit locus*" ("You are everywhere, you whom no place circumscribes").

24. Cf. St. Bernard, *Song* 57,8, *rubigine vitiorum* ("the rust of vices").

25. Cf. Thomas Aquinas, *Summa Theologiae*, IIIa, q.66, art.3, ad 3: "*Ex latere Christi fluxit aqua ad abluendum, sanguis autem ad redimendum*" ("From the side of Christ there flowed water for washing and blood for redeeming").

26. Cf., for example, the "occasional prayer" for the king in the old Roman Missal: "*virtutum etiam omnia percipiat incrementa: quibus decenter ornatus . . .*" ("May he receive also an increase of all the virtues; honorably adorned with these . . .").

27. Philippians 4:4–6; the Introit for the third Sunday of Advent, still known as Gaudete Sunday.

28. The notion of the "wound of love" probably has its origin in the Song of Songs 2:5. The Douay has "I languish with love," and most translations have something similar, but the Septuagint and some early Latin translations have "I am wounded by love." This was the translation St. Augustine knew. There is also a connection with the wounding of our Lord's side on the cross, which is called "the wound of love" in Book I, chapter 16. It is a fairly well-documented mystical phenomenon, described by Richard of St. Victor, Ruusbroec, and Walter Hilton among others, but most clearly by St. John of the Cross and St. Teresa of Avila. St. Teresa lists its three main characteristics. First, it is

sudden. It is not preceded by any particular feelings of devotion, and may indeed occur when the soul is not occupied with God at all. We see this in Gertrude's description. The preliminary grace was received when she was meditating on the wound of love, but the wound itself when she was meditating, apparently with no great fervor, on a quite different subject. The second characteristic is the simultaneous penetrating sweetness and unspeakable suffering. Gertrude does not specify the suffering, but it is evident that her health was seriously affected by her mystical experiences, and there is perhaps a suggestion of it in the references to the necessity of bathing, anointing, and bandaging the wound. Finally, there is the absolute certainty that it has occurred; it is impossible to confuse the experience with any other. Gertrude, despite her awareness of her unworthiness, is emphatic on this point. Some make a distinction between the wound of love, properly so called, and transverberation of the heart, which is a higher grace and is not intended so much to purify, as is the wound of love, as to increase the fervor of love. It is usually accompanied by the vision of a seraph with a burning dart, as in the experience of St. Teresa of Avila. However, Gertrude's experience seems to share some of the characteristics of both, and it is not really possible to "diagnose" her case.

29. Gertrude means the right side of the Lord, not the right side of the picture. It is evident from the description in Book I, chapter 16 that the Lord was seen with the wound in his right side, and this is the constant tradition of iconography. It is interesting to note, however, that in that same description it seems that Gertrude's wound would be in the left side. Stigmatics have varied as to the side in which they have received that wound.

30. Wednesday, Ember Day of Advent, when the gospel *"Missus Est"* was read. (It is now read on 20 December.) In monastic usage there is a special devotion to this gospel, the story of the Annunciation.

31. This was probably St. Mechthild, the close friend and confidant of St. Gertrude. She may also be the person mentioned at the beginning of this chapter.

32. Cf. Is. 12:3; Jn. 7:37–8. "And on the last great day of the festivity, Jesus stood and cried saying: 'If any man thirst, let him come to me; and let him drink who believeth in me. As the Scripture saith: Out of his belly shall flow rivers of living water.' Now this he said of the Spirit which they should receive who believed in him." (The punctuation here does not follow that of the Douay. See CTS translation of *Haurietis Aquas*, AAS vol. 48, 1956.)

33. Cf. St. Bernard, *Song* 18,5 *"unguentum devotionis"* ("the healing ointment of devotion").

34. Cf. Bk. III, ch. 32. Everything she used was considered by Gertrude as a gift of God; hence her remorse when through her carelessness she accidentally broke a thread of flax when she was spinning.

35. Antiphons from the Office of the Blessed Trinity. The saint cites only the beginning of the antiphons proper to the Office in use at that time. It is important to consult the full text of these antiphons in the antiphonaries of the time for the complete expression of the prayers which they suggest.

a) *"Te Deum Patrem ingenitum, te Filium unigenitum, te Spiritum Paraclitum, sanctam et individuam Trinitatem, toto corde et ore confitemur, laudamus atque benedicimus; tibi gloria in saecula"* ("Thee God the Father unbegotten, thee the only begotten Son, thee the Holy Ghost the Comforter, holy and undivided Trinity, with all our heart and mouth we confess, praise and bless; to thee be glory for ever").

b) *"Ex quo omnia, per quem omnia, in quo omnia: ipsi gloria in saecula"* ("From whom are all things, by whom all things, in whom all things: to him be glory for ever and ever"). (These translations are from *Time After Pentecost*, vol. 1 of the *Liturgical Year* by Dom Prosper Guéranger, trans. Dom Laurence Shepherd (Westminster, 1948–50).

c) *"Te jure laudant, te adorant, te glorificant omnes creaturae tuae, o beata Trinitas. ℣. Tibi laus, tibi gloria, tibi gratiarum actio"* ("All thy creatures rightly praise, adore, and glorify thee, O blessed Trinity. ℣. To thee be praise, glory and thanksgiving").

d) *"Tibi decus et imperium, tibi gloria et potestas, tibi laus et iubilatio in sempiterna saecula, o beata Trinitas Deus"* ("To thee honor and dominion, to thee glory and power, to thee praise and joy for all eternity, O blessed Triune God").

e) *"Benedictio et claritas et sapientia et gratiarum actio, honor, virtus et fortitude Deo nostro in saecula saeculorum. Amen"* ("Blessing and fame and wisdom and thanksgiving, honor, power and strength be to our God for ever and ever. Amen"). The antiphons (c), (d), and (e) are no longer in use, and even in the Middle Ages they were not common. For this information and for supplying the full text of the antiphons, I am indebted to Dom H. Dauphin, Librarian, Quarr Abbey. He adds: "I found them in an Antiphonarium of the Library of Karlsrühe, cod. Augiens. LX fo. 227 of the 12th or 13th century; I found also (c) in the Antiphonarium of St. Denys, fo. 169, but not the other ones. Note that in Cod. Aug. LX, the last antiphon is not complete; the line finishes at *forti-*, and the scribe began the following line with another antiphon. I have supplied the rest from the *Capitulum* at Vespers as we have it now."

36. This last sentence comes from a note in the 1412 MS now in the Staatsbibliothek, Munich (CLM 15,332).

37. Cf. Eph. 3:18: "the breadth and length and height and depth." In invoking these Pauline dimensions of divine infinity, Gertrude seems to attribute one to each of the persons of the Holy Trinity. She seems thus, before recommencing her writing, to be making an immense sign of the cross. It is noticeable that she has not retained the fourth dimension of eternity, expressed by the length. That was no doubt in order to emphasize the Trinitarian significance of the theme. St. Bernard, commenting on Ephesians 3:18, sees eternity in the length, charity in the breadth, power in the height, wisdom in the depth; and he uses the same adjectives as Gertrude: inaccessible (*inattingibilis*) height, inscrutable (*inscrutabilis*) depth, immense (*immensa*) breadth (*De Consideratione* 5,13.). William of St. Thierry follows the same interpretation of eternity for the length, power for the height, wisdom for the depth, charity for the breadth. And he adds: "*Et haec est crux Christi*" ("And this is the cross of Christ") (*De natura et dignitate amoris*, ch. 11). St. Augustine attaches a slightly different meaning to the four dimensions, relating them to the human virtues of perseverance, hope, and charity, and to the inscrutable judgments of God. He seems to have been the first to have connected them with the cross. See, in particular, his Epistle to Paulina, called *De Videndo Deo:* Ep. 147,14.

38. 1 Cor. 6:17. St. Bernard frequently quotes this in his sermons on the Song of Songs. See for example 31,6: "*Id loquimur quod Apostolus dicit: quoniam qui adhaeret Deo, unus spiritus est*" ("I am saying only that which the Apostle says: he that is joined to God is one spirit [with him]").

39. Second responsory of Christmas (Monastic Breviary): "*Hodie nobis de caelo pax vera descendit: hodie per totum mundum melliflui facti sunt caeli. ℣. Hodie illuxit nobis dies redemptionis novae, reparationis antiquae, felicitatis aeternae*" ("Today true peace has come down to us from heaven: today throughout the whole world the heavens have dropped honey. ℣. Today there has shone upon us the new day of redemption, of the ancient reparation, of the eternal happiness") (Guéranger, vol. 1).

40. Sequence: *Laetabundus.* "*Sicut sidus radium, profert Virgo Filium.*" Cf. St. Bernard, *Homily on "Missus Est"* 2,17: "*Sicut sine sui corruptione*

sidus suum emittit radium, sic absque sui laesione Virgo parturit Filium"
("Just as the star gives forth its ray without suffering corruption, so did
the Virgin bring forth her Son without losing her virginity").

41. This is reminiscent of the Secret of the Mass of Our Lady on
Saturdays during Advent from the Old Roman Missal: *"ut qui con-
ceptum de Virgine Deum verum et hominem confitemur . . ."* ("that we, who
confess him who was conceived of a virgin to be true God and
man . . .").

42. Cf. St. Bernard, *Song* 35,2: *"Indignam te noveris illa tua familiari et
suavi rerum contemplatione coelestium, intelligibilium, divinarum. Quamo-
brem egredere de sanctuario meo, corde tuo, ubi secretos sacrosque veritatis ac
sapientiae sensus dulciter haurire solebas"* ("You must know that you are
unworthy of that contemplation of things heavenly, spiritual, and divine which is sweet and familiar to you. Therefore, come forth from
my sanctuary, your heart, where you were accustomed to drink with
pleasure deep draughts of the hidden and sacred meaning of truth and
wisdom").

43. Cf. St. Bernard, *De diligendo Deo,* 28: *"Sic affici, deificari est . . .
quomodo solis luce perfusus aer in eamdem transformatur luminis claritatem,
adeo ut non tam illuminatus, quam ipsum lumen esse videatur"* ("To be thus
affected is to be deified . . . as the air, when flooded with the light of
the sun, is transformed into the same clarity of light, so that it seems to
be not merely illumined, but to be light itself").

44. The phrase "spreading out in rivers of charity" originates with
St. Augustine, Sermon 69: *"dilatans rivos charitatis."*

45. Cf. 2 Cor. 4:7. St. Augustine, taking his inspiration from this
text in the sermon cited above, contrasts the somewhat exiguous capacity of poor earthenware vessels with the more capacious dimensions of
charity. It is in the light of this thought that Gertrude sees the essence
of charity spreading out everywhere, and a little further on stresses the
fragility of the earthen vessel which has to contain this treasure. Cf.
also St. Bernard, *De diligendo Deo,* 27: *"Caro et sanguis, vas luteum,
terrena inhabitatio, quando capit hoc? Quando huiusmodi experitur affectum,
ut divino debriatus amore animus, oblitus sui, factusque sibi tamquam vas
perditum, totus pergat in Deum, et adhaerens Deo unus cum eo spiritus fiat"*
("When shall flesh and blood, earthen vessel and earthly dwelling,
grasp this? When it experiences affection like this, that, inebriated with
divine love, unmindful of self, and become to its own self like a broken
vessel, it may utterly pass over into God, and, cleaving to God, become one spirit with him").

46. The earthen vessel, fragile and worthless, symbolizes human nature after the Fall. Through the Incarnation, however, Jesus, in his humanity, was the vessel that was able to contain the precious liquid without losing any of it. The grace for which Gertrude thanks our Lord in the closing words of this chapter is that of having shown her so clearly on this Christmas night the luminous manifestation of his divine power, making it possible for her to receive him as a newborn babe into her soul, as a symbol of the divine indwelling in every soul in a state of grace, together with her own awareness of the fact that through the Incarnation the union of every soul with God is made possible. Gertrude's thought turns naturally toward her own personal mystery: that of the life of God in her soul, the divine indwelling.

47. Deut. 4:24; Heb. 12:29. Cf. St. Augustine, *Confessions* 5:4: *"Tu Deus ignis edax, consumas mortuas curas eorum, recreans eos immortaliter"* ("You, O God, a consuming fire, consume their concerns for this mortal life, and recreate them to the life that never ends"). St. Bernard (*Song* 57,7) says: *"Est enim vere carbo desolatorius, sed qui sic in vitia exerceat vim ignis, ut in anima vicem exhibeat unctionis"* ("He is truly a devastating coal, but one which applies the strength of its fire to vices in such a way as to be at the same time a balm to the soul").

48. Col. 3:10. For a discussion of the idea of "image and likeness" see Bk. I, note 3.

49. Cf. Dan. 3:6. Fire is traditionally the symbol or sign of the presence and action of God and the symbol of divine charity. See, for example, St. Gregory the Great, *Hom. in Ezech.* 1,8. The idea occurs frequently in St. Bernard, for instance, *Song* 31, 4; 57, 7–8.

50. This is reminiscent of the Hymn for the Office of the Dedication of a Church (Monastic Antiphoner): *"Urbs Jerusalem beata/ Dicta pacis visio/ Quae construitur in caelis Vivis ex lapidibus/ Et Angelis coronata"* ("City of Jerusalem the blessed/ Called vision of peace/ Built in heaven of living stones/ And crowned with angels").

51. "The Sunday of *Esto mihi*": The Sunday on which the Introit "Esto mihi in Deum protectorem . . ." (Ps. 30:3,4,2) is sung, now week six in ordinary time. In St. Gertrude's day it was Quinquagesima Sunday, the Sunday before the beginning of Lent. (The two may well coincide.) The Sunday of *Esto mihi* is an important landmark in Gertrude's life of prayer. There are three allusions to it in Book II, her spiritual memorial: chapters 8, 14, and 23. In the Middle Ages the clergy were accustomed to observe a time of penance as a preparation for Lent in reparation for the excesses of the Carnival. This period of

penance commonly coincided with the time from the Thursday before Quinquagesima until Ash Wednesday. Hence it was known as *Esto mihi*, from the opening words of the Introit of Quinquagesima Sunday. It is to this custom that Gertrude was probably alluding.

52. This refers to the first Responsory of Matins of Quinquagesima Sunday, using the text of Genesis 12:1–2: *"Locutus est dominus ad Abram dicens: Egredere de terra tua, et de cognatione tua, et veni in terram quam mostravero tibi: et faciam te in gentem magnam. ℣. Benedicens benedicam tibi, et magnificabo nomen tuum, erisque benedictus"* ("The Lord said to Abram: Go forth out of thy country and from thy kindred, and come into the land which I shall shew thee. And I will make of thee a great nation. ℣. I will bless thee, and magnify thy name, and thou shalt be blessed").

53. The Responsory with this verse is in fact normally the first Responsory at Matins on the Monday after Quinquagesima Sunday: *"Movens Abraham tabernaculum suum, venit et habitavit juxta convallem Mambre. ℣. Dixit Dominus ad eum: Leva oculos tuos, et vide: Omnem terram, quam conspicis, dabo tibi, et semini tuo in sempiternum"* ("So Abram removing his tent came and dwelt by the vale of Mambre. ℣. And the Lord said to Abram: Lift up thy eyes and look: all the land which thou seest, I will give to thee and to thy seed for ever" [Gen. 13:18, 14–15]). No doubt either the verse or the whole Responsory was used for the ninth Responsory of Quinquagesima at Helfta.

54. This is one of the many occasions on which Gertrude echoes the antiphon of St. Agnes: *"Stans beata Agnes in medio flammae, expansis manibus orabat ad Dominum: Omnipotens, adorande, colende, tremende: benedico te, et glorifico nomen tuum in aeternum"* ("Blessed Agnes, standing in the midst of the flames, raised her hands and prayed to the Lord: Almighty, worthy of all adoration, worship and awe: I bless you and glorify your name for ever").

55. The phrase comes from St. Bernard, *Song* 64,10: *"Amor, dignitatis nescius, dignatione dives."*

56. Rom. 1:20. St. Bernard discusses this text in his ninth sermon *De Diversis*.

57. Cf. the invocation *"Cor Jesu, fornax ardens caritatis"* ("Heart of Jesus, burning furnace of charity") from the Litany of the Sacred Heart, largely inspired by the writings of St. Gertrude.

58. Cf. St. Bernard, *Song* 33,6: *"O perenne solstitium quando iam non inclinabitur dies"* ("O perennial solstice, when the sun will never set again").

59. Gen. 2:15. The thought of the earthly paradise may well have inspired this passage. Compare St. Augustine, *Confessions* 10,6.

60. On the five spiritual senses, see Dom Pierre Doyère, "Sainte Gertrude et les Sens spirituels," *Revue d'Ascétique et de Mystique*, no.144 (1960); and Fr. James Walsh S.J., "Guillaume de Saint-Thiérry et les Sens spirituels," *Revue d'Ascétique et de Mystique*, no. 137 (1959).

61. It would be tempting to read here not *calle*, "by way of," but *callo*, "hard skin." The sentence would then run: "Although I have been admitted (to these mysteries) by divine goodness, yet, covered on all sides with the hard skin of my own vices and negligences as though with a thick crust, I have never really been able to grasp any of it." This does read more smoothly in the Latin and seems to make better sense, and some translators have taken this option (for example, the translation made anonymously by the nuns of Wisques and published in 1906). However, there is no MS evidence for it, and the principle that the more difficult—or more unlikely—reading is generally to be preferred is a sound one. We have therefore chosen not to amend the text.

62. The lessons of the Exaltation of the Holy Cross at Matins in the Roman and monastic Breviary suggest nothing of the kind; we have already seen that the liturgy at Helfta did not necessarily correspond with that (see also note 53 above). It may be worth noting that at Matins of the feast of the Holy Trinity is read a text of Fulgentius (*De fide*), which contains a thought very similar to that of Gertrude: "*Apostoli, Spiritus Sancti magisterio instructi, non solum sermone praedicave-runt, verum etiam ad instructionem saluberrimam posteriorum scriptis suis inditam reliquerunt*" ("The apostles, taught by the authority of the Holy Spirit, preached not only by word of mouth, but also left instruction which they set down in writing for the salvation of those who came after them").

63. "In these modern times" (*his novissimis temporibus*): Cf. Heb. 1:2, *novissimis diebus*, "last days." This eschatological perspective, in which all time since the Redemption is considered as the modern or last age of humanity, is a familiar concept in Christian thought.

64. "By repeated inspiration": The Latin, *alternatis vicibus*, literally "by alternating times," seems to suggest a reference to the Lord's heartbeats; each one would thus be a source of inspiration for Gertrude. The point here is that she was unable to receive the unlimited shower of divine grace; it had to be given to her by measure, according

to her capacity. Hence her inability to write more than a certain amount each day.

65. Compare the Prayer from the Rite of Consecration of Virgins now used as the blessing for the cowl of the newly professed: *"Deus aeternorum bonorum fidelissime promissor, certissime persolutor . . ."* ("O God, most faithful in your eternal promises, and infallible in fulfilling them . . .").

66. Cf. Hugh of St. Victor, *Allegories on the New Testament* 3,3, commenting on Mark 6:31: *"Duae sunt vitae: activa et contemplativa. Monemur itaque in his Dominicis verbis ut aliquando ab actione quiescamus et ad secretum contemplationis transeamus"* ("There are two ways of life, the active and the contemplative. These words of the Lord teach us that we must sometimes rest from our activity in order to pass into the hidden life of contemplation").

67. For us, it is rather the sisters Martha and Mary of Bethany who represent the active and the contemplative lives. However, from St. Augustine through the Middle Ages these were seen as symbolized by Lia and Rachel, also sisters, the two wives of the patriarch Jacob (Gen. 29). St. Gregory the Great comments that Rachel is beautiful and infertile because the contemplative life beautifies the soul but does not bring forth offspring through preaching; while Lia is weak-eyed but fruitful because the active life sees less (of spiritual things) but by word and example leads others to imitate its good works (Hom. *in Ezech.* 2,10–11). The theme is a favorite among later monastic writers; e.g., Paschasius Radbert compares Jacob's union with Lia to the love of one's neighbor, which is necessary before one can attain to the love of God, symbolized by Rachel (*Exp. in Mt.* 1,1).

68. Compare the proper *Communicantes* of the Canon of the Mass of the feast of the Ascension: *"Communicantes, et diem sacratissimum celebrantes, quo Dominus noster, unigenitus Filius tuus, unitam sibi fragilitatis nostrae substantiae in gloriae tuae dextera collocavit"* ("United in one communion, we venerate the most holy day on which our Lord, thine only-begotton Son, established at the right hand of thy glory our frail nature which he had taken to himself").

69. Cf. grace after food: *"Agimus tibi gratias omnipotens Deus pro universis beneficiis tuis"* ("We give you thanks, almighty God, for all your benefits").

70. The immediate reference is to John 4:7, where Jesus asks for a drink from the woman of Samaria. St. Augustine comments (*Tract.* 15,12): *"Ille autem qui bibere quaerebat, fidem ipsius mulieris sitiebat"* ("He

who was asking for a drink was thirsting for the faith of the woman herself"). Similarly, here it is the devotion of Gertrude for which the Lord is thirsting. It is not unlikely that she has in mind also the fact that the woman of Samaria was a sinner, as well as being, as a Samaritan, in a "land of unlikeness" to the Lord. There may also be reference to Jesus' cry on the cross: "I thirst." Tradition has been unanimous in interpreting this as a spiritual and not primarily physical thirst.

71. The theme of the cup is an important one in the Bible. It may signify the anger of the Lord (e.g., Jer. 25,15; 49:12), or the Lord himself as the "portion and cup" of the righteous (Ps. 15:5). Jesus spoke of his passion and death as his cup. Perhaps Gertrude here intends to suggest that, as the Lord is her portion and cup, so she is his? She may also have in mind Song 8:2: "I will take hold of thee and bring thee into my mother's house: there thou shalt teach me, and I will give thee a cup of spiced wine and new wine of my pomegranates."

72. Cf. 1 Cor. 10:21. This, especially in the context of what follows, is also reminiscent of the attempt by some of the disciples of St. Benedict to poison him, as related by St. Gregory (*Dialogues* II, 3,4). When Benedict made the sign of the cross over the poisoned cup, it broke at once, thus showing the diabolical origin of the act.

73. Cf. Rev. 12:9; 20:2. There may be a reminiscence to the Preface of the Mass for the Consecration of Virgins; it is worth noting that "the old adversary" (*antiquus hostis*) is a name frequently given to the devil by St. Gregory in his *Life of St. Benedict* (*Dial.* II, 4,3, for example). This sudden temptation to vainglory is not unlike an experience of Benedict himself, who was visited by the devil in the form of a black bird. He made the sign of the cross, the bird disappeared, and he was immediately seized by violent physical desire. In both cases the apparition of the devil is evidently at the origin of the temptation, but does not seem to have any obvious connection with it (see *Dial.* II, 2,1).

74. First Vespers of the Feast of the Holy Trinity: "*Gratias tibi, Deus, gratias tibi, vera et una Trinitas, una et summa Deitas, sancta et una Unitas*" ("We give thanks to you, O God, we give thanks to you, one and true Trinity, only and sovereign Godhead, holy and one Unity").

75. Neither the influence of the devil nor the all-powerful action of God on a soul is able to destroy the essential character of the freedom of the human will. The irreducibility of free will is at the center of the spiritual doctrine and theology of St. Bernard, especially in his treatment of the concepts of "image and likeness" (see note 3 above; see also Thomas Aquinas, *Summa Theologiae*, Ia, q.83, art.I, ad 3).

76. cf. St. Bernard, *Song* 35,2: *"Egredere, et pasci haedos tuos . . . haedos quippe . . . dicit vagos et petulantes corporis sensus"* ("Go forth and feed thy goats . . . by 'goats' he means the wandering and ill-ordered senses of the body"). Gertrude does not specify that the flocks are goats, but this is surely her source. For a very full treatment of the subject of the affections, see vol. 3 of the *Sources Chrétiennes* edition of St. Gertrude's works, Appendix 3, "Affectiones animae," pp. 352–56.

77. *Esto mihi:* See note 51 above. On this occasion the saint, in order to make reparation for the outrages of the Carnival season, welcomes the Lord into her soul with greater devotion. This she does simply—a hint to be remembered—by a more exact fidelity to her vocation.

78. Some translators have understood this to mean that Gertrude has in mind the walls of the room actually giving off steam, perhaps in the form of condensation. It is more likely that she is thinking of the enclosed nature of the room, which makes it seems as if the floor, walls, and ceiling were "giving off" darkness as a pot gives off steam. In this darkness one cannot see more than if one were in a dense cloud or fog. The effect of suffering is the same as that of opening a window—or rather shutters or blinds—to let in light and air. For the image of the boiling pot, compare St. Bernard's "bubbling pot" at *Song* 74,7; the context is, however, very different. St. Gregory Nazianzen speaks of the flesh as a cloud which envelops the soul at *Oration* 21,2 and 39,8.

79. Midnight Mass. As is her custom, Gertrude names the Mass by the opening words of the Introit; in this case *"Dominus dixit ad me: Filius meus es tu: ego hodie genui te"* ("The Lord hath said to me: Thou art my son, this day have I begotten thee") (Ps. 2:7).

80. This is the Collect of the Mass for deceased parents, still to be found in the Roman Missal: *"Deus, qui nos patrem et matrem honorare praecepisti, miserere clementer patri et matri meae, eorumque peccata dimitte, meque eos in aeternae claritatis gaudio fac videre"* ("O God, who commanded us to honor our father and mother, be merciful and have pity on the souls of my father and mother, forgiving them their sins; and give me the joy of seeing them in the light of eternity"). It is interesting, given that Gertrude entered the monastery as a child of four and that nothing is known of her parents, that she should, evidently purely out of filial piety, continue to place them first in her prayers.

81. This Collect, out of use for centuries, has recently been restored and is one of those used in the new Roman Missal for the Mass for several deceased persons. *"Omnipotens sempiterne Deus, cui numquam sine*

spe misericordiae supplicatur, propitiare famulis tuis, ut, qui de hac vita in tui nominis confessione discesserunt, Sanctorum tuorum numero facias aggregari" ("Almighty eternal God, you who are never invoked without hope of mercy, be propitious to your servants, so that they, who have departed this life faithfully confessing your name, may be numbered among your saints").

82. No antiphon *Cum inducerent* has survived. Gertrude may have in mind the second antiphon of the procession on February 2, which runs as follows: *"Responsum accepit Simeon a Spiritu Sancto non visurum se mortem nisi videret Christum Domini: et cum inducerent Puerum in templum, accepit eum in ulnas suas et benedixit Deum, et dixit: Nunc dimittis servum tuum, Domine, in pace. ℣. Cum inducerent puerum Jesum parentes eius, ut facerent secundum consuetudinem legis pro eo, ipse accepit eum in ulnas suas"* ("Simeon had received an answer from the Holy Spirit, that he should not see death before he had seen the Christ of the Lord. And when they brought the child into the Temple, he took him into his arms and blessed God, and said: Now thou dost dismiss they servant, O Lord, in peace. ℣. When his parents brought in the child Jesus, to do for him according to the custom of the law, he took him into his arms"). The ℣., which has been suppressed in the new edition of the Roman Gradual, beginning as it does with a repetition of the words *"Cum inducerent,"* may explain Gertrude's mistake.

83. Cf. Preface of Consecration of Virgins: *"Qui sic perpetuae virginitatis est sponsus, quemadmodum perpetuae virginitatis est filius"* ("He is the spouse of perpetual virginity, just as he is the son of perpetual virginity"). Compare also 1 Thess. 2:19,20).

84. Compare the Hymn *Pange lingua gloriosi* (Hymn at Matins in Passiontide), verse 4: *"Membra pannis involuta/Virgo Mater alligat/et manus, pedesque et crura/Stricta cingit fascia"* ("As his virgin mother binds his limbs in swaddling-clothes enclosed, and ties his hands and feet and legs with tight bands"). The words of this hymn by Venantius Fortunatus would have been familiar to the nun and describe the scene of the Nativity with the infant swaddled like the *bambino* of Italian piety, such as may be seen, for instance, in the frescoes of Giotto. It must have been rarely, if ever, that the saint had witnessed such a scene. In Book III, chapter 30, indeed, she is represented as being unable to remember ever having seen a mother comforting her baby. Despite the attractiveness of the image, Gertrude does not stop at the external details but passes at once to its spiritual meaning.

85. *"Creator alme siderum"* is a variant first line of the hymn more generally known as *"Conditor alme siderum"* ("Creator of the Starry Skies"), the Vespers hymn of Advent.

86. It is most likely that Gertrude takes her "rose without a thorn" from the Sequence *Ave Maria*, known from MSS of the eleventh and twelfth centuries in South Germany. However, this designation of our Lady was known in the earliest Christian centuries. St. Ambrose uses *"Rosa sine spinis"* ("Rose without thorns") and Sedulius *"Rosa spina carens"* ("Rose lacking a thorn").

87. Cf. Antiphon *Gaude Dei Genitrix*. The closing words are *"sis pro nobis, quaesumus, perpetua interventrix"* ("Be for us, we pray, a perpetual intercessor").

88. This "station" (so called according to the time-honored term of monastic usage) after the washing of hands before meals was made, it seems, in the cloisters, where there was a washbasin or fountain with running water (called a *lavatorium*) opposite the entrance to the refectory. Many religious families still retain this custom. The best-preserved *lavatorium* in England is that in the cloisters of Gloucester Cathedral.

89. This is a quotation from an antiphon, from the Office of St. Agnes, used in the ceremony of the Consecration of Virgins: *"Ipsi sum desponsata cui Angeli serviunt: cuius pulchritudinem sol et luna mirantur"* ("I am espoused to him whom the Angels serve; whose beauty the sun and moon admire").

90. The term "gratitude" (*gratitudo*) seems to suggest the attitude of an inferior to a superior, and so would hardly seem suitable to apply to the Persons of the Trinity. However, moral theology makes it clear that gratitude, in that it is a special and distinct virtue (cf. St. Thomas Aquinas, *Summa Theologiae* Ia IIae, q.106) implies that the benefit comes not from a superior but from an equal. Gertrude is therefore right to see in the mutual recognition which the Persons of the Trinity show toward each other the very source of this virtue.

91. Cf. Collect for deceased relatives or benefactors: *"Deus veniae largitor et humanae salutis auctor. . ."* ("O God, the generous giver of mercy and lover of man's salvation").

92. Cf. Prayer before Communion, referring to 1 Cor. 11:29: *"Perceptio corporis et sanguinis tui, Domine Iesu Christe, quod ego indignus sumere praesumo, non mihi proveniat in iudicium et condemnationem: sed pro tua pietate prosit mihi ad tutamentum mentis et corporis, et ad medelam percipiendam"* ("Unworthy as I am, Lord Jesus Christ, I dare to receive thy

body: do not let that bring down upon me thy judgment and condemnation; through thy loving kindness let it be a safeguard and a healing remedy for my soul and body").

93. Cf. Prayer after the oblation of the chalice, after Dan. 3:39: "*In spiritu humilitatis et in animo contrito suscipiamur a te Domine*" ("In a contrite heart and a humble spirit may we be received by thee, O Lord").

94. There is no question here of Gertrude's having a sacramental role, merely graces of enlightenment and of powers of persuasion. It is evident from the echo noted in note 93 that we are still speaking of being judged worthy or unworthy of holy communion; the Lord had specified that only those worthy of it would be sent to Gertrude. It is therefore a question not of absolution but of reassurance.

95. Cf. Prayer for the oblation of the host in the old Roman Missal: "*Suscipe, sancte Pater, omnipotens aeterne Deus, hanc immaculatam hostiam, quam ego, indignus famulus tuus, offero tibi Deo meo vivo et vero, pro innumerabilibus peccatis, et offensionibus et negligentiis meis*" ("Accept, O holy Father, almighty eternal God, this immaculate victim which I, thy unworthy servant, offer to thee, my living and true God, for my sins and offenses and negligences without number").

96. The allusion to eternal preelection seems to be inspired by Ephesians 1:4. The rest of the paragraph is not unlike Romans 8:30, in which St. Paul lists the stages of our life in relation to God: predestination, vocation, justification, glorification. Gertrude, however, has her own list: predilection, vocation, union, enjoyment, consummation. Compare *Haurietis aquas*, CTS 62, p.41: "Love has the nature of the first gift through which all other free gifts are given."

97. Cf. Hymn of the Ascension, *Jesu nostra redemptio*, verse 4: "*Ipsa te cogat pietas ut mala nostra superes*" ("Be moved by this same love to overcome our evils").

98. Cf. St. Augustine, *Confessions* 2,6.

99. Gertrude certainly intends here an allusion to the parable of the Prodigal Son (Lk. 15:11–32), which might be better named the parable of the Loving and Forgiving Father. The son, after having squandered the goods received from his father, falls into the greatest degradation; when he returns home he is completely destitute and can offer nothing to his father of the slightest use or value. But the mere avowal of this misery is sufficient—"Father, I have sinned against you"—for pardon to be instantly granted and his father's riches to be lavished on him in abundance. It is not clear whether in her application of the parable the

saint has in mind the misery of human nature caused by Adam's sin or her own personal misery caused by her own faults. Probably the two are closely connected in her thought, as theologian and mystic.

100. Cf. Collect of the tenth week of Ordinary Time: "*Deus, a quo bona cuncta procedunt*" ("O God, from whom all good things come").

101. Cf. Collect of the seventeenth week of Ordinary Time: "*Protector in te sperantium Deus, sine quo nihil est validum, nihil sanctum*" ("O God, the protector of all who hope in thee, without whom nothing is reliable, nothing holy").

102. "*Vidi Dominum facie ad faciem: et salva facta est anima mea. ℣. Et dixit: Nequaquam vocaberis Iacob, sed Israel erit nomen tuum*" ("I have seen the Lord face to face: and my soul has been saved. ℣. And he said: Thy name shall not be called Jacob, but Israel") (Gen. 32:30, 28).

103. St. Bernard, *Song* 31,6.

104. Cf. Rev. 1:14; also Matt. 17:2: "His face did shine as the sun." The story of the Transfiguration is used as the gospel for the second Sunday of Lent.

105. See James Walsh, S.J., "Guillaume de Saint-Thierry et les Sens spirituels," *Revue d'Ascétique et de Mystique* 137 (1959), p.34. Speaking of the *Exposition on the Song of Songs*, the author comments: "His only precise reference to the *odoratus* does in fact concern the memory of the divine Presence—the traces left in the memory when the Spouse has withdrawn: 'The presence of the Spouse, that is the memory when it is deeply penetrated with his love, is the *mens* illuminated by the light of his Face, that is the unction of the Holy Spirit teaching all things. The odor of his fragrance, now that he is departed, is the trace of his former sweetness lingering in the memory, and, penetrating all other thoughts, the delectable memory which comes from recalling the consolation one has had.' "

106. Cf. Hymn *Tristes erant Apostoli*, Common of Apostles in Paschaltide. In the fourth verse occur the words "*faciem desideratam Domini*" ("the longed-for face of the Lord").

107. The phrase translated "divine eyes" is *deificis oculis*, literally, "deifying eyes." However, Gertrude almost certainly means simply "divine." Compare St. Benedict's use of the phrase "*deificum lumen*" ("the divine light") in the prologue to his *Rule*.

108. Cf. St. Bernard, *Song* 31,6: "*Verbum nempe est, non sonans, sed penetrans: non loquax, sed efficax: non obstrepens auribus, sed affectibus blandiens*" ("The word utters no sound but penetrates; it is not full of words, but full of power; it strikes not on the ears, but caresses the

heart"). Although Bernard is here speaking not of the gaze of the Lord but of his word, yet this is probably Gertrude's source, since this passage occurs immediately before that quoted by her a few lines earlier.

109. Cf. Hymn *Jesu dulcis memoria*, long attributed, almost certainly mistakenly, to St. Bernard. One of the verses runs: "*Nec lingua valet dicere, nec littera exprimere: Expertus potest credere, quid sit Jesum diligere*" ("Tongue cannot say, nor written word express; only he who has experienced it knows what the love of Jesus is").

110. This paragraph is puzzling in places. What, for example, does Gertrude mean here by "if things are with God as they are with humankind"? The alternative reading, *osculi* ("kiss") instead of *oculi* ("eye") is found in some MSS and is rather attractive. The phrase would read "the power of your *kiss* surpasses this vision by far." However, the better MSS, notably that of Munich (see Introduction) have *oculi*, and the present translator has followed the example of *Sources Chrétiennes* in choosing that more difficult reading. In any case, the general line of thought is clear enough: any mystical grace, of however high an order, is a mere shadow of the power of God; if one were to receive more than this shadow, one could not survive.

111. Cf. Collect for the twenty-seventh week in Ordinary Time: "*Omnipotens sempiterne Deus, qui abundantia pietatis tuae et merita supplicum excedis et vota, effunde super nos misericordiam tuam, ut dimittas quae conscientia metuit et adicias quod oratio non praesumit*" ("Almighty eternal God, whose unbounded goodness doth exceed all that thy suppliants desire and deserve, so pour out on us thy mercy that, forgiving what our conscience fears, thou mayst bestow on us what we dare not ask").

112. "The end of my twenty-fifth year": This is a reference to the events described in Book II, ch. 1, concerning Gertrude's "second conversion."

113. "A pagan among pagans" cf. Eph. 4:17–18. Here, and also in chapter 20, Gertrude is probably thinking along the lines of St. Paul. By "pagan" she simply means someone who does not know God and whose mind is clouded and darkened because it has not yet been enlightened by the "true light that enlightens every man" or by divine revelation. Her guilt appears to her the greater as she was living in a religious community and was not surrounded by unbelievers. She was given the opportunity of knowing the truth, although at first her mind was too darkened to see it.

114. "Household": The Latin word is *triclinium*, which normally

means "dining room" or "banquet hall"; however, it is clear that Gertrude has in mind Esther 2:13, where the word is used to mean "the chamber of the women," since she uses the word again in this chapter with the name of Ahasuerus (see note 120 below).

115. Cf. Procession Responsory for the feast of the Nativity: "*Descendit de caelis missus ab arce Patris; introivit per aurem Virginis in regionem nostram*" ("He descended from heaven, sent from the throne of his Father; through [the message spoken in] the Virgin's ear, he entered our region").

116. Cf. the hymn *Optatus* of the feast of the Ascension, attributed to St. Ambrose. The last line of verse 2 runs: "*Magni triumphum praelii, mundi perempto principe, Patris praesentans vultibus victricis carnis gloriam*" ("O triumph of the great battle! Having defeated the prince of this world, Jesus presents to his Father's eyes the glory of his victorious flesh").

117. Cf. third antiphon of the feast of St. Benedict: "*Gloriosus confessor Domini, vitam angelicam gerens in terris*" ("The glorious confessor of the Lord, leading an angelic life on earth").

118. Cf. Book II, ch. 1.

119. This is evidently a reference to Book II, ch. 3.

120. "The palace of Ahasuerus": *triclinium Assueri* (see note 114 above).

121. Cf. St. Bernard, *Song* 52,2: "*Illa maiestas tam familiari dulcique consortio nostrae se inclinare infirmitati minime dedignatur*" ("That divine majesty disdains not to stoop to a familiar and sweet companionship with our lowliness").

122. "*Dator, renovator, conservator omnis boni*": This passage may have been inspired by the prayers for the ceremonial of the Profession and Consecration of Virgins, in which the words "*Bonorum promissor, persolutor, dator*" ("You who promise, fulfil your promise, and give good things") occur; or by various prayers in the Missal where the words *dare* ("to give"), *reparare* (or *restaurare* ("to restore") and *conservare* ("to preserve") are to be found in conjunction.

123. Cf. Hymn *Corde natus*, by Prudentius. The first verse ends: ". . . *Ipse fons et clausula omnium quae sunt, fuerunt, quaeque post futura sunt*" ("He is the source and end of all creatures which are, were, and shall be"). Gertrude uses exactly the same, rather unusual, phraseology.

124. Cf. Rom. 3:4; cf. also the hymn *Rector potens, verax Deus*, attributed to St. Ambrose. St. Augustine also uses the phrase, for example in his *Confessions* 8,10.

154

125. Cf. Prov. 24:12; Gertrude uses the unusual word *inspector*, which is the word used by St. Gregory in his life of St. Benedict (*Dialogues* II,3,5): "*solus in superni inspectoris oculis habitavit secum*" ("He lived alone with himself beneath the gaze of the heavenly one who sees all things"). Some MSS of the *Dialogues* have *spectator*, but when the text is used in the Divine Office, *inspector* is the reading found.

126. Cf. Dante Alighieri, *Divina Commedia: Paradiso* 33,124–127: "*O luce eterna, che sola in te sidi, sola t'intendi, e da te intelletta ed intendente, te ami e arridi!*" ("Eternal light, that in thyself alone dwelling, alone dost know thyself, and smile on thy self-loving, so knowing and so known!"). The spiritual memorial of St. Gertrude ends with an invocation to the Trinitarian life completely filled with its own infinite love. This praise, in the form of a magnificent epitome, derives from the same source of inspiration as that with which Dante closes the last Canto of the *Paradiso*. Before setting in motion the whole creative activity of the infinite love which moves "the sun and the other stars," he adores, like Gertrude, this same love in the mystery *ad intra*.

Book III.
The Herald of Divine Love

Prologue

The grace of a great humility together with the power of the divine will were compelling her with a sort of urgency to make known to another person the confidences that follow. She thought she was herself so unworthy that her gratitude would not be a sufficient response to God's magnificent gifts. And so, when she had revealed them to another person, she rejoiced in God's praise, which, as it seemed to her, would then, like a precious stone, be lifted out of the dark mud and worthily set in gleaming gold. Finally, it was at the command of her superiors that this confidant wrote the following pages.

Chapter 1. The Special Protection of the Mother of God

She had learnt by a spiritual revelation that she was about to suffer some adversity that would increase her merits, and in her human frailty, she was afraid. The good Lord, taking pity on her timidity, himself charged his merciful mother, the august empress of heaven, to be a gracious mediatrix for her, so that whenever the weight of this adversity became more than she could bear, she could always have recourse to the Mother of mercies who, she knew, would come to her aid.

156

Not long after this, she was much troubled because a person who was devoutly consecrated to God[1] wanted to make her disclose the special gifts which God had conferred on her during the preceding feast, and for various reasons, she deemed this would be very difficult; yet she did not like to refuse altogether, because she feared that this might be contrary to the will of God. She turned to the Consoler of the afflicted, desiring to be taught what it was most expedient for her to do in this case. From her she received this answer: "Give away all that you have, for my son is more than rich enough to repay you for all you expend for his glory." But as she had wrapped her secret round with so many concealments of her own invention, she could not easily disclose it; in this situation she flung herself down at the Lord's feet, imploring him to give her some indication of what would be most pleasing to him and to grant her the grace to accomplish that will of his. Then she obtained of the divine goodness this reassuring reply: "Put my money in the bank, and when I come back I will take it out with interest" (cf. Lk. 19:23). Thus she was taught that what she had considered to be good reasons, sent her by the Spirit of God, were but human in origin, coming from herself. And so from that time she began to relax her intention of strict secrecy, and rightly so, as Solomon testifies: "It is the glory of kings to conceal the word, and the glory of God to search out the speech."[2]

Chapter 2. The Rings of the Spiritual Espousals

While she was offering to God in a short prayer all the pain she had to endure, of body or soul, and all the joys, spiritual or physical, which were denied her, the Lord appeared. He was wearing this two-fold offering she had made him—namely, of joys and of sufferings—in the form of two jeweled rings, one on each hand. When she had understood the meaning of this, she often repeated the same prayer. After a little while, she was reciting it when she felt the Lord stroking her left eye with the ring on his left hand, which she understood to be a symbol of physical pain. And from that time, that same eye which she had seen the Lord touching spiritually, suffered so much physically that it never regained its former health. From this she understood that, just as the ring is the symbol of espousals, so any trial, whether of body or soul, is the truest sign of divine election and is like the espousals of the soul with God; so that those who suffer can say truly, and even with confidence: "My Lord Jesus Christ has espoused me with his ring."[3] And so in all her adversities she never lacked this gift of grace, and she could truly raise her mind in grateful praise and thanksgiving to God and in consequence could joyfully add these words: "And like a bride he has adorned me with a crown."[4] Gratitude in adversity is like being adorned with the most beautiful crown of glory, more precious far than gold and topaz (cf. Ps. 118:127).

Chapter 4. Contempt for Temporal Comforts

Around the feast of St. Bartholomew[5] she was overwhelmed by inordinate sadness and impatience; her soul was invaded by such darkness that it seemed to her that she had almost entirely lost the joy of the divine presence. This lasted until the following Saturday, when she had the happiness of seeing the darkness disperse through the intervention of the Virgin Mother of God during the singing of the antiphon "Stella Maris Maria" in her honor.[6] Next day, which was Sunday, in her joy at being so caressed and cherished through the goodness of God, she remembered her previous impatience and all her other defects. She began to be very dissatisfied with herself and, in a spirit of dejection—indeed, almost in despair, so many and so great were the defects which she discovered within herself—she besought the Lord to help her to improve, in these words: "Alas, most merciful Lord, make an end of my wickedness, for I know not how to correct it or to put an end to it. Deliver me, O Lord, and set me beside thee, and let any man's hand fight against me" (Job 17:3). Taking pity on her desolation, the merciful Lord showed her a very small and extremely narrow garden,[7] where flowers of various kinds were growing in profusion. It was surrounded by a hedge of thorns and a feeble trickle of honey was flowing through it. And he said to her: "Would you prefer the pleasure you take in these pretty flowers to me?" "Never, Lord God!" she answered. Then he showed her a little garden with muddy soil, covered with unattractive greenery interspersed with a few worthless but fairly colorful little flowers. He questioned her about this as well, saying: "Now, would you prefer this one to me?" She turned away from it indignantly and answered: "Far be it from me to prefer what is false and worthless (I do not call it good but positively bad) to you, the only true, the supreme, solid, lasting, and eternal good!" He said: "Why, then, this lack of confidence, as though you were not in charity,

158

although anyone who has received such an abundance of gifts must surely be convinced of it? Does not Scripture bear witness that charity covers a multitude of sins (1 Pet. 4:8)? That is why you do not prefer your own will to mine, when you could live without any adversity, comfortably and honorably, finding favor with men and with a reputation for great holiness. Now I showed you this in the similitude of the flower garden; and I set before you the pleasures of the life of the flesh in the verdure of this muddy place." To which she rejoined: "Oh, I wish, a thousand times I wish, that I had entirely renounced my will in despising the flower garden which you showed me; but I am afraid that the narrowness of the garden led me too easily to reject it." And the Lord said: "But it is my overflowing love for my chosen ones that makes me usually restrict their temporal satisfactions and comforts through the prickings of conscience, so that they may the more easily despise them."

Then she proceeded with constancy to renounce all pleasure, both heavenly and earthly. Reposing on the breast of her Beloved, cleaving firmly to him, it seemed to her that no creature would be powerful enough to remove her, ever so little, from this refuge where she was always ready to draw with joy (cf. Is. 12:3) from the Lord's side and taste of the flood of life-giving sweetness, far surpassing the sweetness of balm.

Chapter 5. How the Lord Came Down to Her in Her Humility

On the feast of St. Matthew, Apostle,[8] God came to meet her with great blessings of sweetness. At the elevation of the chalice she was offering this same chalice as a thanksgiving to the Lord; and she began to reflect in her heart that her offering of the aforesaid chalice would not be complete unless she offered herself to endure tribulations for Christ. And so, in this state of holy elation, she tore herself away from the place where she seemed to be reclining delightfully on the Lord's breast and threw herself down on the ground, like a wretched corpse, with these words: "Lord, I offer myself to bear everything that may be to your praise!" The Lord at once made haste to rise and, lying down on the ground beside her, as if gathering her to himself, he said: "This is my own!" As though revived by the virtue of the divine presence, she raised herself up before the Lord and said: "Yea, my Lord, I am the work of your hands."[9] And the Lord said: "You have received this further grace because my love is so intertwined with you that I could not live in complete blessedness without you." Marveling at the excessive condescension of these words, she said: "O my Lord, why do you speak thus, since having deigned to find your delight in your creatures (cf. Prov. 8:31), you have an infinite number of others, both on earth and in heaven, with whom you could live in complete blessedness, even had I never been created?" To which the Lord replied: "He who has always lacked a limb does not suffer the same affliction as someone who has one of his limbs cut off when already an adult. So, from the moment I set my love upon you, I could never suffer us to be separated from one another."

Chapter 6. The Soul's Cooperation with God

On the feast of St. Maurice[10] while Mass was being celebrated and the priest was proceeding to the silent words of the consecration of the host, she said to the Lord: "This act, Lord, that you are about to perform deserves a perfect and infinite respect; and that is why I, who am so insignificant, dare not even raise my eyes to it. Rather, I shall plunge myself down and lie in the deepest valley of humility I can find, there to await my portion of it; for from it comes the salvation of all the elect."

To which the Lord answered: "When a mother wants to do some embroidery with silk or pearls, sometimes she puts her little one in a higher place to hold the thread of pearls or help her in some other way. And so I have put you in a higher place with the intention of making you participate in this Mass. Because, if you will raise yourself up to help me of your own free will in this work, even if it is hard; if you want to be of service so that this oblation may have its full effect on all Christians, whether living or dead, in accordance with its dignity and excellence; then you will have given me the best possible help in my work, according to your possibilities."

Chapter 7. The Lord's Compassion

On the feast of the Holy Innocents,[11] as she was being hindered in her preparation for communion by wandering thoughts, she sought divine aid to overcome them. This was the answer she received from

God in his kindness and mercy: "Anyone assailed by human temptations who takes refuge with me, firmly trusting in my protection, is the one of whom I can say: 'One is my dove (Song 6:8), chosen from among thousands (5:10) who has wounded my divine heart with one look of her eyes (4:9)'—so much so that if I thought I could not come to her aid my heart would be desolated by such sadness that all the joys of heaven could not ease my distress. For in my body, which is united with my divinity, my elect always have an advocate[12] which compels me to have compassion on their various needs."

And she said: "O my Lord, how can your pure body, in which there has never been anything whatever to reprove, compel you to have compassion on us in our various states of distress?" To which the Lord replied: "It is easily demonstrated to anyone who uses his intelligence. Did not the Apostle say of me: 'It behooved him in all things to be made like unto his brethren, that he might be merciful' (cf. Heb. 2:17)?" And he added: "This one look of the eyes of my chosen one by which she pierced my heart means the sure trust that she needs must have in me, because I have the power, the knowledge and the will to be faithfully at her side under all circumstances; this confidence has such influence over my love that I can never be far from her."

And she rejoined: "O my Lord, if this sure confidence is a good thing, and if no one can have it except as a gift from you, how can one who lacks it be at fault?" The Lord replied: "Anyone can overcome a lack of confidence to some extent, as the Scriptures bear witness. And even if not with their whole heart, yet with their lips they can repeat to me the words of Job:[13] 'And if I should be plunged into the deepest abyss, thou shalt deliver me' (cf. Job. 30:23–24), or 'Although thou shouldst slay me, yet will I trust in thee' (Job 13:15), and the like."

Chapter 9. Dispensation of Divine Grace

It was divinely revealed to a certain person that through the prayers of the community the Lord would vouchsafe to release a great number of souls from their punishment in purgatory, and for this intention a special prayer was prescribed for the whole community. The one about whom this book is written was fulfilling the obligation to pray one Sunday with the others in order that this multitude of souls might be released from their pains; as devoutly as she could, she offered herself to the Lord for the salvation of the souls. Then she drew nearer to the Lord and beheld him as a king in his majesty, distributing gifts. As she could not see or discover exactly what it was that the Lord seemed to be doing so busily, she said to him: "O most benevolent Lord, last year, on the feast of St. Mary Magdalen,[14] you confided in me, although unworthy, how you were compelled by your own mercy to lay all your benignity at your feet, because it was at your feet that so many souls, following the example of the blessed sinner, your true lover, humbly prostrated themselves that day.[15] Now mercifully deign to enlighten the eyes of my understanding and show me what it is that you are so occupied in doing at this moment; for it is hidden from me." To which the Lord answered: "I am distributing gifts." From these words she understood that the Lord was distributing the prayers of the community for the relief of souls who were present and yet were quite invisible to her. Then the Lord added: "Don't you want to offer me all that your merits could have gained for you to increase the value of this gift of mine?" Moved by the touching sweetness of these words, and not knowing that, persuaded by the person we have mentioned to whom the promise of liberating the souls had been made, the community was doing just that, she thankfully agreed, as though the Lord were asking a particular favor of her; and with a cheerful heart,[16] she replied happily: "Lord, with immense joy (1 Chron. 29:17) I gladly offer you, in union with your perfection, not only my own spiritual goods, which are almost nothing, but also those of the whole community to which I belong; for I have a share in these and through your grace I can make them all fully mine and freely offer them to you." And the Lord most graciously accepted the offering.

Then the Lord, as if captivated, spread as it were a cloud[17] over himself and her alone. Stooping down and lifting her tenderly up toward him, he said: "Give your attention to me alone and enjoy the sweetness of my grace." Then she said: "Why, my Sweet, my God, have you accorded this favor of the revelation about the souls to this person and entirely deprived me, when you lovingly deign to show me so many of your secrets?" To which the Lord replied: "Remember how often you have despised yourself, thinking yourself utterly unworthy of the gifts of my grace, and even thinking that you have been given them as an incentive, like a hireling who serves for wages, almost as though you could not be faithful to me without this gift? It is for that reason that you esteem others more highly than yourself; others who have been led by no such inducements and yet appear to be faithful to me in everything. I have dealt with you as I do with them so that, without knowing any more about the souls than the others did, you yourself do not lack that merit which you admire in them."

In the state of rapture caused by these words she understood the admirable and ineffable condescension of God's love,[18] sometimes coming down to man and generously and copiously flooding him with grace, and yet sometimes refusing him lesser favors in order to preserve humility, the fundamental grace which preserves all the others; and how in both these ways the Lord makes everything work together unto good for loving souls (cf. Rom. 8:28). Transported by gratitude and admiration for God's infinite goodness to her, she became faint and beside herself, almost as if out of her mind, and she rushed to throw herself on the Lord's breast with these words: "O my Lord, I am too small to bear this weight!" Then the Lord began to diminish the greatness of the revelation which she was experiencing. Her strength having returned, she said to him: "Kindest Lord, since through the incomprehensible and inexplicable wisdom of your providence you require that I should lack this gift, I do not intend ever to desire it again."

Then she added: "All the same, Lord, are you not going to hear me when I pray for any of my friends?" To which the Lord replied, as though confirming it with an oath: "By my divine power, I shall certainly do so!" And she said: "Then I shall pray now for that person who has been so often recommended to me." At once she saw a little river, pure as crystal, issuing from the Lord's breast and flowing into the heart of the person for whom she was praying. Then she questioned the Lord, saying: "Lord, as this person does not feel the influx of grace, what good can it do her?" To which the Lord answered: "When a doctor makes a sick person drink a cup of medicine, it is not when the person swallows the draught that those who are looking after him can see that he is restored to health; neither does the sick person feel at once that he is cured, and yet the doctor, who knows the healing power of the draught of medicine, knows very well in what way it will be beneficial to the sick person." And she said: "Why, Lord, do you not take away her unreasonable ways and other defects about which I have so often prayed to you?" To which the Lord said: "It was said of me, the child Jesus: 'And Jesus advanced in age and wisdom before God and man' " (cf. Lk. 2:52). This person grows gradually and improves from hour to hour; she will turn her vices into virtues. I will forgive her all her human failings so that she may see after this life all that I have prepared for man in decreeing to exalt him above the angels.

Now the time was approaching when she was to go to communion. She asked of the Lord that, in addition to the number of souls which he was that day to release from their pains to join the heavenly choirs through the prayers of the person who has been several times mentioned, he would also anticipate the hour of his grace for the same number of sinners who were destined to be saved. She did not presume to pray for those who were destined to be damned, but the Lord chided her for her timidity, and said: "Surely the dignity of the presence of my immaculate body and of my precious blood is such that even those who are in a state of mortal sin might through its merits be recalled to a better way of life?" Pondering on the extent of the generosity in these words, she said: "Since your inestimable love condescends to hear my unworthy prayers, I implore your Majesty, in union with the love and desire of all your creatures, that, whatever the number of souls may be which you will now release from purgatory, you may grant me that the same number of sinners still living in this world in a state of mortal sin may attain to your grace—those for whom you particularly desire prayers to be offered. Let it be granted to whomever you desire, at any time, and in any place. I do not choose to pray specially for my friends or relatives or those near me." This the kind Lord graciously accepted and gave her his assurance about it.[19]

Then she said: "I would like to know, Lord, what it would please you that I should add to these prayers." Receiving no reply to this, she said: "I know, Lord, that in my unfaithfulness I do not deserve to receive a reply to this question, because you, to whom all hearts are known, know me to be so negligent that perhaps I would not do as you tell me." The Lord with a serene countenance[20] tenderly replied: "Confidence alone is sufficient to obtain everything easily; but if in your devotion you really desire to add something over and above, then recite the psalm 'O praise the Lord all ye nations' (Ps. 116) three hundred and sixty-five times to make up for any negligence of theirs in my divine praise."

Chapter 10. Three Offerings

It was the feast of St. Matthias.[21] She resolved that she would not go to holy communion, for she felt herself hindered for several reasons. During the first Mass, she was thinking of God and of her own soul; the Lord showed her more affection, with greater tenderness, than any friend could ever feel for his friend. She was but little pleased, however, because she was accustomed to receiving more sublime favors in a more sublime way. She would have like to have been rapt entirely out of herself and, passing utterly into her beloved, who is called a consuming fire (Heb. 12:29), to have been melted, as it were, by the burning ardor of charity, to have been united intimately and inseparably with him. As this time she could by no means contrive to do as she would have liked, she diverted her thoughts, turning her attention to God's praise, praising him in another way that was customary to her: first, by exalting the immense goodness and condescension of the ever-adorable Trinity for every grace which, from the abyss of its own inexhaustible abundance, flows down to benefit all the saints; second, for every grace bestowed on God's most holy mother; third, for every grace infused into the most sacred humanity of Jesus Christ, imploring all the saints, each and every one, to offer in sacrifice to the resplendent and ever tranquil Trinity, in reparation for her negligence, all the zeal and care with which they had come before the Lord of glory to receive their eternal reward, on the day when, having attained to their ultimate perfection, they were taken up into heaven. With this she recited three times the psalm "O praise the Lord all ye nations" (Ps. 116), first in honor of all the saints; second, in honor of the Blessed Virgin; and third, in honor of the Son of God. At which the Lord said to her: "And how are you going to reward my saints who offer such intercession for you, since today you are proposing to abstain from this holy communion in which you usually offer me in return your thanksgiving for them?" At this, she was silent.

Then, at the oblation of the host, she desired with great desire (cf. Lk. 22:15) to find an oblation which she could worthily offer to God the Father to his eternal praise. She received this answer from the Lord: "If you were to prepare yourself today to receive the sacrament of my life-giving body and blood, you would certainly receive the threefold benefit which you were longing for in this Mass; namely, to enjoy the sweetness of my love and, as though melted by the ardor of my divinity, to flow into me, as gold merges with silver, so that from this amalgam you would have the most precious alloy which you could then worthily offer to God the Father to his eternal praise; and all the saints would be fully remunerated." Convinced by these words, she was enflamed by such desire that it would not have seemed hard to her to fly toward the sacrament of salvation even though she had had to brave drawn swords.

After having received the body of the Lord, while she was making her thanksgiving to God, the true lover of humankind said to her: "Today you, by your own choice, had intended to serve me like the rest, with straw and clay and bricks (cf. Exod. 1:14); but I chose you to be one of those who were to be refreshed by the sweet delights of my royal table." And when on the same day she noticed another person abstaining without reason from holy communion, she said to the Lord: "Why, most merciful God, do you permit her to be tempted like this?" To which the Lord answered: "Am I to be blamed if she covers her eyes with the veil of her own unworthiness, so that she cannot see anything of my fatherly love and affection?"

Chapter 11. Of an Indulgence, and the Desire for the Will of God

Hearing one day an indulgence of several years being preached, as was the custom for obtaining offerings, she said to the Lord with heartfelt devotion: "Now if I had great riches, Lord, I would gladly offer much gold and silver (Ezra 8:30) in order to be absolved from sin by this indulgence, to the praise and glory of your name." To which the Lord replied kindly: "By my divine authority, you have full remission of all your sins and failings." Instantly, she saw her soul shining without a stain, as white as snow (cf. Ps. 50:9; Is. 1:18).

Some days afterward, when she came to herself, she found her soul shining and white as she had seen it before, and she began to fear that there might be some illusion in such a show of innocence, thinking to herself that such purity, if it had been genuine, would by now appear somewhat darkened through the continual lapses into negligence and levity which often occur through human frailty. The Lord lovingly consoled her in her despondency with these words: "Do you not think that I keep to myself a greater power than that which I accord to my creatures? Now, if I gave the sun such power that if a white cloth is soiled by some stain, through the warmth and power of the sun's rays the stain instantly vanishes and the former whiteness is restored, bleached even brighter than it was before, how much more can I, who am the creator of the sun, keep a soul on whom I direct my merciful glance free from the contamination of every sin or failing, purifying her, by the power and the glowing warmth of my love, from every stain?"

Another time, the consideration of her own unworthiness and lack of trust so much discouraged her that it was not possible for her to accomplish any exercise to the praise of God or to long for the delights of contemplation in her usual way. At last, however, the gratuitous mercy of the Lord, through communion with the most holy life of Jesus Christ, so encouraged her that she seemed to herself to be advancing, according to her desire, into the presence of the Lord, the King of kings, as it is said that Esther came into the presence of King Ahasuerus.[22] Then the Savior deigned to speak graciously to her in these words: "What is your bidding, Lady Queen?" To which she replied: "I beseech you, O Lord, and I desire with all my heart that your most blessed will be accomplished in me in the way that is most in accordance with your good pleasure."

Then the Lord, naming one after another all the people who had specially recommended themselves to her prayers, said: "What, then, do you ask for her, and for this other, who specially recommended themselves to your prayers this day?" And she said: "I do not wish to ask anything for them save that in them all your most peaceable will may be accomplished." After that the Lord said again: "And what would you like me to do for you?" To which she answered: "First and foremost among all delights, I long that in myself and in all your creatures your most peaceable and praiseworthy will may be accomplished. And in order that this may come about, I am perfectly ready to expose every member of my body to suffer any pain whatever."

God in his great kindness and love first anticipated these words by inspiring them and afterward rewarded her for them by saying: "Since you seek the accomplishment of my will with such devoted affection, behold: in my customary benevolence I shall reward your efforts with this gift: I shall grant you to appear as pleasing in my sight as if you had never in the slightest transgressed my will."

Chapter 14. Two Ways of Making Reparation

Ever zealous for the salvation of his chosen ones, the Lord sometimes permits them to feel as a burden something which in itself is small, so that the treasure of their merit might thereby be increased to no small extent. Once she found it so burdensome to make her confession that it seemed to her she could never do it by her own efforts. And so she prayed to the Lord about it with all the devotion and fervor of which she was capable. This was the answer she received: "Now, would you like to entrust this confession to me with the fullest confidence so that you need make no further effort to do it?" To which she replied: "Truly, my most loving Lord, I have full—and more than the fullest—confidence in your omnipotence and goodness. But I think that, if I have offended you by my sins, it would be wrong not to make the effort to meditate upon it in the bitterness of my soul to show you some reparation." The Lord was pleased with this answer and she applied herself to the recollection of her sins. Soon her skin appeared to her somewhat scratched, as though she had rolled among thorns.[23] And having disclosed her miseries to the Father of mercies (2 Cor. 1:3,4) as to an experienced and trustworthy doctor, she heard him say, lovingly bending down toward her: "With my divine breath, I will warm the bath of confession for you. When you have been washed to your liking, you will be presented to me all spotless." Eager to strip for this bath, she said to the Lord: "Out of love of your glory, my Lord, I lay aside all fear of human respect so that, if it were necessary, I would not hesitate to show all my wretchedness to the whole world." Then the Lord covered her as though with his own mantle, stripped naked as she was, and made her repose on his breast while she waited for the bath to be prepared.

The time for confession was at hand. Much troubled by conflicting thoughts, she said to the Lord: "Since the fatherly mercy of your loving heart is not unaware of the extreme difficulty I have in making this confession, why, kindest Lord, do you allow me to be so exceedingly troubled by conflicting thoughts?" The Lord replied thus: "Maidens who take a bath usually have attendants to rub them down; so, in like manner, the things which trouble you will be of advantage to you. Soon there appeared to her, on the Lord's left, as it were, a very hot bath from which steam was rising. On his right, the Lord showed her a most delightful garden full of all sorts of flowers. In this garden were to be seen some very beautiful roses without thorns; from the brightness and vigor of their scented blossoms they wafted a refreshing fragrance and by some marvelous charm attracted all who came near. He was beckoning her that she was at liberty to go into this pleasant garden if she preferred it to the bath of which she was complaining so unduly. At which she said: "Never, Lord, but without further ado I will get into the bath which you have warmed for me with your divine breath." And the Lord said: "May it avail for your eternal salvation!"

Therefore she understood that this garden signified the intimate sweetness of divine grace which, borne softly on the light south wind

168

of love (cf. Song 4:16), besprinkles the faithful soul with the precious dew of loving tears making it instantly whiter than snow (cf. Ps. 50:9), fully assured not only of the remission of sins but also of the increase of an abundant store of merits. By this she learned that it was pleasing to the Lord for her to choose the bitterer and leave the sweeter, for his love. And when, after confession, she went to her place for prayer, she felt that the Lord was very graciously deigning to favor her with his presence, although he had ordained the painful troubles and difficulties of the confession, in which she had had the greatest reluctance to pronounce what others would not have been ashamed to say almost boastingly before everybody, passing it off in jest.

It is to be noted that the soul is cleansed from all sin in two principal ways. The first is through the bitterness of repentance and all that goes with it, which is signified by the bath. The second is by the gentle fire of divine love and all that goes with it, which is what is meant by the garden of delights.

After confession, she fixed her mind on the contemplation of the wound in the Lord's left hand, as one might rest while still perspiring after taking a hot bath, until she could complete the penance which the priest had given her. However, it was of such a kind that it had to be postponed for a time, and she felt this to be a great trial and feared lest her sweetest and dearest Lord might not grant her the free and intimate enjoyment of his presence until it was completed. During the Mass, therefore, when the sacred host was being immolated by the priest, most truly the most efficacious reconciliation with sinful humanity, she made of it her own offering to the Lord in thanksgiving for the benefits of the bath and as a pleasing reparation for all her faults. The offering was received, and she herself was received in the bosom of the kindest of fathers; in experiencing this, she was truly visited by the Dayspring from on high, through his tender mercy and truth (Lk. 1:78).

Chapter 16. Progress in Times of Desolation, and Spiritual Communion

While the community was singing the Mass *Salve Sancta Parens*[24] in honor of the Mother of God on the last day before the suspension of the divine mysteries,[25] Gertrude said to the Lord as she prayed: "How are you going to console us, most gracious Lord, in our present trial?" The Lord replied: "I shall increase my pleasure in you. Just as the

169

bridegroom can take more pleasure in the the bride in private than in public, so likewise your sighs and desolation will be my pleasure. The love you have for me will be increased in you, just as pent-up fire burns more extensively. Moreover, just as a swollen torrent of water breaks forth and overflows its banks, gaining greater force by having been held back, so my delight in you and your love for me will break forth and overflow."

Then she said: "And how long is this interdict going to last?" To which the Lord answered: "As long as it lasts, these things of which I have spoken will also last." She rejoined: "Great princes would consider it shameful to confide their secrets to worthless persons of the lowest rank. In the same way it might seem improper to you, O King of kings, to disclose the secrets of your divine providence to me, the offscouring of all creatures (1 Cor. 4:13). That is why, I think, you have not given me a clear and complete answer, although the end of all things is known to you from the beginning."

And the Lord said: "Not so; but I act in this manner for your greater good and for your salvation. For if, at times, I raise you up by contemplation to a share in the knowledge of my secrets, I exclude you from them sometimes to preserve your humility, so that in receiving them you may find out what you are by my grace, and again, when you lack them, you may know what you are of yourself."[26]

At the Offertory of the Mass, *Recordare, Virgo Mater,*[27] at these words "that you may plead in our favor," as she was concentrating her attention upon the Mother of all grace, the Lord intervened with these words: "You and your sisters do not need anyone to plead in your favor, for I am myself entirely favorably disposed toward you." Turning over in her mind certain imperfections both in herself and in some of the others, she was at a loss to know how the Lord could assure her that he was entirely favorably disposed toward them. The Lord made her understand by saying gently: "My own natural goodness leads me to look on the better side; embracing this with the whole of my divinity, the imperfect is concealed by the perfect." Then she said: "O most bountiful, how can you now give me, so unworthy and so ill-prepared, such great and such consoling gifts of your grace?" He replied: "Love compels me."[28] She pursued: "Where are now those stains which I contracted from the fit of impatience into which I fell a short time ago, and showed to some extent by my words?" The Lord answered: "They are totally consumed in the fire of my divinity (cf. Heb. 12:29); for I consume every deforming imperfection in any soul to whom I stoop by the free gift of my benignity."

Then she said: "O most merciful God, since your grace so frequently forestalls my unworthiness, I would gladly know whether, after death, my soul will have to be purged of the faults of impatience and the like?" As the kind Lord feigned not to hear this, she added: "Truly, Lord, were the beauty of your justice (Jer. 50:7) to require it, I would willingly and gladly go down even into hell, that in this way I might make you more worthy reparation. But if your innate goodness and mercy were really to find greater glory in all these faults being consumed by your love, I would take the liberty to demand that that love, which is far more than I deserve, may purify my soul from every stain!" This the Lord graciously granted, in the power of his divinity and his love.

The next day, while Mass was being celebrated for the lay people,[29] at the time of communion she said to the Lord: "Do you not pity us, most merciful Father, seeing that, on account of these temporal goods by which we have to be sustained for your service, we are deprived of so precious good as your body and blood?" He replied: "And how can I feel so very sorry? It is as if I were leading my bride into a pleasant and festal banquet hall (cf. Song 2:4) and, just before entering, I were to take her aside into a less attractive place to arrange with my own hand some slight disorder either in her dress or her ornaments, that I might lead her into the banquet hall with more honor." Then she said: "O my Lord, how can they find favor with you who have brought on us this heavy trial?" But the Lord said: "Let them be, for I shall settle that with them."

On another day, at about the time of the oblation of the saving Victim, when she was offering this same host to the Lord for his eternal praise and for the salvation of the whole community, the Lord himself received the host within himself, and then, breathing life-giving sweetness from his inmost being, said: "With this breath I will feed them with divine food." Then she said to him: "Now, my Lord, are you giving communion to the whole community?" He replied: "No, but only to those who desire it or who would wish to have such a desire. As for the others, because they belong to the community, they will be granted the grace to receive that strong desire for it; as in the case of a person who, while taking little interest in food, is finally attracted by the savory smell to take pleasure in eating."

On the feast of the Assumption,[30] at the elevation of the host, she heard the Lord saying: "I am coming, that I may offer myself to God the Father for my members." She replied: "Shall you, most loving Lord, suffer us, your members, to be cut off from you by the excommunication which those who are trying to rob us of our goods inflict on us?" To which the Lord said: "If anyone is able to take from me the very marrow of my bones—for so closely do you cleave to me—let him cut you off from me. This excommunication which has been imposed on you will do you no more harm than would someone trying to cut you with a wooden knife, which cannot penetrate at all, but only leave some slight impression made by its blade."

Then she said: "O Lord God, you who are unfailing Truth, have you not told me, in spite of my unworthiness, that you are purposing to increase your pleasure in us and our love for you? How is it that some people complain that they feel themselves cooling in their love for you?" He replied: "I contain within myself all good things; and at the time appointed I give to everyone the portion that is best for him."

Chapter 17. The Lord's Condescension and the Sharing of Grace

It was the Sunday on which the feast of St. Lawrence fell,[31] together with the anniversary of the dedication of the church. During the first Mass she was praying for some people who had devoutly asked for her prayers, when she saw the trunk of a green vine reaching from the throne of heaven down to the earth; by means of its spreading foliage ascent could be made from the bottom to the top. She understood this ascent to mean the faith whereby the chosen are raised up to heavenly things. She recognized several of the community in high places at the top, to the left of the throne, as it were, and the Son of God standing with due reverence in the presence of his heavenly Father; it was at the time when the community would have been going to communion, had they not been prevented from doing so by the interdict. She greatly desired that she as well as the others there present might be spiritually favored with the life-giving sacrament, through the divine mercy which no human power can withstand. Then she saw the Lord Jesus holding in his hand a host which he seemed to plunge into the heart of God the Father; then he withdrew it, rosy red, as though it were stained red with blood. Very much at a loss, she asked herself what this might signify, since red is the symbol of suffering, and God the Father could never be marked by any trace of the red color of suffering. And while she was preoccupied with these thoughts, she failed to notice whether the desires she had expressed had been fulfilled, except that after a time she was aware that the Lord had found a peaceful resting-place in the heart and soul of those of the community whom she had recognized before in the high places. But she had no idea how this had come about.

Meanwhile, she remembered someone who had asked for her prayers just before Mass with humble devotion, and she prayed for her that the Lord might give her a share in the honor already mentioned. To this she received the following answer: "No one can make the ascent of faith I showed you who is not raised by confidence; and the one for whom you are praying is lacking in it." She answered: "Lord, it seems to me that the want of confidence in that soul proceeds from humility, which you usually reward with more abundant grace." To which he answered: "I will come down and I will communicate my gifts to her and to all those who are in the valley which is humility." Then she saw the almighty Lord descending by a sort of scarlet ladder and, shortly afterward, he appeared in the middle of the altar of the church, clad in pontifical vestments. In his hands he was holding a pyx like the one in which consecrated hosts are usually reserved. During the whole of the Mass until the Preface, he continued seated, turned toward the priest. And such a multitude of angels[32] were present for his service that the whole of the church to the right of the Lord, that is to the north, seemed to be filled with them. These angels showed the special joy they felt, enveloping with extreme affection this place in which their fellow-citizens,[33] that is, the nuns of the community, were so continually offering their prayers to God. Whilst to the left of the Lord, that is, to the south, a choir of angels was standing; near, but apart from them, the choir of apostles, and apart from them, that of martyrs; then the choir of confessors, and lastly the choir of virgins. While she was observing this wonder, she remembered that, according to the Scriptures, "Incorruption bringeth nearer to God" (Wisd. 6:20), and she understood that between the Lord and the holy virgins there shone a particular ray of light of snow-white brilliance, which united the virgins with the Lord more closely than all the other saints, seeming to caress them with the sweetest love and a wonderfully joyous intimacy. She also understood that some rays of admirable brilliance were falling directly onto some members of the community, as though there were no obstacle between them and the Lord; although she knew that in reality several solid walls separated them from the church in which she beheld the vision.

In the joy of this wonder she was yet mindful of some of the other members of the community and said to the Lord: "Since you, O Lord, in your infinite love, favor me with this grace of incredible sweetness, what are you going to do for those who labor in exterior employments and enjoy hardly any such graces as these?" To which the Lord replied: "I pour my balm upon them, although they seem to sleep." She began to consider what power this balm might possess, and marveled to think that it was equally profitable for those who practice spiritual exercises and for those who do not; because this balm renders the bodies anointed with it incorruptible, and the same result is produced no matter whether they are asleep or awake. Then she was enlightened by a clearer analogy: when a man eats, his whole body is strengthened in every member, although he enjoys the taste of the food with his mouth only. So it is when some special graces are conferred on chosen souls; God's boundless love accords an increase of merit to all his members— and especially to those who belong to the same community—except in the case of those who deprive themselves through jealousy or ill-will.

Meanwhile, as the "Glory to God in the highest" was being intoned, the Lord Jesus, the Sovereign High Priest, sent forth toward heaven, to the glory of God the Father, a divine breath like a living flame. And at the words "and on earth peace to men of good will" he breathed forth this same breath, like gleaming snow, over all those who were present. Afterward, at the "Lift up your hearts," the Son of God arose and through his powerful attraction drew to himself the desires of all those present. Then, turning toward the east, surrounded by the countless angels who were ministering to him, he stood with raised hands and offered to God the Father, through the words of the Preface, the prayers of all the faithful. After this, when they began to intone the "Lamb of God," the Lord raised himself up on the altar, with all his majesty. At the second "Lamb of God," the inscrutable influence of his wisdom flowed into the hearts of each individual who was present. At the third "Lamb of God," concentrating himself toward heaven, he offered in his own person to God the Father the prayers and aspirations of all. Then, in the abundance of this overflowing sweetness, whilst giving the kiss of peace with his divine lips to all the holy ones there assembled, he accorded to the choir of virgins, in preference to all the others, the privilege that, after the mouth's kiss, he laid his tenderest kiss upon their heart. After this, the Lord poured forth, as it were, all the honeyed torrents of his divine love, giving himself to the community with these words: "I am wholly yours; let each of you enjoy me to her heart's content."

After this she said to the Lord: "Lord, although I am now filled with the most incredible sweetness, yet it seems to me that when you were on the altar you were too far from me. Grant me, therefore, during the Blessing of this Mass, the favor of feeling that my soul is united to you." This the Lord accomplished in such a way that she felt herself clasped to his breast and firmly held in divine union in an embrace that was as sweet as it was close.

Chapter 18. The Gift of Preparation for Receiving the Body of Christ, and Several Other Points

She was approaching one day to receive the life-giving sacrament while the antiphon *Gaude et laetare*[34] was being sung. At the words "Holy, holy, holy," she prostrated herself on the ground with heartfelt humility and prayed the Lord that he would deign to prepare her so that she might worthily share in his heavenly banquet, for his glory and for the welfare of all. At that the Son of God, suddenly bending down like a sweet lover, imprinted on her soul the sweetest kiss. While the second "Holy" was being sung, he said: "Behold, in this kiss, and with this second "Holy," which is addressed to my person, I will give you all the holiness of my divinity and my humanity, that you may be worthily prepared to come up to receive holy communion."[35]

The following Sunday, while she was thanking God for the gift which we have mentioned, behold the Son of God, more beautiful than a thousand angels (cf. Ps. 44:3), took her in his arms, seeking to glory in her, and joyfully presented her to God his Father in that perfection of sanctity which he himself had bestowed on her. Then God the Father, through his only-begotten Son, was so well-pleased with her soul that he seemed to be unable to contain his love and, together with the Holy Spirit, granted her the first and third "holy" belonging to them, so that she might receive the perfect blessing of all holiness; of almighty power, of wisdom, and of goodness.[36]

On another occasion, when going to communion, she saw that several persons were hindered from doing so for different reasons. Rejoicing in spirit, in the affection of her inmost heart, she said to the

Lord: "Thanks be to you, my beloved God, my sweetest Lover, for having placed me in such a state that neither my relatives nor any other cause can hinder me from sharing in your most joyful banquet." The Lord replied with his usual sweetness and kindliness: "Since you declare that you have nothing to hinder you, know also that there is nothing in heaven or on earth, not even the judgment or the requirements of justice, which could hinder me from doing you all the good which my heart desires."

Again, on another occasion when she was going to communion, she was most desirous that she should be properly prepared by the Lord. Gently and lovingly he comforted her with these affectionate words (Est. 15:11): "Behold, now I am clothing myself in you so that I can stretch forth my delicate hand among prickly sinners, for their good, without being harmed; and I clothe you with myself so that all those whom you may bring mentally into my presence—indeed, all those who have a like nature to yours—you will raise to such dignity that I may be able to do good to them, according to my royal munificence."

Another day when she was going to participate in the divine mysteries, while she was recalling God's goodness to her, there came into her mind this quotation from the book of Kings: "Who am I or what is the house of my father?" (1 Sam. 18:18). Rejecting the words "the house of my father," since she assumed that her ancestors had been people who had lived their lives according to the law of God, she considered herself, a frail little plant, placed close to the inextinguishable furnace of the divine heart, receiving the benefit of its warmth, burning within herself as if naturally, yet fading away from hour to hour through her faults and negligences till at length she was brought almost to nothing, lying there like the smallest of burned-out coals. Turning then to Jesus, the Son of God, her loving Mediator, she prayed that he would deign to present her, just as she was, to be reconciled to God the Father. Her most loving Jesus seemed to draw her toward himself by the breath of love of his pierced heart, and to wash her in the water flowing from it, and then to sprinkle her with the life-giving blood of his heart (cf. Jn. 19:34). With this action she began to revive, and from the smallest cinder she was invigorated and grew into a green tree, whose branches were divided in three, in the form of a fleur-de-lys.[37] Then the Son of God took this tree and presented it with gratitude to the glory of the ever adorable Trinity. When he had presented it, the whole blessed Trinity with great graciousness bowed down toward the offering. God the Father, in his divine omnipotence, set in the upper branches all the fruit that this soul would have been able to produce, were she to correspond aright to divine omnipotence. In the same way, she saw the Son of God and the Holy Spirit setting in the other two sections of the branches the fruits of wisdom and goodness.

Afterward, when she had received the body of Christ, she beheld her soul, as was said above, in the likeness of a tree fixing its roots in the wound of the side of Jesus Christ; she felt in some new and marvelous way that there was passing through this wound, as through a root, and penetrating into all her branches and fruit and leaves a wondrous sap which was the virtue of the humanity and divinity of Jesus Christ. Thus, through her soul, the work of his whole life took on more splendor, like gold gleaming through crystal. Hereupon not only the blessed Trinity, but all the saints, rejoiced with delight and wonder. They all rose up[38] in reverence and, as though on bended knee, offered their merits, represented like crowns, hanging them on the branches of the tree we have mentioned, to the praise and honor of him the splendor of whose glory now shone through her and gladdened them with fresh delight. As for her, she besought the Lord that all those in heaven and on earth and even in purgatory (for indeed, all would have benefited from the fruits of her works, had she not been negligent) might now have at least some share in those fruits with which she had just been enriched by his divine generosity. As she was praying, each single one of her good works (symbolized by the fruits of the tree) began to distill a beneficent liquid. Part of this liquid spread over the blessed, increasing their bliss; part of it spread out over purgatory, easing the pain of souls; another part of it spread over the earth, increasing the sweetness of grace for the just, and for sinners the bitterness of repentance.

During Mass one day, at the elevation of the host, as she was offering this same sacred host to God the Father as a worthy reparation for all her sins and to make up for all her negligences, she understood that her soul, presented to the divine majesty, was as pleasing to him as was Christ Jesus, the splendor and image of his Father's glory (Heb. 1:3), the spotless Lamb of God, who was offering himself to God the Father at the same moment on the altar for the salvation of the world. For it was through the perfectly innocent humanity of Jesus Christ that God the Father beheld her cleansed from every sin, pure and immaculate, enriched by his most excellent divinity and adorned with the same fullness of virtue with which the glorious divinity blossomed forth through his most holy humanity.

While she was making her thanksgiving to the Lord as best she could, rejoicing in the admirable benevolence of divine love, he gave her to understand that as often as anyone assists at Mass with devotion, in union with God who offers himself there in the sacrament for the salvation of the whole world, God the Father truly regards him with the same satisfaction as that with which he looks upon the sacred host that is being offered to him; so that person is like a man who comes out of the darkness into full sunlight, and is suddenly bathed in light. Then she questioned the Lord, saying: "And if one falls into sin, my Lord, does one immediately lose this blessedness? Just as one who leaves the sunlight to go back into darkness loses the lovely brightness of daylight?" The Lord answered: "No; although by sinning he does shade himself to some extent from the light of God's clemency, yet my loving kindness always preserves in him a vestige of that blessedness unto eternal life, which increases in him each time he takes care to assist with devotion at the reception of the sacraments."

One day, after having received communion, she was meditating on the care with which we should watch over the tongue, since it is the tongue more than all the other members of the body which receives the most precious mystery of Christ. She was instructed by this comparison: that anyone who does not restrain his tongue from uttering vain words, false, shameful, slanderous words and the like, and goes unrepentant to communion, receives Christ (as far as he can do so) as if he were receiving a guest by pelting him on his arrival with the stones which were heaped up around the door or by dealing him a blow on the head with a heavy bar. Let anyone who reads these lines ponder them with tears of deep compassion, considering how so much kindness can be met with so many injuries, and how he who came with gentleness for the salvation of humanity can be so cruelly treated by the very ones he came to save. The same could be said of any other sin.

Another day when she was to go to communion she felt herself insufficiently prepared; and when the time came she thus addressed her soul: "Behold, now the Bridegroom is calling you and how can you go to meet him when you are not adorned with the merits with which you ought to be prepared?" Then, shrinking back still further in her great unworthiness, wholly mistrusting herself but placing all her hope in God alone, she said to herself: "What is the use of delaying? If I were to spend a thousand years in trying, left to myself I could still never prepare myself worthily, since I am not able to provide anything which would serve for the appropriate lavish preparation. Yet I shall set out to meet him with humility and faith; and when he sees me from a long way off, moved by his own love, he is powerful enough to send to meet me everything that I need in order to present myself, fittingly prepared, to him." With these despositions she went forward, keeping the eyes of her heart fixed on her deformities and disorders.[39]

And after she had gone a little way, she beheld the Lord looking at her with pity, or rather, with love; and sending forth to meet her as a suitable preparation his Innocence, which clothed her as with a soft white gown; his Humility, whereby he deigns to unite himself to souls that are anything but worthy of such a favor, which covered her like a violet tunic; his Hope also, whereby he longs and thirsts for the soul's embrace, which adorned her like a mantle of green color; his Love, whereby he is wounded for souls, wrapping it around her as with a cloak of a golden color; his Joy, which makes him find his delight in a soul, setting it on her brow like a jeweled diadem; and finally, his Confidence, whereby he deigns to trust in the fragile clay of our humanity, making it his delight to be with the children of men (Prov. 8:31), which he gave her for shoes; and so she was worthy of being brought into his presence.

She had received communion, and while she was recollecting herself, the Lord showed himself to her in the form of a pelican, such as it is usually represented, piercing its heart with its beak. Looking at it in wonder, she said: "O my Lord, what are you trying to teach me by this similitude?" The Lord replied: "That you may consider what ineffable ardor of love compels me to offer such a precious gift; and, if it does not sound too paradoxical to say this, that I should prefer that this gift would lead to my death, rather than that I should deprive a loving soul of this gift of myself. Moreover, you must consider the excellent way in which your soul, in receiving this gift, is invigorated and receives the life which lasts eternally; just as the little pelican is invigorated with blood from the father's heart."[40]

Another day, the preacher had given a long sermon on divine justice, which made such an impression on her that she was alarmed and trembled to approach the divine sacrament. God in his loving kindness encouraged her with these words: "If you forget to see with the eyes of faith the signs of the goodness I have shown you in many, many ways, do at least see with the eyes of your body this small pyx in which I am enclosed in order to come to you; and be assured that the strictness of my justice is quite as completely enclosed in the meekness of my mercy; and it is that mercy which I show to all in this visible sacrament."

On another occasion, at a similar hour and in the same manner, the divine Love invited her to taste of his gentle sweetness with these words: "Observe the smallness of the material form in which I show you the whole of my divinity and my humanity, and compare this size with the size of the human body; judge, then, to what extent I stoop in my benevolence; for just as the size of the human body exceeds the size of my body—that is, my body under the species of bread—it is my mercy and my charity which induce me in this sacrament to permit the loving soul in some sort to prevail over me."

On another day, when the saving host was being distributed in communion, the Lord explained to her once again his exceedingly great condescension in these words: "Don't you see how the priest who is distributing the hosts has taken care to turn back the sleeves of the vestment he is wearing out of reverence for the sacrament while he celebrates and handles my body with his bare hands?[41] I want you to understand that although, as is but right, I look with affection on the works done for my sake, such as prayers, fasts, vigils, and the like, however—though it does not seem so to the less spiritually minded—I am drawn toward my Elect with greater compassion when they are forced by their human weakness to have recourse to my mercy, just as you see that the bare flesh of the priest's hand touches me more closely than do his vestments."

When, on another day, the bell was sounding for communion and the chant was being intoned, she, feeling herself insufficiently prepared, said to the Lord: "O my Lord, you are coming to me! Why did you not send me, as you easily could, some ornament of devotion with which I might come to you becomingly prepared?" To which the Lord replied: "Sometimes the Spouse is better pleased at seeing the fair neck of his bride unadorned than when it is covered by a necklace; and he is more pleased also to take her delicate and lovely hands (Song 5:14) in his own than to see them covered by long gloves. So I sometimes take more pleasure in an act of humility than in the grace of devotion."

It happened once that many of the community had been obliged to abstain from going to communion; and she, after having received the sacred mystery, was the more devoutly making her thanksgiving, saying to the Lord: "You invited me to your banquet and I came giving thanks."[42] The Lord rejoined with these most tender words, sweeter than honey and the honeycomb (Ps. 18:11): "Know that I desired you with my whole heart." Then she said: "And what delectable glory, O Lord, could accrue to your divinity from me, when in my unworthiness I break up your immaculate sacrament between my teeth?" To which the Lord answered: "The heart's love makes the words of the loved one sound sweet. And so my own love makes me take delight sometimes in what my chosen ones would find little to their taste."

On another occasion, while the sacrament was being distributed, she felt an ardent desire to see the host and was prevented from doing so by the crowds of communicants who were approaching. She understood that the Lord was affectionately inviting her and saying: "It is inevitable that those who remain far from me know nothing of the sweet secret which we share. But if you would experience its delights, come and do so, not by seeing but by tasting the savor of that hidden manna (Rev. 2:17).

One day she noticed one of the nuns approaching, trembling with timidity, to receive the life-giving sacrament; as she turned away in annoyance and almost in indignation, the Lord reproved her gently for this, saying: "Do you not see that the honor of reverence is due to me no less than the sweetness of love? But since the deficiency of human nature means that both of these cannot be equally present in the dispositions of one person, and as you are all members one of another (Rom. 12:4,5), it is but right that what is lacking in one should be supplied by another. For example, one who is more affected by the sweetness of love shows me less reverence; she should be glad when her deficiency is made up for by another who is more reverent, and in her turn should desire that the other should have the consolation of divine unction."

When on another occasion she saw a different person very timid and fearful for the same reason, she began to pray for her. The Lord said: "I wish my chosen ones did not think me so cruel, but would believe that I accept as good, or even perfect, every act which costs them something. For example, it involves a personal sacrifice to carry out the worship due to God if one feels no sweetness of devotion, and yet serves him nonetheless by the recitation of prayers, by genuflections, and the like, and, above all, trusts in his loving mercy. This homage God will be pleased to accept."

Again, praying for someone who was complaining that she received the grace of devotion much less frequently on the days when she went to communion than on certain other days, even ferial days, the Lord gave her this answer: "That is no accident, but comes about by my providence: because when on ferial days and also at unexpected moments it happens that I favor the soul with the grace of devotion, I intend thus to raise her up to me, when perhaps she would otherwise have remained in a state of tepidity. But when, on the other hand, on feast-days or at the moment of communion, I withdraw this grace, the hearts of my chosen ones are more stimulated by voluntary desires or by humility; and this effort of attention or this contrition is often of more advantage to their salvation than is the grace of devotion."

When on another day she was praying for someone who had abstained from receiving the Lord's sacrament because she had committed some slight fault and feared lest she might be a cause of scandal to those who saw her, if she were to receive communion, Gertrude received in response this similitude: "She is like a person who, noticing a stain on their hands, at once washes them. After washing, not only are they cleansed from that obvious stain, but their hands have been made wholly clean. This happens with my chosen ones whom I permit sometimes to fall into some little fault, so that they may repent, and by their humility become more pleasing to me. But there are some who oppose this benevolent design because they fail to appreciate the interior beauty which pleases me after their repentance, and strive only after exterior cleanliness, according to the judgment of men. This happens, for example, when, for fear that they will be held guilty by men for lack of preparation for reception of the sacrament, they care less about losing the grace which they could have received from me through this sacrament."

Another day on which she was to go to communion, she felt interiorly that she was being invited by the Lord. Almost as though she were already in the heavenly palace, seated by God the Father reigning in all his glory, and about to feast with him at his table, she saw herself to be ill-prepared for this, and in such a state of disorder that she was anxious to withdraw. The Son of God approached her and seemed to be leading her to a place apart to prepare herself in private. And first he seemed to be washing her hands for the remission of her sins, making over to her the purifying effect of his passion. Then, taking off his own ornaments, the chain which was around his neck and the rings from his arms and fingers, he adorned her with them, putting them upon her with the advice that she should walk with dignity and in a becoming manner, and not like a foolish woman who, through awkwardness and lack of experience, is not able to move in a fitting way, and so attracts contempt and ridicule instead of respect for her modesty. By these words she understood that they walk like fools who, having put on the Lord's ornaments, are indeed aware of their own imperfections and pray the Son of God to make up for them; and

THE HERALD OF DIVINE LOVE

yet, after accepting his favors, remain as timid as ever, because they do not have perfect confidence in the complete satisfaction which the Lord has made for them.

On another communion day, as she was offering to the Lord the victim which is the Lord's body for the alleviation of souls in purgatory, she perceived that by this offering the sufferings of the faithful souls had in fact been much relieved. Then, full of wonder, she said to the Lord: "O my most loving Lord (and I can say this only through your grace), although I am, alas, so very unworthy, yet you always deign to honor me with your presence, or, rather, to dwell within me; how is it that you do not always bring about in me the same effect as that which I now experience after having received your most sacred body?" To that the Lord replied: "Just as when a king is dwelling in his palace access is not always easy for everyone, but when, overcome by his love of the queen who dwells nearby, he deigns to quit his palace in order to pass through the city to visit her, then all the citizens and inhabitants of the city (thanks to the queen) may more easily and more fully enjoy his royal liberality and wealth. And so it is with me when, moved by the tenderness and sweetness of my heart, through the life-giving sacrament of the altar, I incline toward a faithful soul who is without mortal sin: all the inhabitants of heaven as well as of earth and of purgatory receive an increase of priceless benefits."

As she was preparing for communion on another day she felt a great desire to abase herself in the lowliest valley of humility and to hide herself in it out of reverence for the amazing graciousness of the Lord in communicating his precious body and blood to his chosen ones. And now the profound humiliation of the Son of God when he descended into limbo to overthrow it became clear to her. By trying to unite herself to him in his humility, it seemed to her that she had descended into the very depths of purgatory. Then, abasing herself as much as she could, she understood that the Lord was saying to her: "When you receive me in the sacrament, I will draw you so close to myself that you will draw with you all those who have inhaled the priceless fragrance of your desire which clings to your garments" (Song 1:3).

After this promise, whenever she was desirous of receiving the sacrament, she asked that the Lord would grant her as many souls from purgatory as there were particles into which the host broke in her mouth[43] and, as she tried to divide it into as many pieces as she could, the Lord said to her: "That you may know that my mercies are over all my works (Ps. 144:9) and that there is no creature that can exhaust the abyss of my love, behold I am ready to grant you, through the merits of this life-giving sacrament, a much greater number than you would presume to ask me for."

On another day before communion she abased herself according to her frequent custom on account of her unworthiness, imploring the Lord to receive his most sacred host for her himself in his own person in her place and to incorporate it into himself; and then to breathe into her each hour with his sweet and noble breath just as much as he knew to be suitable to her small capacity. After that, she reposed for a time in the bosom of the Lord, as it were beneath the shadow of his arm (cf. Ps. 90:4). She was so placed that her left side seemed to be held against the Lord's blessed right side.[44] After a little while, raising herself, she perceived that through the contact with the wound of love in the Lord's most sacred side, her left side had been drawn into a sort of ruddy scar. Then, as she was going to receive the body of Christ, the Lord himself seemed to receive the consecrated host in his divine mouth. It passed through his body and proceeded to issue from the wound in the most sacred side of Christ, and to fix itself almost like a dressing over the life-giving wound. And the Lord said to her: "Behold, this host will unite you to me in such a way that on one side it touches your scar and on the other my wound, like a dressing for both of us. You must cleanse it, as it were, and renew it every day by turning over in your mind with devotion the hymn "*Jesu nostra redemptio.*"[45] After this it pleased him, as if to show the growing intensity of her desire, to increase this practice of piety every day; so that one day she recited the hymn once, the second day twice, and the third day three times, and so on until the day when next she was to go to communion.

Chapter 19. How to Pray to the Mother of God

It was the hour of prayer and, coming into the presence of God, she asked him what subject he would most like her to apply herself to during that hour. The Lord answered: "Keep close to my mother who is seated at my side, and strive to praise her." Then she devoutly hailed the Queen of heaven with the verse: "Paradise of pleasure . . . ," praising her for having been the most pleasant abode which God's inscrutable wisdom, to whom all creatures are known, chose as his dwelling from among all the delectable pleasures of his Father. She prayed that she might obtain for her own heart such attractive and varied virtues that God might be pleased to dwell there also. At that, the blessed Virgin seemed to bend down, as though to plant in the heart of the supplicant various flowers of virtue, such as the rose of charity, the lily of chastity, the violet of humility, the heliotrope of obedience, and others of the same sort, showing by this how eager she always is to hear the prayers of those who call upon her.

Then, as Gertrude hailed her again with the verse: "Rejoice, O you who guide our ways . . . ," she praised her for having ordered, better than all other human beings, the whole household of her affections, ways, and senses, and all her other emotions, with such diligence that the Lord who dwelt within her could be given the most seemly service; for she never committed any fault, in thought, word or deed. Gertrude prayed that she too might obtain the same grace. At that, the Virgin Mother seemed to send her own affections in the form of noble damsels, commanding them to join themselves to those of the supplicant, and to strive to serve the Lord with them and make up for any shortcomings that might be found in their service. In this way our Lady let it be known how eager she is to aid those who call upon her.

After a little time had passed, Gertrude said to the Lord: "O my brother,[46] since you were made man to make up for all human defects, now deign to make up to your blessed Mother for what may have been lacking in my praise of her." When he heard these words, the Son of God arose and most reverently went to kneel before his Mother; bowing his head, he saluted her most courteously and affectionately, so that she could not but be pleased with the homage of one whose imperfections were so abundantly made up for by her most beloved Son.

The following day, as she was praying in this way, the Virgin Mother appeared to her in the presence of the ever adorable Trinity, which appeared in the form of a fleur-de-lys, as it is usually shown, with three petals, one erect and two turning downward. Thus she was given to understand that the blessed Mother of God is justly called the White Lily of the Trinity, because she has received into herself, more fully and perfectly than any other creature, the virtues of the adorable Trinity; virtues which she never stained with even the least speck of venial sin. The erect petal denotes the omnipotence of God the Father; the two turning downward, the Wisdom and Love of the Son and the Holy Spirit, whom she most resembles. Wherefore she understood from the blessed Virgin that if one were to salute her devoutly with the words: "White Lily of the Trinity and fairest Rose of heavenly bliss," she would show how great is her power through the omnipotence of the Father; and with what ingenuity she knows how to work for the salvation of the human race, through the wisdom of the Son; and how immeasurably her heart abounds in tenderness, through the love of the Holy Spirit.

The blessed Virgin added: "Besides this, at the hour of death I shall appear to the soul who salutes me in this way in a blossoming of such beauty that she will be wondrously consoled as I reveal to her the bliss of heaven." From that time Gertrude resolved to salute the blessed Virgin, or her images, with these words: "Hail, white Lily of the resplendent and ever tranquil Trinity! Fairest Rose of heaven's bliss! The King of heaven chose to be born of you, to be fed with your milk! Oh, feed our souls on the outpourings of divine grace!"

Chapter 20. Of Her Special Love of God and of a Salutation of an Image of the Blessed Virgin

She was wont, as lovers are, to refer to her Beloved everything that she liked or savored. Whatever she heard read or sung, any praise or homage of the blessed Virgin or some other saint, whatever moved or charmed her, always made her turn her thoughts to the King of kings, who was rightly the Lord of her choice and her one delight, rather than to the saints whose feast or memorial was being celebrated. And so on the feast of the Annunciation[47] of the Lord, when the blessed Virgin was so often extolled by the preacher and no mention was made of the Lord's Incarnation, which brought about our salvation, she was grieved and, after the sermon, as she was passing in front of the altar of the glorious Virgin, in saluting her she did not feel moved exclusively by sweet affection toward the mother of every grace, but instead every time that she saluted and praised her, her loving thoughts always went out toward Jesus, the blessed fruit of her womb. She began to fear that by this she had incurred the displeasure of so powerful a queen. Her fears were set at rest by the kindest of consolers, who said: "Fear not, dearest, because it is this kind of salutation or praise of my beloved mother, directed more to me than to herself, which is the most agreeable to her. All the same, if your conscience is troubled by this, next time you are in front of the altar of my immaculate Mother, try to salute her image with greater devotion, without saluting mine." To this she replied: "Far be it from me, my Lord, my only—or rather all—my good; for my heart could never consent to forsake you, my whole salvation, the very life of my soul, and to direct my attention elsewhere in making such a salutation." To this the Lord fondly answered: "Consent to me now, my love. And as often as you salute my Mother and not me, I shall not only accept, but will reward this act of perfection whereby one truly faithful, with a ready heart, has forsaken me, the hundredfold of all hundredfolds, for my greater glory."

Chapter 22. How Sickness Excuses Apparent Negligence

Once sickness prevented her from following the regular observance, and she remained seated during Vespers. Her heart filled with longing and sadness, she said to the Lord: "Would I not be praising you better, Lord, if I were in Choir with the community, praying and strenuously following all the other regular exercises instead of being kept here now through this infirmity, wasting so much time doing nothing?"

The Lord answered: "Do you think that the spouse takes less pleasure in his bride when he is alone with her in the privacy of the nuptial chamber, and they can delight one another with the charm of intimate converse and tender embraces, than when he leads her forth in all her beauty to be seen by the crowds?" From this she understood that a soul goes out, as it were, adorned, in public, when she sets herself to do good works for the glory of God; whereas she remains quietly alone with her spouse in the nuptial chamber when she is prevented by bodily suffering from doing such works. Because, when she is thus deprived of all pleasure arising from external senses, she is left entirely to God's good pleasure. And so the Lord takes all the more delight in a person, in proportion as they find within themselves less and less motives for self-satisfaction and vainglory.

Chapter 23. The Threefold Blessing

She was assisting at Mass one day as devoutly as ever she could; they had reached the "Kyrie eleison" when it seemed to her that her guardian angel had taken her up into his arms like a little child and was presenting her to God the Father for his blessing, saying: "Bless, O Lord God, Father, your little daughter!" God the Father was silent for a time, as though it were beneath him to bless such a little thing; coming to herself again, she was covered with confusion and began to consider her wretchedness and unworthiness. Then the Son of God arose and made over to her all his most holy life on earth to supply for her shortcomings. And then she saw how splendidly she was attired in rich clothing as if she were grown up into the measure of the age of the fullness of Christ (Eph. 4:13). Then God the Father was appeased and, bending lovingly toward her, gave her a threefold blessing together with a threefold remission of all the sins, whether of thought, word, or deed, whereby she had offended against his almighty power. Then she offered to God the Father by way of thanksgiving all the most perfect life of his only-begotten Son. At this, the gems with which her garments were adorned seemed to vibrate together, giving out the sweetest and most delectable melody in eternal praise of God the Father. By this, she understood how very pleasing it is to God the Father when one offers up to him the most perfect life of his Son. After this, the angel we have mentioned presented her in like manner to the Son of God, saying, "Bless, Son of the King, your sister." After she had received from him a threefold blessing in remission of everything she had committed against the wisdom of God, she was finally presented by the angel to the Holy Spirit with the words: "Bless, O Lover of humankind, your betrothed!" At this she received as a dowry a threefold blessing in remission of all the sins whereby she had offended against the goodness of God.

Therefore, let anyone who likes to do so strive to gain these nine blessings at the "*Kyrie eleison*."[48]

Chapter 25. **The Service of the Divine Heart**

Another time, when she was striving to pay the greatest attention to each single note and word and seeing that in this she was very often hindered by human frailty, sadly she said within herself: "And what profit can there be in a labor in which I am so inconsistent?" The Lord could not bear her sadness and gave her, with his own hands as it were, his divine heart in the form of a lighted lamp, saying: "Behold, here is my heart, the sweetest instrument of the ever adorable Trinity. I hold it in front of the eyes of your heart; it will supply all that you lack, faithfully making up for all that you entrust to it. And so everything will appear most perfect in my sight. Because, like a faithful servant who is always ready to do what his lord pleases, from now onward my heart will always cleave to you, so that it may make up at any time for all your negligences."

Awestruck in her amazement at such unheard-of condescension on the Lord's part, she deemed it most incongruous that the heart of the Lord, the unique, most precious treasure-house of the divinity, containing all goodness, should be placed at the service of such a little creature, waiting, like the servant of a lord, to supply for all her negligences.

The Lord kindly came to the rescue of such faintheartedness and deigned to encourage her with this similitude: "Suppose," he said, "that having a very musical and supple voice, and moreover a great love of singing, someone near you who had a very loud and harsh voice were singing very badly so that even after making great efforts she could hardly sing a note correctly, wouldn't you be indignant if she would not let you sing what you are able and most ready to render, and what she would do with so much difficulty? So, without any doubt, my divine heart, recognizing the frailty and inconstancy of human nature, always waits with ineffable longing to supply for whatever you entrust to it, if not by words, at least by a sign, so as to do for you whatever you are unable to do for yourself. Its omnipotence makes it act with ease; its impenetrable wisdom enables it to know what is best; and the goodness which is natural to me makes me desire with sweet and joyous benevolence to accomplish this end."[49]

Chapter 26. Of the Abundant Grace Flowing into the Soul from the Heart of God

After this, while she was thinking with gratitude of the more-than-magnificent gift just mentioned, she asked the Lord how long he would graciously deign to let her keep it. The Lord answered her: "As long as you wish to keep it I shall not cause you to suffer by withdrawing it from you." Then she said: "O God, author of inestimable marvels, how is it that I am aware of your divine heart hanging in the form of a lamp in the midst of my heart (alas, so unworthy), and yet, whenever, by the favor of your grace, I may dare to approach you, I have the joy of finding it within yourself, offering me an abundance of all delights?" He replied: "Just as you stretch out your hand when you want to take hold of something and, when you have taken it, you draw it back toward you; so, languishing for love of you (Song 2:5), when you are distracted by exterior things, I stretch out my heart to you to draw you to myself; and, again, when, your inmost thoughts in harmony with mine, you recollect yourself, and again attend to me, then I draw back my heart again, and you with it, into myself, and from it I offer you the pleasure of all its many virtues."

Then, pondering within herself with the greatest wonder and gratitude the gratuitous kindness of God to her, and considering her wretchedness and her many and varied defects, in the greatest dejection she plunged herself, as was her custom, into the lowliest valley of humility, deeming herself to be utterly unworthy of all grace. She kept herself secretly hidden for a time. The Lord who, though he inhabits the highest heaven, loves to impart his grace to the humble (Ps. 112: 5–6), seemed to send down a sort of golden tube, like a drinking-straw, from his heart which was hanging suspended like a lamp over the soul who was cowering in the valley of humility. Through this tube he caused to flow into her in a wonderful way all that she could desire. For instance, if she, remembering her defects, were to humble herself, the Lord would have pity on her at once and from his most blessed heart there would flow into her the spring-like flowering of his divine virtues. These, blotting out all her faults, did not let them appear anywhere in the sight of his divine benignity. In like manner, if she desired to have some spiritual ornament, or anything which the human heart conceives of as desirable and pleasant, instantly all the sweetest and happiest thoughts and sensations flowed into her through the tube we have mentioned.[50]

After some time, during which she had been enjoying such sweet delights and, not without the cooperation of divine grace, when she was becomingly adorned with every virtue—not hers but the Lord's—and appeared to be absolutely perfect (cf. Ez. 16:14), she heard as though in her heart a most sweet voice, as sweet as the lovely melody of a skillful harpist playing on his harp (cf. Rev. 14:2), a voice singing these words: "Come to me, my own! Enter into me, my own! Remain with me, my own!" Sweet as honey, the Lord helped her to understand the true meaning of this song: "Come to me, my own; because I love you as the cherished bride of my heart, I want you always present; therefore I am calling you. Again, because I find my delight in you, I want you to enter into me; as a young man desires to find perfected in himself the delight of his heart. Again, as I, your God, who am Love, have chosen you, I desire that you remain indissolubly united with me, as a living man is unwilling to let go the breath of life without which he could not exist, even for an hour."

During the infinitely sweet delight which this caused her, she felt herself to be drawn in an indescribable way, through the tube we have mentioned, into the heart of the Lord, and she had the happiness of finding herself within the very being of her spouse and lord. What she there felt, saw, heard, tasted, touched,[51] is known to her alone, and to him who deigned to admit her to such a union, so excellent and so sublime, with him, Jesus, the spouse of the loving soul, who is God, blessed above all, for ever and ever.

Chapter 28. The Cloister of the Lord's Body

At Vespers, while they were singing "*Vidi aquam egredientem*"[52] the Lord said to her: "Behold my heart; now it will be your temple. And now look among the other parts of my body and choose for yourself other places[53] in which you can lead a monastic life, because from now on my body will be your cloister.[54] To this she said: "Lord, I do not know how to seek further or how to choose, because I find such sweet plenty in your sweetest heart, which you deign to call my temple, that apart from it I am unable to find any rest or refreshment, both of which are necessary in a cloister." Then the Lord said: "If it pleases you, you may find both these things in my heart; for you have heard about others who, like Dominic,[55] never left the temple, eating and even sleeping there. Do choose, however, some other places which you think it would be expedient to have in your cloister."

Then, at the Lord's bidding, she chose the Lord's feet for a hall or ambulatory; his hands for workshop; his mouth for parlor and chapter house; his eyes for library where she might read; and his ears for confessional. Then the Lord taught her that she should always go up to it after each fall, as though ascending the five steps of humiliation, which are to be remembered by these five expressions: "I, a wretch, a sinner, a beggar, evil, unworthy, come to you as to the overflowing abyss of mercy, to be washed from every stain and to be cleansed from every sin. Amen."

Chapter 30. Of the Use of Free Will, of the Offering of the Heart, and of Various Other Points Which She Understood Through the Words of the Divine Office

During the Mass *Veni et ostende*[56] the Lord appeared, all mellifluous, as it were, with the sweetness of divine grace, breathing forth his divine and life-giving breath as he descended from his high throne of imperial glory[57] as though to flood more plenteously those who were desirous of his divine grace, for the sweet feast of his Nativity. Then she prayed for those who had commended themselves to her that the Lord might give to each of them an increase of his grace. She received this reply: "I have given to everyone a golden tube of such power that he may draw whatever he desires from the infinite depths of my divine heart.[58] This tube she understood to mean free will, through which a man may claim for his own every spiritual good, both heavenly and earthly. For example, if anyone ardently longs to be able to give God praise, thanksgiving, service, and fidelity equal to that which any saint has ever given him, such a desire is as agreeable to the immense goodness of God as though it had actually been carried out. But this tube takes on its brilliant gold color when a person thanks God for having given him a will of such nobility that with it he can gain infinitely more than the whole world could achieve with all its powers.

Then she perceived that the members of the community standing round the Lord were drawing draughts of divine grace for themselves, according to the ability of each, through the tube which had been given them. And some appeared to be drawing directly from the interior of his divine heart, while what others were imbibing came from the hands of the Lord. And the further away from the heart they drew, the more difficult it was for them to obtain what they wanted. And the closer they were trying to get to the heart of the Lord, the more easily, sweetly, and abundantly could they draw from it. Those who were close to the heart of the Lord and drew directly from it signify those who were always conformed and subdued to the will of God, desiring above all else that the most laudable will of God be fully perfected in their regard, in matters both spiritual and temporal. And these touch the depths of the divine heart so efficaciously that, at the time predestined by the Lord, they shall surely receive in themselves the torrents of divine sweetness (Ps. 35:9), the more fully and sweetly, the more entirely they rely on his will. Those who try to draw graces from the

192

Lord's other members are those who desire to obtain, according to their own wishes, the gift of grace, or practice of virtue, which attracts them most. And they have the greater difficulty in striving for what they desire, the more they depend on their own will and the less they rely on Providence.

Now she offered her heart to the Lord with these words: "See, Lord, here is my heart, empty of all creatures. I offer it to you with my whole will, praying that you will wash it in the sanctifying water from your most sacred side, and that you will adorn it becomingly with the precious blood of your most sweet heart, and that you may prepare it for yourself most fittingly in the fragrant ardor of your divine love."

Then the Son of God appeared, offering to God the Father her heart united with his divine heart, in the likeness of a chalice, made of two parts, joined with wax. Seeing this, she said to the Lord in devout supplication: "Grant, most loving Lord, that my heart may cleave always to you, like a flagon which is offered for the refreshment of lords, that you may always, at your pleasure, have it at hand, clean, and ready to pour into it or out of it at any time you please, and for whomsoever you please." The Son of God kindly accepted this and said to his Father: "To your eternal praise, O holy Father, may that heart pour forth all that my human heart contains for distribution."

After this, she often offered her heart to the Lord in the aforesaid words and seemed to see it filled in such a way that its outpourings of praise and thanksgiving sometimes increased the joys of these dwelling in heaven, and sometimes contributed to the perfection of those who still dwell on earth, as will be seen in what follows. For it was from this time that she understood that it pleased the Lord that she should have these things written down for the good of many.

In Advent, at the responsory *"Ecce veniet Dominus protector noster, sanctus Israel,"*[59] she understood that if someone applies himself with all his heart to desire that his whole life be governed, in prosperity and adversity, according to the most laudable will of God, then by such thoughts, with God's grace, he would be giving as much honor to God as one would give to an emperor in placing the imperial crown on his head.

Again, she understood from the words which we read in Isaiah: "Arise, arise, stand up, O Jerusalem" (Is. 51:17) the advantage which the church militant here on earth derives from the devotion of the elect. Because, that is, when one loving soul turns to the Lord with her whole heart and will, ready, if she could, to compensate to God for all offenses detrimental to his honor, and so shows him her tenderness as she prays, aflame with the torches of love, it pleases him so much that sometimes he will be reconciled to, and forgive, even the entire world. And this is what is meant when it is said: "Thou hast drunk even to the bottom of the cup" (ibid.); because in this way the rigor of justice is completely changed to the serenity of mercy. But to that is added: "Thou hast drunk even to the dregs" (ibid.). From this it is understood that for the damned, who can expect only the dregs of justice, no redemption is possible.

Again, in the words of Isaiah: "Thou shalt glorify him, while thou dost not thine own ways" (Is. 58:14), she understood that if a man decides in advance what he will do or say, and then, seeing that it is of no profit, refrains from doing what perhaps he would have liked to do, he will derive from it three benefits. The first is that he will be given sweeter delight in God, as it is said: "Thou shalt be delighted in the Lord" (ibid.). The second is that harmful thoughts will have less power over him, as it is said: "I will lift thee above the high places of the earth" (ibid.). The third is that in eternal life the Son of God will, among other things, communicate the fruits of his own holy life to him, since he has resisted nobly and gained a glorious victory over all temptations, as it is said: "And I will feed thee with the inheritance of Jacob thy father" (ibid.). Again in Isaiah's words, "Behold, his reward is with him" (Is. 40:10), she understood how the Lord himself in his love is the reward of the elect; so sweetly does he insinuate himself into them that a loving soul can truly say she is rewarded far beyond her merits. "And his work is before him" (ibid.), that is, when a soul puts her whole trust in divine Providence, desiring the will of God in all her actions, then, by God's grace, she already appears perfect in his sight.

Again, by these words: "Sanctify yourselves, children of Israel,"[60] she understood that if a soul is ready to repent of all her sins, whether of commission or of omission, and intends with all her heart to obey God's commandments, as truly will she be found holy before God and made ready as was the leper who was cleansed, to whom the Lord said: "I will, be thou made clean" (Matt. 8:3).

Again, by these words: "Sing ye to the Lord a new song" (Is. 42:10), she understood that a new song is sung to the Lord by all who sing with the intention to be devout, for, since it is from God that they have received the power to form this intention, they are renewed and made pleasing to him.

Again, by these words: "The spirit of the Lord is upon me" (Is. 61:1) and, further, "to heal the contrite of heart" (ibid.), she understood that the Son of God, sent as he was by the Father to heal the contrite of heart, usually tries his chosen ones by suffering, which may sometimes be quite slight, or come from external circumstances, in order to have an opportunity to heal them. However, when he turns to the soul on such occasions, it is not the troubles which are causing the heart to break which he heals, since that may not be so harmful, but rather anything injurious that he finds in the soul.

Then through these words: "In the splendors of the holy places,"[61] she realized that so great, so incomprehensible, is the light of the divinity,[62] that even were each one of the saints from Adam down to the last man to have a personal knowledge of it as luminous, as exalted, and as vast as any creature may have, and if no one of them were to share what they knew with another—even if the number of the saints were a thousand times greater than it is—the divinity would still remain inexhaustible and infinitely beyond all intelligence. And that is why it is not said: "In the splendor of the holy places," but 'In the splendors of the holy places, from the womb before the day star I begot thee.' "

Once, when they were singing in honor of a martyr, "*Qui vult venire post me,*"[63] she saw the Lord walking along a path, pleasant to behold, with fairest flowers and verdure, but narrow and lined with dense hedges bristling with sharp thorns. She saw that he seemed to be preceded by a cross which parted the thorns and made the way wider and easier. With a serene expression on his face, turning toward those who belonged to him, he invited them to follow him, saying: "Whoever wishes to come after me, let him deny himself, and take up his cross, and follow me." From this, she knew that the cross of each is his own personal trial. For example, for some souls obedience is a cross, when they are obliged to do what is contrary to their wishes; for others, to be burdened with infirmity, which acts as a restraint; and so on. We should all carry our crosses and apply ourselves with a good will to suffer adversity gladly, and in addition to do all that is in our power, neglecting nothing which we know to be for the greater glory of God.

When they were singing the verse of the psalm: "The words of the wicked . . ." (Ps. 64:4), she understood that if anyone who commits a sin through human frailty is too severely reprehended for his fault, the mercy of God is provoked, and the merits of the culprit are increased.

During the singing of the "Hail holy Queen," at the words "eyes

195

of mercy," she asked for health of body for herself, at which the Lord, fondly smiling, said: "Don't you know that I look on you most mercifully when you are being chastened by bodily or mental suffering?"

Again, on the feast of several martyrs, while they were singing "The glorious blood . . . ,"[64] she realized that although blood is in itself an unpleasant thing, it is praised in Scripture because it is shed for Christ; similarly, the neglect of religious duties, for motives of obedience or fraternal charity, pleases God so much that it too might well be termed glorious.

On another occasion she understood how God, by a hidden dispensation of his judgment, sometimes permits wicked people, when they try to tempt chosen souls by deceitfully asking them to disclose secrets, to receive a reply which only serves to make them persist in obstinacy and error. And this is to the detriment of the wicked, but to the advantage of the just. That is why we find in Ezekiel: "If anyone place his uncleanness in his heart and set up a stumbling-block of his iniquity before his face and shall come to the prophet inquiring of me by him, I the Lord will answer him according to the multitude of his uncleannesses; that he may be caught in his own heart . . ." (Ez. 14: 4,5).

Through these words, which are sung of John, "He drank the mortal poison . . . ,"[65] she understood that, as John was preserved from mortal poison by the virtue of faith, so the fidelity of the will keeps the soul immaculate, however poisonous what is insinuated into the heart against the will may be.

By the versicle "Vouchsafe, O Lord this day,"[66] she understood that whenever a man commends himself to God, praying that he will keep him from sin, then, even if it seems to that man, by the hidden designs of God, that he has fallen into some grave sin, yet he will never sin in such a way that he lacks the grace of God, which will support him like a staff and lead him easily to repentance.

While they were singing the Responsory, *"Benedicens . . . ,"[67]* she presented herself to the Lord as though she were Noah in person, imploring him to give her his blessing. After this was done, the Lord himself in his turn seemed to be asking her for a blessing. Then she understood that a man is blessing God when he says in his heart that he repents of having offended his creator and implores his help to prevent him from falling again into sin. At this blessing the Lord of heaven bowed low, showing her that this was as acceptable to him as though that blessing had been responsible for all his beatitude.

196

Again, by these words, "Where is thy brother Abel?"[68] she comprehended that God requires every religious to give an account of whatever is done against the *Rule* by his fellow religious, if such a fault could have been prevented in some way, either by personal admonition or by reporting to the superior. The excuse which some people give, "It is not my duty to correct my brother," or "I am worse than he is," will be no better received by God than were the words of Cain, "Am I my brother's keeper?" (Gen. 4:9) Everyone is held responsible before God for restraining his brother from evil and encouraging him to do good. And each time that he fails in this, against his conscience, he sins against God. And it is in vain that he claims that he did not receive the charge to do so, because the charge is truly from God, as his conscience tells him. If he neglects this duty, God will require an account of it from his soul, and perhaps more from his soul than from the soul of the superior, who was either not present or, if he was, perhaps did not notice. Wherefore there are the menacing words of Scripture: Woe to those who do evil, woe, woe to those who consent (cf. Rom. 1:32). He who consents to evil practices deceit in concealing it when, by disclosing it, he could show forth God's praise.

From the Responsory *"Induit me Dominus,"*[69] she understood that anyone who works, in words or deeds, to promote the cause of religion, and who fights in the lawful cause of justice, clothes the Lord, so to speak, in a rich garment of honor and glory. And the Lord will reward him in eternal life according to the riches of his royal liberality, clothing him with joy as with a garment and, as an additional reward, he will deck his brow with a crown of spiritual glory (cf. Is. 61:10). But in particular she understood that if in advancing the cause of good or of religion one suffers adversity, it is more acceptable to God, just as a garment is more acceptable to a pauper if it warms as well as clothes him. And if someone who tries to promote the cause of religion is prevented by others from having any success, his merit is not in the least diminished in God's sight.

While they were singing the Responsory *"Vocavit angelus Domini,"*[70] she realized how hosts of angels surround the elect and are fully sufficient to protect them. But if the Lord in his fatherly providence sometimes suspends this protection and lets his chosen ones be tried in some way, it is in order that they may be the more gloriously rewarded; their reward will be all the greater if they have triumphed by their own virtue while the custody and protection of their guardian angels have, so to say, been withheld.

197

Again, as a consequence of that Responsory, she understood that, just as holy Abraham stretched forth his arm in obedience and so deserved to be called by an angel, so the elect, when he bends his mind wholeheartedly to do some difficult work for God, is instantly smiled on by the sweetness of divine grace and deservedly consoled by his own conscience. And so in the boundless liberality of God he is given this consolation even before his eternal reward; for each will receive a reward appropriate to his labor.

Once, when she was reflecting on the adversities of her past life, she asked the Lord why he had allowed her to be troubled by certain persons. To that she received the following reply: "When a fatherly hand is raised to chastise the child, the rod cannot resist. And so I could wish that my chosen ones would never blame the persons by whom they are tried, but should always consider that, in my fatherly affection, I would never let the faintest breath of wind blow against them if I were not looking to the eternal salvation they will receive as their reward; rather let them have compassion on those who stain their own souls for their purification."

One day she was having difficulty with a certain task, and she said to God the Father: "Lord, I offer you this work through your only Son, in the power of the Holy Spirit, to your eternal praise." She knew the power of these words to be such that in a marvelous way they elevate any work done with that intention far beyond human estimation, so that whatever is offered is made pleasing to God the Father. Just as that which is seen through a green glass appears to be green, or red, if seen through a red glass, and so on, whatever is offered to God the Father through his only-begotten Son becomes most pleasing and acceptable to him.

Once as she was praying she asked the Lord what good it did her friends to pray for them all the time, while she saw in them no improvement as a result of her prayers. The Lord instructed her by this comparison: "When a little child is brought back from the presence of an emperor who has enriched him with vast possessions and an immense revenue, which of those who look at his childish form can see any effect of what he has been given, although his future wealth and greatness are no secret from those who were witnesses? Do not be surprised, therefore, that you see no material result from your prayers, for I, in my eternal wisdom, will dispose of them in the most useful and perfect way. And no faithful prayer is without fruit, although the way in which it bears fruit is hidden from humankind."

Desiring to know what fruit there was in directing her thoughts to God, she was thus enlightened: When a man meditates or simply turns his attention to God, it is as though he were standing before the throne of glory holding up to God a mirror of marvelous luster, in which the Lord rejoices to see his own image reflected, because it is he who sends and directs all good things. As through his own limitations a man sometimes has difficulty in doing this, the harder he strives to do it, the more delectably does the mirror seem to shine before the face of the ever adorable Trinity and all the saints. And this will be for the abiding glory of God and for the everlasting bliss of the soul.

One feast-day, when she was prevented from singing by a bad headache, she asked the Lord why he so often let this happen to her on a feast-day. She received this reply: "Lest perchance you are carried away by the pleasure of singing the sacred melody and become less receptive of grace." And she said, "Your grace, Lord, can protect me from that." He rejoined: "But it is easier for a person to be perfect if an occasion of falling into sin is taken away from him by his being brought low by some affliction or trouble. This brings him a twofold growth in merit, for he increases in both patience and humility."

Carried away by her love, she said to the Lord one day: "How I wish, O Lord, that my soul might burn with such a fire that it might melt and be like some liquid substance, so that it could be entirely poured out into you!" He answered: "Your will is to you such a fire." By these words she saw that it is by his will that a man receives the full effect of all the desires he has as regards God.

She had often sought by prayer to obtain from the Lord the rooting out of vices in herself and others; and had often felt that one could not do better than to ask God in his mercy to loosen the bonds which come from bad habit, so that it would be as easy to resist a vice as if the difficulty were not increased by the force of habit which we call second nature. Now she came to recognize in this the admirable plan of divine love for the salvation of humankind, which, for the increase of our eternal glory, permits us to be attacked by many and violent temptations to evil, so that we may be able to gain a more glorious victory over them.

During a sermon she heard the preacher say that no one could be saved without the love of God, and that everyone must have at least enough to be brought to repent and to abstain from sin for the sake of the love of God. She considered in her heart that, in departing this life, more people seem to repent through a fear of hell rather than for love of

God. To this the Lord made answer: "When I see the death agony of those who have at any time found my remembrance sweet, or who have done some meritorious work, even if on the point of death, I show myself to them so full of kindness, love, and mercy that they repent from the bottom of their hearts for having ever offended me, and through this repentance they are saved. And so I would like my chosen ones to praise me for this benefit, among the general benefits for which they give me thanks."

Sometimes when meditating she began to see her interior deformities and to be so displeased with herself that with anxiety she would wonder how she could ever be pleasing to God, who would see so many stains in her, for where she saw only one stain, the all-penetrating eyes of the divinity would see an infinite number. She was reassured about this by the divine reply: "Love makes pleasing." By this she understood that if on earth human love has such power that sometimes it makes the deformed pleasing, for love's sake, to those who love them, and even at times so pleasing that the lovers, through the power of love, want to resemble their loved ones, how then be distrustful of God, who is Love itself? Cannot he, through the power of love, make pleasing those whom he loves?

Again, like the Apostle, she longed to be dissolved and to be with Christ (Phil. 1:23–24). Many a time she sighed from the depths of her heart about this, and once she received this consoling answer: That as often as she expressed with her whole heart the desire that she might be freed from this deadly prison, and yet with a firm will was ready to remain as long as it pleased God to keep her in the body, so often would the Son of God unite the merit of his most holy life to hers so that, in a wondrous way, she might appear perfect before the face of God the Father.

One day she was reflecting on the numerous and wonderful graces she had received so freely from God's love, deeming herself to be most wretched and unworthy of every good thing, since she had accepted such innumerable gifts from God and had wasted them so carelessly that they seemed to have borne no fruits—for neither had they increased her enjoyment or her thanksgiving, nor had they helped others, to whom, had they been made known, they might have tended to some edification or been a means of bringing them to know God better. She was consoled by being enlightened thus on the subject: The Lord does not bestow his gifts of grace on his chosen ones in order to exact from each a worthy fruit, for he knows that human frailty often prevents that. But the overflowing love and generosity of God cannot restrain itself; although he knows a man is not able to make use of all of them, he assiduously pours forth a great quantity of extra graces, in order that the man may at least receive a great quantity of blessedness in the future. It is just like this with the earthly things which are sometimes given to a child who has, at the time, no idea of the use they will be to him; when he is grown up, he will derive much profit from them. Similarly, the Lord, in giving graces to his elect in this life, is preparing them and making them suited to the things in whose enjoyment will consist their eternal beatitude in heaven.

When she was bemoaning in her heart that she could not desire to praise God as much as she should have done, she was divinely taught that God is best satisfied when we are not able to do more than want to have this great desire; our desires are great before God in proportion to our desire that they should be great. And when the heart has this desire—that is, the will to have the desire—God takes more delight in dwelling in the soul than a person could have in dwelling among flowers of springtime loveliness.

On another occasion she was prevented by bodily infirmity from giving her attention fully to God for some days; when she came to herself, her conscience was troubled. With devout humility she set herself to confess her fault to the Lord. And although she feared she would have to toil for a long time to regain the sweetness of divine grace, suddenly, in an instant, she felt the gentle kindness of God, who was bending over her with the tenderest embrace, and saying: "Daughter, you are always with me and all I have is yours" (Lk. 15:31). These words made it clear to her that if sometimes out of human frailty we neglect to direct our attention to God, his loving mercy never fails to consider all our works to be worthy of an eternal reward, so long as the will does not turn away from God, and one makes frequent acts of contrition for everything for which the conscience feels remorse.

As a feast was approaching, she began to feel unwell, and she desired that the Lord might keep her well until after the feast, or at least to mitigate the infirmity, that she might not be prevented from celebrating the feast; she would, however, submit herself entirely to the divine will. She received this answer from the Lord: "By asking for this, and above all because you submit your will to mine, you lead me into a little garden of delights, planted with flowers and very lovely in my sight. But, you know, if I hear your prayer that you may not be hindered in my service, then I shall be following you to the part of the garden which you yourself prefer. While, if I do not grant your prayer, and you persevere in patience, then you will be following me to the part of the garden which I like better, because I take more pleasure in you if you have this desire in spite of your trouble than if you had devotion together with sensible pleasure."

She was considering the judgment of God in giving some souls great consolation in his service, while other souls remain in a state of aridity, and was enlightened thus by God: "The heart has been created by God to hold delight, just as a vessel for holding water. Now if the vessel holding water lets it seep out through any small cracks, the vessel will gradually empty and become dry; so if the human heart that is filled with spiritual delight lets it seep out through the senses of the body, by seeing and hearing, or by allowing any of the other bodily senses to be freely indulged, it could leak out in such a way that the heart would become wholly emptied of delight in God. And anyone can experience this for himself. If one desires to see something, or to say some word in which there is little or no profit, and one does it at once, one thinks it is of no importance, because it slips away as easily as water. But if one proposes to restrain oneself for God's sake, the spiritual delight will increase so much that soon the heart will be too small to contain it. Thus it is that when a man restrains himself in such matters, he comes to experience delight in God; and the harder he has to strive to do it, the more pleasure he will find in God, and the more fruitful will be his devotion.

One day she was feeling very depressed about some little matter of no importance. At the elevation of the host she offered this feeling of desolation to God's eternal praise. Then the Lord seemed to attract her soul through the most sacred host as through a gateway and, making her rest sweetly on his bosom, he tenderly spoke these words: "See, in this resting-place you will breathe free from all troubles, but every time you leave it, bitterness will invade your heart again, and this will be a saving antidote."

On another occasion she was feeling worn out and said to the Lord: "O my Lord, what is to become of me? What do you want of me?" The Lord answered: "As a mother comforts her child, I will comfort you."[71] He added: "Haven't you ever seen a mother caressing her child?" At this, she was silent, not being able to remember. The Lord recalled to her mind that scarcely six months before she had seen a mother fondling her little child, and he reminded her especially of three things which she had not noticed at the time. First, the mother often asked her little child to kiss her, at which the little one was obliged to raise himself with an effort on his weak little legs. The Lord added that it was necessary to raise oneself with a great effort by means of contemplation to the enjoyment of the sweetness of his love.[72] Second, the mother tested the will of her child, saying: "Do you want this? Do you want this or that?" and let him have nothing. So God tries a man when he makes him foresee great troubles which never come to anything. However, when a man submits willingly, God is fully satisfied and makes him worthy of an eternal reward. Third, when the child spoke, no one present could understand a word the little boy said, save only his mother. So only God can understand man's intention and judges him accordingly, far otherwise than man, who sees only exterior things.

Another time, when she was downcast at the memory of her former sins to such an extent that she desired only to hide herself completely, the Lord deigned to incline with such gracious condescension toward her that the whole court of heaven seemed to be trying to restrain him as if in astonishment. The Lord responded thus: "Nothing can restrain me from following her when she so powerfully attracts my heart by the cords of her humility."

Asking the Lord what he would like her to apply her thoughts to at that time, she received this reply from him: "I want you to learn patience." It chanced that just then she was very much upset about something. She said to him: "And how and by what means can I learn this?" Then the Lord, lifting her up like a kind teacher who holds his little pupil close to his breast, proposed to her three ways of acquiring patience, as if he were teaching her three letters, saying in the first place: "Consider how great is the affectionate intimacy with which a king addresses the person who above all others is most like him in every way; judge, therefore, how my affection for you grows when you suffer with patience for my sake contempt like that which I suffered." In the second place, he said: "Again, consider with what respect the friend of a king, who resembles him in everything, is treated by all his subjects; and judge what glory your patience is laying up for you in the court of heaven." Then, in the third place, he said: "Consider what comfort can be given by the consoling caresses of a faithful friend; judge, therefore, with what sweet tenderness I shall console you in heaven for the least of the things which afflict your mind here."

Chapter 32. Constant Desires, Troubled Dreams, and the Temptations of the Enemy

During the Mass for the Dead, while they were singing the Tract *Sicut cervus,*[73] at the words, "My soul thirsts," trying to rouse herself from her tepidity, she said to the Lord: "Alas, my Lord, how lukewarm are my desires for you, my true good, since I can so seldom truly say to you that my soul thirsts for you." The Lord replied: "Say to me not seldom but very often that your soul thirsts for me; for the merciful love with which I desire man's salvation compels me to believe that, whenever my chosen ones desire some good thing, it is really myself that they desire, since all good things are in me and come from me. For example, if a man desires health, ease, wisdom, and the like, in order to increase his merit I often consider that it is myself that he desires, unless he deliberately turns away from me, that is, if he desires to have wisdom that he may boast of it, or health that he may do amiss. And for that reason I frequently afflict those who are specially dear to me with infirmities of the body or distress of the mind and so on, so that, when they desire the good which is the opposite of these ills, the ardent love of my heart causes me to reward them more abundantly, with the generosity which is my delight."

On another occasion something similar was made known to her by divine inspiration; that is, the Lord, who delights to be with the children of men (Prov. 8:31)—although he may find in men nothing that could make them sufficiently pleasing to be worthy of his presence—sometimes sends them troubles or sorrows, either of body or of spirit, precisely in order to have the opportunity to stay with them, as the Scriptures truly say: "The Lord is nigh unto them that are of a contrite heart" (Ps. 33:19). And again: "I am with him in tribulation" (Ps. 90:15).

When we consider this and similar things, we are forced to cry out from the depths of our hearts with all the gratitude and love of which our human frailty is capable, the words of the Apostle: "Oh, the depths of the riches of the wisdom and of the knowledge of God! How incomprehensible are his judgments, and how unsearchable his ways!" (Rom. 11:33). How inventive he is in working for the salvation of humankind!

One night she had fallen asleep when the Lord visited her in a dream so sweetly that she seemed to be as much refreshed by the intimate fellowship of the Lord's presence as by the most delicious banquet. On awaking she said to him in gratitude: "How is it, Lord God, that I, most unworthy, should receive this, rather than others who are often so much troubled in dreams that their cries terrify those who hear them?" He answered: "If those whom my fatherly providence disposes to sanctify through suffering seek, while they are awake, to procure comfort for their bodies and so deprive themselves of occasions of merit then, in my divine love, I trouble them with dreams which I send them so that they may merit at least something." She asked: "But Lord, how can they acquire merit if they have no intention of suffering and do so, as it were, against their will?" He explained: "My goodness accomplishes this. In the world, those who wear ornaments of glass or copper do indeed appear to be adorned, but those who wear gold and real gems must be considered to be very much wealthier; the same applies in this case."

Once, when she was reciting the Canonical Hours with less attention than usual she saw at her side the ancient enemy of humankind who, in mocking guise, recited the rest of the psalm "thy testimonies are wonderful . . ." (Ps. 118:129), hastily slurring over and suppressing words and syllables. When he had finished, he said: "Well has your creator, your savior and your lover, employed his gifts in giving you such facility of speech! You can make eloquent discourses on any subject whenever you want, but when you speak to him your words are so hasty and careless that just now in this psalm you left out this number of letters, this number of syllables, and this number of words." Then she realized that if this wily enemy had counted so exactly the letters and syllables, it was so that after death he could bring grave accusations against those who tend to say the Hours of the Divine Office in a hurry and without real attention.

Once, when she was spinning rather hurriedly, she happened to let some small threads of wool drop, all her attention being turned toward the Lord to whom she was offering her work. She saw the devil picking up the threads, as if to bear witness to her fault. But when she called upon the Lord he chased the enemy away, reproaching him for having dared to interfere with a work that had been offered to God from the very beginning.

Chapter 33. The Faithful Service of the Lord

Burning with a very great longing for the Lord, she said to him: "Now, my Lord, may I pray to you?" The kindest Lord replied with tenderness: "Come, my lady and queen, you may well command me, because I shall comply with your will and desires in everything, more promptly than any servant could serve his mistress."

To this she said: "I have absolute trust in every word you address to me in your most loving condescension; but, as you show yourself so eager to hear me (so unworthy), why, I ask, are my prayers so often without effect?" He replied: "When the queen is spinning and says to her servant, 'Give me the thread which is hanging down over my left shoulder' (thinking it is so, since she cannot see behind her back), and he, seeking to obey her command and seeing that the thread is hanging down over her right shoulder and not her left, takes it where he finds it and gives it to his lady, deeming this more advisable than to fulfill her orders literally by pulling a thread out of the left side of her gown. It is the same with me, who am inscrutable wisdom; if I do not grant your prayers to the letter, without doubt I always grant you instead something more profitable, for you are sometimes prevented by your human frailty from understanding what is best."

Chapter 35. Effects of Receiving the Body of the Lord

She prayed to the Lord that at the time of her death he would grant that her last food on earth might be the life-giving sacrament of the body of Christ, and in the spirit she was told that what she had asked was not entirely for her good. For there is no bodily necessity which can diminish the effects of that sacrament; how much less, then, that food which a sick person receives unwillingly and as if a punishment were being inflicted upon him, merely to sustain life for the glory of God. Therefore if, when one receives this sacrament, that union whereby man is united to God ennobles all the good that is in one, far more is it true at the moment of death, then, when one has received the sacrament, everything that is thenceforth done with a pure intention, such as suffering with patience, or taking food, drink, and the like, can become meritorious and, through union with the body of Christ, will increase the treasure of one's eternal merits.

Chapter 36. The Value of Frequent Communion

When, on another occasion, she was about to go to communion, she said to the Lord: "O Lord, what is it that you are about to give me?" He replied: "My whole self, with all my divine power, just as my virgin mother received me." Then she asked: "In what way shall I have more than those who received you with me yesterday and today omit to do so, since you always give yourself wholly?" He explained: "If in ancient times anyone who had twice been made consul always preceded someone who had only once held that dignity, how could anyone who had received me more often on earth not have much greater glory in eternal life?"

Then, sighing, she said: "Oh, how much greater than mine is the glory of priests, who communicate daily by reason of their priestly office!" And the Lord said to her: "Indeed, the glory of those who come to me worthily shines very brightly. And yet, the experience of interior delight is a very different thing from the exterior glory. And so there is one reward for someone who comes with desire and love, another for one who receives with awe and reverence, and yet another for one who makes great efforts to be prepared for receiving. But none of these is given to a priest who celebrates merely out of habit."

Chapter 38. The Effect of God's Look of Love

Her great devotion to the body of Christ made her desire to receive it frequently. Once, when she had been preparing herself more fervently than usual for several days beforehand, during the night before the Sunday she felt her strength failing and saw that she would not be able to go to communion. As was her wont, she consulted the Lord about what she could best do to please him. The Lord replied to her gently: "Just as the spouse who has eaten his fill of various dishes prefers to rest for a while quietly in the nuptial chamber with his bride rather than to sit beside her at table, so it will please me more that you should abstain from communion this time, through prudence, rather than receiving." She said: "And how, my most loving Lord, can you really say that now you have eaten your fill?" He replied: "Each one of the restraints you have placed upon your words and all your senses, and also the good desires, prayers, and intentions to which you have applied yourself in preparing for the reception of my most precious body and blood are for me like various most exquisite dishes served to me, with which I am well satisfied."

When she came to Mass, very weak and longing for spiritual communion, it happened that the priest who had taken the body of Christ to a sick person was returning from the village. At the sound of the bell, she was filled with desire and said to the Lord: "Oh, how gladly would I receive you now, life of my soul, at least spiritually, had I but a little time in which to prepare myself!" He replied: "The eyes of my divine love will prepare you most fittingly. Upon which she saw the Lord looking at her, directing rays as of sunlight into her soul and saying, "I will fix my eyes upon thee" (Ps. 31:8). By these words she understood that three things were effected in the soul by the divine gaze, which was like the sun, and that there were three ways in which the soul should prepare to receive them. First, the look of divine love, like the sun, takes away all stains from the soul, purifying it and making it whiter than snow (cf. Ps. 50:9). And this effect can be gained by the humble recognition of one's own defects. Second, the look of divine love melts the soul and fits it to receive spiritual gifts, just as wax is melted by the sun's heat and made ready to take the imprint of a seal. And this effect the soul obtains by devout intentions. Third, the look of divine love makes the soul fruitful, so as to bring forth flowers of virtue, just as the sun gives fecundity to the earth so as to bring forth and multiply its various fruits. And this effect is obtained by faithful trust; for if a person abandons himself wholly to God, faithfully trusting in God's boundless love, everything, whether in adversity or in prosperity, will work together unto good (cf. Rom. 8:28).

At both the Masses at which the community was to receive communion,[74] the Lord showed himself to be graciously present there and seemed to be offering the saving host with his own adorable hand[75] to each one who came to receive, while the priest made the sign of the cross over each host. Moreover, the Lord Jesus seemed with each host that he offered to the other nuns to bestow a most efficacious blessing on her. At this she said in wonder: "Do those who have already received you sacramentally have greater profit, or is it I, who have so freely received so many divine blessings?" He replied: "Is one who is adorned with precious stones and jewelry considered wealthier than one who possesses a great hidden treasure of fine gold?" By these words he gave her to understand that although those who communicated sacramentally would undoubtedly receive a greater abundance of grace for both body and soul as a consequence, according to the belief of the church, yet one who, purely out of the virtues of obedience and prudence and for the glory of God, abstained from sacramental communion, but communicated spiritually, aflame with desire and love of God, would deserve of his divine goodness the blessing which she then received, followed by much more efficacious fruits in God's sight, in a manner which is, however, hidden from human understanding.

Chapter 40. How the Son of God Appeases God the Father

On another occasion she was trying to choose from among all the gifts which the Lord in his generous love had graciously bestowed on her the one which would be most useful to show to other people for the sake of their progress. The Lord, entering into her thoughts and desires, gave her this answer: "It is very profitable for people to remember this: That I, the Son of the virgin, stand ever before God the Father to intercede for the salvation of the human race. And whenever, through human frailty, they fall into some sin in their hearts, I offer my immaculate heart to God the Father for their amendment; when they sin with their lips, I offer my most innocent lips; when they sin with their hands, I show my pierced hands. And so on in a similar way, whatever their sin may be, at once my innocence appeases God the Father, so that penitents may always easily obtain forgiveness. And so I would like my chosen ones, whenever they have prayed for the forgiveness of their faults, always to give me thanks for having obtained for them that this should be so easily granted.

Chapter 41. How She Looked at a Crucifix

One Friday, as evening was falling, she was looking at a crucifix. Moved to compunction, she said to the Lord: "Ah, my sweetest Lover, how many and how cruel sufferings you endured this day for my salvation, and I, alas, in my infidelity have made so little of it that I have passed the day occupied with other matters; I have not spent this day calling to mind with devotion what you, my eternal salvation, suffered for me at each hour, and that you, who are life itself and give life to all things, died for love of me!"[76]

The Lord replied to her from the cross: "That which you were neglecting, I myself have supplied for you. For instance, every hour I gathered into my heart what you should have been recollecting in your heart, and afterward my heart was exceedingly full. Almost bursting with great desire, I have longed for this hour when you would make this intention your own. Now, with that intention of yours, I want to offer to God my Father all that which I have supplied for you throughout this day, for without your intention my action could not be so conducive to your salvation."

In this can be seen how very faithful is the love of God for humankind. In return for this single intention, whereby a man recognizes and is sorry for what he has neglected, the Lord makes amends to God the Father and supplies fully, in the highest degree, for every defect, for which it is right that everyone should praise him.

Again, as she was holding a crucifix in her hand with devout attention, she was given to understand that if anyone were to look with a similar devout attention at an image of Christ crucified, the Lord would look at them with such benign mercy that their soul, like a burnished mirror, would reflect, by an effect of divine love, such a delectable image, that it would gladden the whole court of heaven. And as often as anyone does this on earth with affection and due devotion, it will be to his eternal glory in the future.

Another time she received this instruction: That when a person turns toward a crucifix, he is to consider in his heart that the Lord Jesus is saying to him in gentle tones: "See how I hung upon the cross for love of you, naked and despised, my body covered with wounds and every limb pulled out of joint. And now my heart is moved with such sweet charity toward you that, if it were expedient for your salvation, and if you could be saved in no other way, I would bear for you alone all that you may imagine I bore for the whole world." By such meditations the heart of man is incited to gratitude, because truly one cannot look at a crucifix without being touched by God's grace. Therefore a Christian so lacking in gratitude as to underestimate the immense price of his salvation could not be considered blameless; for never can one look devoutly upon a crucifix without receiving some fruit.

On another occasion, when she was occupied in thinking about the Lord's passion, she understood that meditations on the prayers or passages of Scripture which deal with the Lord's passion are infinitely more efficacious than any others. As it is impossible to touch flour without getting dusty, so no one can think about the Lord's passion with any devotion and not derive some fruit from it. Indeed, even if one only reads something about the passion, one is preparing one's soul to receive at least some of its fruits; for the intention of a person who calls to mind the passion of Christ bears more fruit than the many intentions of another who pays no heed to the Lord's passion. Let us try, therefore, to turn over in our minds more frequently the subject of Christ's passion, so that it may be for us honey in the mouth, music in the ear, gladness in the heart.[77]

Chapter 42. The Bunch of Myrrh

It happened one night that a crucifix hanging near her bed seemed to be leaning down toward her, as though about to fall. She at once set it to rights and caressingly spoke these words: "O my sweetest little Jesus, why are you leaning down?" He answered her at once: "The love of my divine heart impels me toward you." Then, seizing the crucifix, she pressed it to her heart; embracing it and covering it with kisses, tenderly she said: "A bundle of myrrh is my beloved to me" (Song 1:12). The Lord, as if taking the words from her lips, added: "He shall abide between my breasts" (ibid.). By this he gave her to understand that a person should diligently wrap all his adversities and sufferings, whether of mind or of body, in the most sacred passion, as one inserts a dried sprig in the middle of a bunch. For example, when a man troubled by adversity is provoked to impatience, let him recall the admirable patience of the Son of God, who was led as a meek lamb to the slaughter to be sacrificed for our salvation and did not open his mouth (Is. 53:7) to utter one impatient word. If a man has occasion to avenge himself on someone who has injured him in word or deed, let him try to consider again the sweetness of the heart of his Lover who never rendered evil for evil (1 Pet. 3:9), never revenging himself by so much as a word, but rewarding all that he had to bear with the greatest good, he redeemed by his passion and death those who persecuted him even unto death. And so, following the Lord's example, one should always render good for evil. Again, if hatred for those who have injured one rises in the breast, one should always remember the exceeding sweetness with which the most loving Son of God, among the indescribable anguish of his passion and the pains of death, prayed for those who crucified him, saying: "Father, forgive them," and, in union with his love, one should make an effort to pray for one's enemies.

And the Lord added: Anyone who wraps his adversities and sufferings in the bundle of my passion, inserting them into it, and tries to imitate closely the example of my passion in every way, he it is who really abides between my breasts.[78] For him I shall have a special affection, and all that I have merited through my patience and other virtues I shall give him to increase his merits."

Then she said: "And in what way, my Lord, will you receive the great emotion with which certain persons are moved by the representation of your cross?" The Lord replied: "I shall receive it with pleasure. However, as for those who are greatly moved by the image and yet do not imitate the example of my passion, I shall look on them as a young girl might look upon her mother who gives her various garments and ornaments chosen to gratify her own pleasure and desire for worldly ostentation, without consulting the girl as to what she might prefer and, indeed, harshly refuses to give her what she likes. As the mother's wishes differ from those of the daughter, the daughter will hardly be grateful for what is spent on her, because she knows that her mother makes her wear these ornaments to satisfy her own vanity and not out of sweet affection for her. In the same way, all the honor and reverence shown by a person to my cross cannot give me complete satisfaction if he is not trying to imitate the example of my passion."

Chapter 43. The Crucifix

She was most anxious to acquire an image of the holy cross so that she might venerate it often for love of her Lord. But she refrained for conscience's sake, because she feared that such an occupation might hinder her enjoyment of the interior gifts of God. She was reassured by this answer from the Lord: "Have no fear, dearest, because this cannot in the least hinder what is spiritual, since I alone am the cause of your occupation. And I must say that I am not a little pleased by such devotion shown to the crucifix. When, as sometimes happens, a king cannot always remain with his beloved wife, he leaves with her some particularly dear relative of his in his place. If she shows dutiful affection for this person, her spouse will receive it as if it were shown to himself, for he knows that this is not an illicit affection for a stranger, but chaste zeal for love of him. In the same way, I delight in seeing my cross venerated out of pure love for me. That does not apply, of course, if a person takes pleasure in the mere possession of a crucifix and does not try by means of it to meditate on the love and fidelity with which I underwent the bitterness of my passion for his sake, or in some other way follows his natural inclinations rather than striving to imitate the example of my passion."

Chapter 44. How Divine Sweetness Attracts the Soul

It happened one night that whilst she was occupied in meditating devoutly on the Lord's passion, she was thrown into a state of agitation by the vehemence of her emotions. She felt her heart[79] much inflamed within her by the exceedingly great thirst of her desires, and said to the Lord: "My sweetest lover, if anyone knew what I now feel, that person would say that I should abstain from such fervor in order to recover my bodily health. As, however, no secret thoughts of mine are hidden from you, you perceive and know how, with all the efforts of my will and my senses, I am powerless to resist the emotion caused by your sweetness, penetrating and thrilling every fiber of my being." To which the Lord replied: "Who, unless he were altogether devoid of feeling, could be unaware of how ineffably the stirring of the sweetness of my divinity exceeds by far all human and carnal pleasures? Every carnal delight, compared with divine sweetness, is like a tiny drop of dew compared to the vastness of the ocean. For all this, however, men are so often carried away by human pleasures that they can scarcely resist them, although they know that they are endangering not only their physical health but their eternal salvation as well. How much less can the soul that is penetrated with the sweetness of my divinity resist the attraction of my love, from which she will procure eternal felicity?"

Then she said: "Perhaps people might say that, having made profession in a monastic Order, I should moderate my fervor in order to be able to observe the *Rule* with greater exactitude?" The Lord graciously deigned to instruct her with this comparison: "It is as though some serving men were placed by the king's table to wait on the king and to serve him with sedulous care and reverence. If this king, enfeebled by age or infirmity, called on one of those who stood by to support him for a moment, and leaned on his breast, it would be very inappropriate if the serving man whom the king had chosen to support him suddenly got up and let him fall on the pretext that his orders had been to stand and wait at table. In the same way, it would be very much more inappropriate if she whom I attract freely in my love to the enjoyment of contemplation were to withdraw in order to follow more exactly the

213

Rule of the Order in which she had made profession. I am the Creator
and Renewer of all things; I take infinitely more pleasure in one loving
soul than in any labor or bodily exercise, such as may be performed by
anyone even without love or a pure intention." He added: "If someone
who is not specifically drawn by my spirit to the peace of contemplation, and yet neglects to follow her *Rule* because she desires to attain to
contemplation, then she is like a person who seats himself at the king's
table when he has not been ordered to do that, but rather to serve at the
king's table. If a servant seats himself uninvited at the king's table, he
gains not honor but rather contempt on account of his disrespectful
behavior. Similarly, one who neglects the *Rule* of her Order, trying by
her own devices to attain to divine contemplation (which is something
no one can have without a special gift from me) will find in this course
more harm than profit, since not only will she never succeed in her
attempt, but besides she becomes lax in doing what is, in fact, her
duty. And if anyone neglects the *Rule* of her Order out of mere bodily
convenience, without necessity, seeking exterior pleasures, she is like
someone who, called to wait at the king's table, goes away and makes
himself disgracefully dirty cleaning out the horses' stable."

Chapter 46. The Seven Hours of the Blessed Virgin

Keeping vigil one night, exerting herself to think with love about
the Lord's passion, she became very tired, and although she had not
yet said Matins, she felt all her strength failing. She said to the Lord:
"Ah, my Lord, as you know that, through my human frailty, I cannot
do without a little rest, show me what I can do to honor and serve your
most blessed Mother, since I am not able to recite her Hours[80] as I
ought."

The Lord said to her: "Praise me by the sweet sounding harmony
of my heart, in the innocent integrity of her virginity in which she, a
virgin, conceived me, bore me, and after my birth remained a virgin
inviolate.[81] She imitated the innocence which led me to permit myself,
at the hour of Matins, for the redemption of the human race, to be
taken captive, bound, struck, and given blows, and to be mercilessly
subjected to all kinds of misery and outrage." While she was doing
this, she saw the Lord offering his divine heart to his virgin Mother, in
the likeness of a golden cup, whence she might drink. And when she

had drunk of the honey sweetness of this draught, she seemed sweetly and abundantly satisfied—inebriated, rather—and, penetrated to the marrow, she was seen to rejoice with exceeding gladness.

Then she praised the blessed Virgin, saying: "I praise and salute you, Mother of all blessedness, most worthy tabernacle of the Holy Spirit, through the sweetest heart of Jesus, God the Father's most loving Son and yours, praying that you may help us in all our necessities and at the hour of death. Amen." And she understood that if anyone praises the Lord as has just been described, and at the same time praises the blessed Virgin by adding the verse "I praise and salute you, Mother . . ." as above, each time, they would, so to speak, offer to the virgin Mother a drink from the sweetest heart of Jesus Christ, her most loving Son.[82] The royal Virgin will gladly accept this offering and will kindly deign to reward it with the liberality of her maternal affection.

Then the Lord continued: "Praise me for Prime with the sweetly sounding harmony of my heart, for the serene humility with which the immaculate Virgin was ever more ready to receive me. She imitated the humility which led me, the judge of the living and the dead, to stand, at the hour of Prime, before a man like a Saracen[83] to be judged, for the redemption of the human race.

At Terce, praise me for the fervent desire which drew me, the Son of God, from the bosom of the Father into her virginal womb. She imitated me in that fervent desire with which I desired the salvation of man as I was being struck with hard scourges, crowned with thorns, and, at the hour of Terce, deigned to bear upon my tired and bleeding shoulders with such meekness and patience a most infamous cross.

At Sext, praise me for that firm and most secure hope with which the heavenly Virgin always aspired with good will and holy intentions to seek my glory. She imitated me when, hanging on the tree of the cross on high, in the harshness of a most bitter death, I longed with all my strength for the redemption of the human race, so that I cried: "I thirst" (Jn. 19:28). I thirsted so much for the salvation of human souls that, had it been necessary, I would have borne harder and more bitter torments; I was ready to offer myself freely and entirely for the redemption of man.

At None, praise me for that most ardent mutual love of the divine heart and the immaculate Virgin, which joined and inseparably united the most excellent divinity with tender humanity in the Virgin's womb. She imitated me, the life of the living, as I died of the immensity of my love on the cross at the hour of None, succumbing to a most bitter death for man's redemption.

At Vespers, praise me for that most constant faith in which the blessed Virgin alone, at the time of my death, when the apostles had fled and everyone despaired, remained unshaken in true faith. She imitated me in the fidelity with which I, now dead, taken down from the cross, followed man down even to the confines of hell, to limbo, snatching him thence in my mercy with my all-powerful hand and transferring him to the joys of paradise.

At Compline, praise me for that most laudable perseverance with which my sweetest Mother persevered to the end (cf. Matt. 10:22) in goodness and virtue. She imitated me in performing so lovingly the work of human redemption that, after obtaining man's true liberation from the bonds of sin by the most bitter death, I even wanted my incorruptible body to be buried according to human custom, in order to show that there was no indignity I would refuse to undergo for the sake of man's salvation."

Chapter 48. The Effect of Compunction

The community was once dreading the approach of enemies said to be strongly armed and advancing on the monastery.[84] For such dire necessity, it was decreed that the psalter should be recited in common, with the repetition after each psalm of the verse "O most blessed light"[85] and the antiphon "Come Holy Spirit."[86] While she was praying fervently with the others she understood in the spirit that the Lord wanted to touch certain hearts with compunction through the Holy Spirit by means of this prayer, so that they would recognize their own faults and repent with a good will, taking care, as far as possible, to avoid all sin in the future. While they were all pouring forth their contrite prayer, she saw a vapor, as it were, being exhaled from each heart, as though it had been touched by the very spirit of compunction. This vapor surrounded the cloister and its vicinity, repulsing to a distance the hostile forces.[87] And the greater the contrition of heart and the stronger the inclination to good will, the more efficacious was the vapor exhaled from those persons in repulsing the hostile forces. From this she understood that the Lord's chief intention, by means of such dread and trials caused by the enemy, was to draw the hearts of his chosen community more closely to himself so that, while trembling with fear and purged from all their faults, they might the more effectually take refuge in his fatherly protection and find help in his divine consolations.

Having comprehended this, she said to the Lord: "Why, most loving Lord, does it frequently happen that those things which you deign to reveal to me so freely in your love are so different from what you reveal to others, so that by this very difference it often happens that what you reveal to me is noticed by some, though I would much rather it were kept hidden than made known?" He replied: "If a learned man were to be questioned by people of different nationalities and replied to them all in the same language, it would be pointless; he would be understood by no one. But if he replies to each in his own language, that is, in Latin to the Latins, Greek to the Greeks, then he would give more admirable proof of his great learning, as his replies would be in the tongue most suited to each. It is the same with me: The greater the diversity with which I communicate my gifts to each person, the more clearly do I show the unsearchable depths of my wisdom. For my gifts are adapted to each person in the way that is most appropriate to the intelligence of each, and reveal what I wish to reveal according to the capacity of each one to whom I give the revelation. For example, to the more simple I demonstrate ideas by more corporeal similitudes, and to those of greater intellectual capacity I propound analogies that are more hidden and obscure."

Chapter 50. The Delight of the Lord's Senses in the Soul

One day when she was to go to communion she was overcome by illness and felt all her strength failing. Fearing lest this might cause her to have less fervor, she said to the Lord: "O sweetness of my soul, alas, I know only too well my utter unworthiness to receive your most sacred body and blood, and, if I could find anything to give me pleasure or alleviation in any creature apart from you, I would abstain today from holy communion. But, from east to west, from south to north, I know that there is nothing which could please me and refresh both body and soul apart from you. Burning and panting, therefore, hurried along by the thirst of desire, I come to you, the fountain of living water." This the Lord in his kindness graciously accepted. Requiting her in his turn with the same loving tenderness, he replied: "Since you assure me with such certainty that you can find no delight in any creature apart from me, so, in virtue of my divinity, I assure you that I have no desire to find delight in any creature apart from you."

In her heart of hearts she wondered whether, although the Lord in his kindness had deigned to say that he desired to take no delight in any creature apart from herself, yet this might some day be changed. Entering into her thoughts, the Lord replied: "For me, my will is the same as my power; therefore I can only do what I will to do."[88] And she said: "And what, O kindest lover, do you find in me, the very off-scouring of all creation, to delight you?" He answered: "My divine eyes rejoice ineffably in looking at you, for by bestowing upon you so many and so varied gifts of my grace, I made you beautiful in my sight. My divine hearing, also, is moved as though by the sound of the sweetest musical instruments by each and every word uttered by your lips, whether you are murmuring soft words of love to me, or praying, either for sinners or for souls in purgatory, or correcting or instructing someone, or speaking any words for my glory. Even if no other advantage to any person results, all the same, because of your good will and your intention firmly directed toward me, your words sound sweetly in my ears and move my divine heart to the very depths. The hope with which you are always panting after me I breathe in, and it is to me a scent like the sweetest fragrance of delight. Your every sigh and desire tastes to me better than any aromatic thing. Your love gives me the delight of the tenderest embrace."

Then she began to desire that the Lord would restore her former health, so that she might observe the *Rule* of her Order with greater exactitude and fervor. To which the kind Lord replied: "And why should my spouse seek to displease me by opposing my will?" She asked: "But does this desire of mine seem to you to be contrary to your will, since it seems to me that in it I do but seek your glory?" The Lord replied: "These words of yours are but childish babblings, and so I shall not pay any attention to them, but if you go on insisting more importunately, I shall not be pleased."

She understood by these words that if one desires good health in order to serve God, one does well; but that it is more perfect by far to commit oneself entirely to the divine will, trusting that God ordains for each one whatever is best for him and his salvation, whether it be prosperity or adversity.

Chapter 51. The Heartbeats of the Lord Jesus

When she saw the others assembling for the sermon, she complained within herself and said to the Lord: "You know, my dearest, how gladly I would now hear the sermon with all my heart, were I not held back by sickness." To which the Lord answered: "Would you like me to preach to you, my dearest?" She answered: "I would, very much." Then the Lord made her lean against his heart, with the heart of her soul close to his divine heart. When her soul had sweetly rested there a while, she heard in the Lord's heart two wondrous and very sweet pulsations.[89]

The Lord said to her: "Each of these two pulsations brings about man's salvation in three ways. The first pulsation effects the salvation of sinners; the second, that of the just. With the first pulsation, first, I address God the Father, ceaselessly appeasing him and leading him to have mercy upon sinners. Second, I invoke all my saints, excusing the sinner with fraternal fidelity, and urging them to pray for him. Third, I address the sinner himself, calling upon him to repent, and awaiting his conversion with ineffable longing.

"With the second pulsation, first, I address God the Father, inviting him to rejoice with me for having shed my precious blood to such good purpose for the redemption of the just, in whose hearts I now find so many delights. Second, I address all the heavenly hosts, inviting them to praise the lives of the just, and to thank me for the benefits I have already bestowed upon them, and for those I will bestow in the future. Third, I address the just themselves, lavishing various favors on them for their salvation and admonishing them to progress from day to day and from hour to hour. And just as the pulsations of the human heart are not impeded by seeing or hearing or by any manual work, but always maintain their regular motion, so the government and disposition of heaven and earth and the whole universe can never affect in the very least these twofold pulsations of my divine heart, still them, modify them, or in any way hinder them, till the end of time."

Chapter 52. How the Lord Receives the Sleeplessness of His Dear Ones

After this it happened that she spent an almost sleepless night. This made her so weak that, all her strength failing, she offered that weakness to the Lord, according to her usual custom, to his eternal glory and for the salvation of the whole world. The Lord, kindly taking pity on her, taught her to call upon him in these words:

"By the most tranquil sweetness in which you have reposed from all eternity to the bosom of God the Father, and by the loveliest rest that you took in the womb of the Virgin, your mother, where you stayed quietly for nine months, and by the most glad delight you deign to find in all souls that love you, I pray you, most merciful God, not for my convenience but for your eternal glory, deign to grant me some rest so that my wearied limbs may recover their strength."

As she said these words, it seemed to her as though they were so many steps ascending to bring her close to the Lord. Then the Lord showed her at his right side a very lovely sitting-place which had been prepared there, saying to her: "Come, my chosen one,[90] repose on my heart and see how my unresting love may be your rest." While she was thus sweetly reclining on the Lord's heart, source of all sweetness, she could distinctly hear its most sweet beating. She said to the Lord: "O my sweetest lover, what are these heartbeats saying to me now?"

"They are saying this: That when someone who is tired and destitute of strength through keeping vigil with me prays to me, in the three phrases which I have just inspired you to say, that I might give him rest for my glory and to restore his strength, and I do not grant this, then, if he takes hold of patience[91] and humbly bears his weakness, I shall the more graciously accept that from him, in my divine gentleness and kindness. If a person wakes his special friend from a pleasant sleep, although aware that he was very sleepy, simply in order to have the pleasure of conversing with him, and that friend rises quickly and gladly to afford him that satisfaction even at the cost of great effort to himself, the person will be more grateful to that friend than he would be to another who stays up all night, as he is used to doing, not only for his friend's benefit but also for his own. Just so, it is infinitely more agreeable to me if someone who is sick spends all his strength in vigils and offers me the suffering he endures humbly and patiently, than if someone who is quite healthy and strong watches all night in prayer with no difficulty."

Chapter 53. Contentment with God's Will

Once she was ill with a fever, and sometimes after she had been perspiring profusely the fever increased, while sometimes it decreased. One night, bathed in perspiration, she began to wonder with some anxiety whether her sickness would take a turn for the worse or for the better. The Lord Jesus appeared to her, lovely as a flower; in his right hand he held health and in his left hand sickness. He held out both hands to her at once so that she might choose whichever she preferred. She, however, pushed them both aside and, making her way in the fervor of her spirit, she passed between the two outstretched hands of the Lord to reach his most sweet heart, where she knew that the plentitude of all good things is hidden, seeking only his adorable will, worthy of all praise. The Lord received her tenderly and gently enfolded her in his embrace; she reclined for a while on his heart. Then, with her face turned away from the Lord and the back of her head still leaning on his breast, she said: "See, Lord, I turn my face away from you, desiring with all my heart that you pay no heed to my will, but that, in all that concerns me, your adorable will be done."

By this let it be seen that a faithful soul commits herself and everything that is hers entirely and with such secure trust to the divine will that she actually delights in her ignorance of what the Lord may do in her regard, so that the divine will may be more purely and perfectly accomplished in her.

At this the Lord caused to flow down from both sides of his sweet heart, as though drawn from a full cup, two rivulets flooding into her bosom, saying: "Because you have renounced your own will entirely, turning your face away from me, I am sending all the sweetness and delight of my divine heart into you." To which she replied: "As you, my sweetest lover, have given me your divine heart so often and in so many ways, I should like to know now what profit I may have in consequence of what you are again so generously giving me?" He explained: "The Catholic faith teaches, does it not, that I give myself, with all the good things contained in the treasury both of my divinity and of my humanity, to a person who communicates even a single time, for his salvation. And yet, the more often a person communicates, the more will that person's blessedness be increased and multiplied."

Chapter 55. Languishing for Love

A short time after this she was ill in bed for the seventh time, and one night was thinking about the Lord when he approached and, bending toward her with the most tender gentleness, he said: "Tell me, my beloved, that you languish for love of me" (Song 5:8). She said: "Ah, how should I, so unworthy, presume to say that I languish for love of you?" He replied: "Anyone who willingly offers to endure suffering for my sake can truly glory in that, and so may tell me that he is languishing for love of me in that he is suffering with patience and is meditating perseveringly on me." Then she said: "But what could you, dearest, gain from such an assurance?" He answered: "Such an assurance is joy to my divinity, honor to my humanity, beauty to my eyes, praise to my ears." And he added: "Whoever brings me this message shall receive great consolations. Moreover, the unction of my love is so powerfully moved that I am vehemently impelled to heal the contrite of heart, that is, those who are desirous of grace; to preach release to captives, that is, sinners; and deliverance to them that are shut up, that is, the souls in purgatory" (cf. Is. 61:1).

Then she said to the Lord: "Father of mercies, are you not going to deign to restore my former health, after seven attacks of this sickness?" He replied: "If during the first attack of the sickness I had intimated to you that you were to to fall ill seven times, perhaps, because of the frailty of your human nature, you might have been afraid and have given way to impatience. And so, if I were now to promise that this sickness would be the last you would have to endure, it is certain that, in your hope, you would lose much of your merit. Therefore the fatherly providence of my uncreated wisdom disposed that you should experience this twofold ignorance so that you should always be obliged to long for me with your whole heart, trustfully commending to me all your troubles, whether interior or exterior. I regard you with such sweet faithfulness, and I take such care of you, that I shall never permit you to suffer more than you can bear (cf. 1 Cor. 10:13), for well I know the delicacy and frailty of your patience. You may see this clearly in the fact that after the first attack of sickness you were weaker than you are now after the seventh, for in my divine omnipotence I am able to accomplish what human reason would deem impossible."

Chapter 56. Why Life and Death Were One and the Same for Her

One night, when she was showing her love for the Lord in many different ways, she asked him, among other things, how it was that although she had been ill now for a long time, yet she had never once desired to know whether her sickness would end in death or in health, for life and death were all the same to her (cf. Rom. 14:8). The Lord replied: "When a spouse leads his bride into a rose garden, there to gather roses to twine into a garland, the bride finds such charm in sweet converse with her spouse that she never thinks of asking him which rose he is going to pick for her. But when they are come into the rose garden, she takes at once whatever rose her spouse picks and hands to her for the garland, and that she twines into the garland without further ado. So it is with the faithful soul whose greatest joy is to do my will and to delight in it as in a rose garden. And whether it pleases me to restore her to health, or whether I end her life on earth immediately, she will surely take it as one and the same, because she commits herself with full confidence to my fatherly care."

Chapter 57. The Devil's Hatred for Refreshment Taken in Moderation

Another night, quite exhausted by the many consolations afforded by the presence of the Lord and by her own exertions in applying her understanding to spiritual things, she took some grapes to refresh herself, with the intention of giving some refreshment to the Lord in herself. Graciously accepting this loving intention, the Lord said: "Now I am recompensed for that bitter draught which I drank from the sponge on the cross for love for you (Matt. 27:48), since now instead I taste in your heart ineffable sweetness. And the more purely you consider my glory in taking refreshment for your body, the sweeter is the refreshment that I shall take in your soul."

Having collected the skins and pips of the grapes in her hand, she threw them down in the middle of the room, and Satan, the enemy of all good, tried to gather up the refuse in order to show the crimes of a sick person who, contrary to the *Rule*, had eaten before Matins. No sooner had he taken one of the grape skins between his fingers than he felt such a sensation of burning pain that, uttering terrible shrieks, he rushed at full speed out of the house, taking care not to touch with his foot anything else that might cause him such intolerable pain.

Chapter 59. Bodily Comfort Taken for the Lord's Sake

When through infirmity she was unable to take part in the choral Office, she often went to Choir to hear the Hours, so that at least thus she might exercise her body in the service of God. And as she considered that her devotion to God was less fervent than she could have wished, she frequently complained of this to the Lord, saying in a spirit of dejection: "How, my dearest Lord, can you derive any honor from me while I sit here negligent and useless, scarcely attending to one or two words or notes?" To which the Lord at length made this answer: "What good would you derive from it if a friend offered you once or twice some sweet, freshly made mead from which you might hope for much relief? Know, then, that I take far greater pleasure in each single word or note[92] that you are now able to concentrate upon for my glory."

During Mass she was so weak that she hesitated to rise for the Gospel; she reproached herself for this, since she did not know whether there was any point in such prudence, for even if she were to spare herself in that way, she had no hope of regaining her former health. As was her wont, she asked the Lord what would be to his greater glory. He replied to her: "If you want to make an effort to do something for my glory when it is beyond your strength, I accept that from you as though I needed it for my honor to be complete. If you abstain from doing it, and accept comfort for your body, for my sake, then you are offering me something which I will accept as though I were myself sick and unable to do without this comfort. And so I shall reward you either way, for the glory of my divine munificence."

Chapter 60. Renewal of the Sacraments

One day she was examining her conscience and found there something she would like to have confessed. As she could not have recourse to a confessor, following her usual custom she took refuge with her only solace, the Lord Jesus Christ, and bewailed her difficulty. To which he responded in these words: "Why are you troubled, my love? As often as you ask it of me, I who am myself High Priest and true pontiff (Heb. 3:1, etc.), I shall be ready to renew in your soul all seven sacraments at once, more effectively than any priest or bishop could do one at a time. I will baptize you with my precious blood; I will confirm you in the strength of my victory; I will espouse you to me in my faithful love (Hos. 2:20); I will consecrate you in the perfection of my most holy life;[93] in my loving mercy I will absolve you from the bonds of every sin; in my overflowing charity, I will feed you with myself, and will myself be refreshed by you. And the sweetness of my spirit will penetrate your whole being with such beneficent unction that through every sense and movement devotion will be, so to speak, distilled, and so, without ceasing, you will be ever more prepared and sanctified for eternal life."

Chapter 61. The Effect of Charity

Another time, although still very weak, she had got up for Matins. She had just finished one Nocturn when she was joined by another sick person with whom she had the charity to recommence Matins, not without great fatigue. During Mass, when she was praying still more devoutly to the Lord, it seemed to her that she saw her soul very marvelously adorned with precious jewels and shining with a wonderful brightness. Divinely instructed, she understood that she had merited this adornment because she had humbly and charitably recited again with the younger nun that part of Matins which she had recited before, and that the shining ornaments were equal in number to the words she has thus repeated. Then she remembered some negligences which she had not yet confessed, being prevented from doing so by the absence of a confessor, and bewailed this to the Lord. He answered: "Why are you complaining of your negligence, seeing that the robe of charity, which covers a multitude of sins, so gloriously envelops you?" (1 Pet. 4:8). She said: "How can I be consoled by the fact that charity covers my faults, when I know that I am stained by so many of them?" To this he replied: "Charity not only covers sins, but by its warmth, which acts like that of the sun, it consumes and utterly destroys all the negligences of venial sins and even confers extra merit."

Chapter 63. The Lord's Fidelity to the Soul

Injuries inflicted by a friend are usually harder to bear than those inflicted by an enemy, as the psalm has it: "If my enemy had reviled me, I would verily have borne with it" (Ps. 54:13–14). When Gertrude learned that a person to whom she had tried with more special zeal and fidelity to give help for the good of her soul had not corresponded with due fidelity—indeed, was acting in a contrary manner as though she disdained what had been done for her—in her distress she took refuge with the Lord. He consoled her with these kind words: "Do not be sad, daughter, for I allowed this to happen for your greater spiritual welfare. I take the very greatest delight in your company and in being always with you, and I want to enjoy this more often. If a mother has a little boy whom she tenderly loves and wants to have always at her side, and the boy wants to run off and play with his friends, she places a scarecrow or something alarming nearby, so that the frightened boy runs back quickly to take refuge in her arms. I too want you always at my side, never to leave me, and so I permit your friends sometimes to cause you pain so that, never finding perfect fidelity in any creature, you will come running back the more eagerly to me, knowing that with me alone you will find an unchanging abundance of joy and fidelity."

Then the Lord lifted her on to his breast, like a very small child. With many caresses he placed his divine mouth close to her ear, and soothed her in various ways, saying: "As a tender mother kisses away the troubles of her little child, so I want to soothe away all your troubles and adversities by whispering soft words of fondest love."

When she had been enjoying for a time the infinite sweetness of divine consolations and repeated caresses in the bosom of the Lord, he offered her his heart, saying: "Look, my beloved, at the very core of my heart, and consider carefully with what fidelity I have disposed and managed everything you have ever asked me to do for you, in the way that is most profitable for the perfection and salvation of your soul. And now consider whether you can reproach me for the least infidelity to you." Then she saw the Lord making, out of the tribulation of which we have spoken, a sort of splendid ornament of golden flowers. Then, remembering some people whom she knew to be suffering affliction, she said to him: "Oh, how much more worthy are they and deserving of recompense and of being decorated with even more precious ornaments of your love, merciful Father, than I am, for they suffer such grievous troubles and do not have any such consolations as I often have, in spite of my unworthiness, alas, and often I do not bear all that happens to me with becoming patience." He answered: "In this and in every circumstance I show the most delicate care and tender love for you, like a mother tenderly loving her delicate little child. As she knows he could not easily bear the weight of silver and gold ornaments (with which she would like to deck him out) she adorns him with light flowers which do not weigh him down and yet impart a certain air of brilliance. So I too moderate your troubles, so that you may not sink beneath their weight, and yet may not entirely lack the merit of patience."

At this, when she considered the sublimity of divine love in all that concerned her salvation, in her profound gratitude, she broke forth into devout praises. Then she saw that the ornaments she had been given for her tribulation, which looked like flowers and were very light in weight although brilliant, took on a certain weight when, in her gratitude, she sang praises to God for her adversity. And from this she understood that the grace which God gives to make us able to praise him in adversity compensates in a nobler way for what is wanting in the weight of our affliction, just as an ornament of pure gold is more precious than a silver ornament gilded only on the surface.

Chapter 64. The Fruit of Good Will

A certain nobleman sent to the monastery to ask for some of our community to establish the monastic life in some other monastery,[94] and Gertrude got word of it. She was full of good will and always ready to do whatever was pleasing to God, although she was not at all strong, and was always motivated by zeal for the glory of God. Kneeling before a crucifix, she fervently offered her heart to God to his eternal glory, ready to do with body and soul whatever might be according to his good pleasure. The Lord appeared so deeply moved and pleased by this offering that, as though coming down from the cross, with great joy and loving gentleness he caught her up in the sweetest embrace, with an ineffable transport of joy; he was like a sick person who, having almost despaired of any cure, receives with gladness the medicine long desired and hoped for, from which he expects to recover his former health completely. Gently holding her against the wound in his sacred side, he said: "Welcome, my dearest; you are a soothing balm to my wounds, the sweet alleviation of all my sufferings." By these words she understood that when anyone abandons his will without reserve to God's good pleasure, whatever adversity he knows to be imminent, the Lord accepts this homage exactly as if, at the time of his passion, this person had put soothing balm on all his wounds.

Then, continuing her prayer, she reflected in her heart on the many ways in which she would have liked to promote the glory of God and the expansion of the monastic life, as far as in her lay, should occasion arise for her to go on the foundation. While these and other thoughts were occupying her mind, she recollected herself and reproached herself for wasting time with such idle thoughts which would probably come to nothing, since she was so weak that death seemed nearer than their fulfillment, and moreover, if they were to be fulfilled, there would be time enough then to make plans. Then the Lord Jesus appeared to her, as it were in the midst of her soul, in great glory, surrounded by fresh spring flowers, roses and lilies,[95] and said to her: "See how I am glorified by the dispositions of your good will, like the splendor of shining stars and golden candlesticks—for John says in his Apocalypse that he saw the Son of Man in the midst of golden candlesticks (Rev. 1:13), having in his right hand seven stars (Rev. 1:16). The other thoughts which came into your head gave me as much pleasure in the delightful freshness of roses and lilies."

Then she said: "Alas, God of my heart (Ps. 72:26), why do you put into my head so many different desires which are never to be fulfilled? Only a few days ago you put into my head the thought of hastening the reception of the sacrament of extreme unction and kindled my desire for it. While I was occupied with various thoughts about this, you filled me with joy and gave me many consolations concerning it. And now, on the contrary, you provoke me to desire to go away to a new religious foundation in another place, when I am so weak that I could hardly walk as far as would be required."

The Lord replied: "According to what I have already said at the beginning of this book,[96] I have planned to give you to be a light to the Gentiles (Is. 42:6, 49:6), that is, to enlighten many souls. It is necessary that in your book everyone should find instruction and consolation, each according to his capacity. Besides, friends often enjoy talking together about many things which will never come to pass. And sometimes, too, a friend will propose to another some difficult project, so that he may have a certain proof of his friend's fidelity and, more particularly, of the generosity of his good will toward himself. I, too, delight in proposing to my chosen ones many difficult projects which will never come about, in order to have proof of their love for me and their fidelity, so that I may reward them afterward for these great things which they will in fact never have the opportunity of doing, because I look upon their good will alone as though it were the accomplishment of their good intentions. And so, in a way, it was I who suggested to you a desire for death and so for hastening the reception of the sacrament of extreme unction. So all the devout and earnest preparations which you made then, both interiorly and exteriorly, I have already laid up for you in the secret depths of my heart, in view of your eternal salvation. You are therefore to know that, as it is said, 'But the just man, if he be prevented with death, shall be in rest' (Wisd. 4:7), if it should happen to you, through some accident, to be taken unawares by sudden death, or to receive the sacrament of extreme unction after losing consciousness (as often happens with very great saints) you would come to no harm thereby. For all the things you have done for so many years past to prepare yourself for death shall grow green again and blossom in the unfading springtime of my eternity, and produce fruits for your eternal salvation, in union with the power of my divine action."

Chapter 65. The Efforts Required to Obtain Benefits

At the request of a certain person Gertrude was offering the Lord all the things which, through the free gift of his love, he had deigned to do in her, and was asking him to grant a share to this person. Suddenly, this person for whom she was praying appeared to her in the presence of the Lord who, seated on a glorious throne, was holding on his knees a robe, very marvelously embroidered, which he was presenting to this person without, as yet, clothing her in it. In astonishment Gertrude said to the Lord: "When a few days ago I made you a similar offering for the soul of a poor deceased person for whom I was then praying, you deigned to raise her without delay to the supreme joys of heaven. Why, kindest Lord, through the merits of these same graces which you have accorded to me, most unworthy, do you not clothe this person, who so much desires it, with the robe you are presenting to her?" He answered: "When I am offered something in charity for the souls of the faithful departed then, out of the love which is natural to me (for it is in my nature always to be merciful and to spare),[97] since I know that they can no longer help themselves in any way, I take pity on their misery

229

and immediately grant to them whatever has been offered for them, in absolution of sins or in alleviation of their sufferings, or to increase their eternal felicity, according to the state and merit of each. But when a similar offering is made for the living, certainly I use it for their salvation, but since they themselves may still work for their own salvation by good works, good desires, and good will, it is but fitting that what they wish to obtain through the merits of others, they should try to merit through their own labors. That is why, if the person for whom you are praying wishes to be clothed with the benefits which I have bestowed upon you, she should try to apply herself spiritually to three things: first, let her bow down in humility and gratitude to receive the robe, that is, let her confess humbly to needing the merits of others and give me heartfelt thanks for being willing to make good her poverty through the riches of others. Second, let her take this robe with hope and trust, that is, hoping in my goodness, and trusting that great profit will come of it for the progress of her soul. Third, let her put on this robe by exercising herself in charity and in other virtues. And let all who desire to have a share in the blessings and merits of others do likewise; in this way they will be able to receive profit from them."

Chapter 67. Of Humiliation Under the Scourge of God

She was praying one day for people who had harmed the community by pillaging,[98] and were causing great trouble in other ways also, when the loving and merciful Lord appeared to her. It seemed to her as though one of his arms were causing him pain; it was twisted as though it were dislocated and almost helpless. And the Lord said: "Consider what torture I should feel now if someone were to hit me with a blow of the fist on this arm. I am afflicted by just such pain by all those who, without compassion on the peril to which the souls of your persecutors are exposed, frequently recount the defects of these their enemies and the injuries they have inflicted. They do not remember that these people too are members of my body (cf. 1 Cor. 12). All those, on the other hand, who are moved by loving compassion and who implore me in my mercy to convert them and to reform their lives from error, are like those who put soothing ointment on this arm. And as for those who are kind enough to advise them to amend their ways, they are like skillful doctors who gently manipulate the arm and restore it to its natural position."

Then, in admiration at the Lord's incomparable goodness, she said: "And how, most loving Lord, can you justify the comparison of such infamous people to your arm?" He said: "Because they belong to the body of the church, of which it is my glory to be the head" (cf. Eph. 5:23). To this she protested: "My Lord, they are now separated from the church by an interdict, having been publicly denounced and excommunicated because of the injury they have inflicted on our community."[99] To which the Lord replied: "Nevertheless, as long as they can still be reconciled to the church by absolution, my love obliges me to take care of them, as I have an ineffable desire for their repentance, and I long for their conversion to me."

Then she prayed the Lord to deign to keep the community safe, in his fatherly care, from their molestations. He responded: "If you humble yourselves under my mighty hand (1 Pet. 5:6), acknowledging before me in your hearts that you merit this chastisement on account of your negligences, then in my fatherly mercy I will protect you from injury caused by hostile incursions. But if you rise up in pride and anger against those who ill-treat you, threatening them or wishing them evil for evil, then, through a just decree of my judgment, they will prevail against you, injuring you and molesting you in many ways."

Chapter 68. That Exterior Labors Are Acceptable to God

One year when the community was heavily burdened by debt, Gertrude prayed more devoutly and insistently to the Lord that in his kindness he might help the administrators of the monastery to pay what they owed. Gently and tenderly he replied: "And in what way is it to my advantage to help them in this?" She said: "That they may thenceforth be free to apply themselves with greater fervor and attentiveness to spiritual duties." He answered: "And how would I benefit from that, since I have no need of your goods (Ps. 15:2) and it is all the same to me whether you give yourselves to spiritual exercises or to the toil of exterior labor, so long as your will is freely directed toward me? For if I took pleasure in spiritual exercises only, surely I would have so reformed human nature after the Fall that there would no longer be any need for either food or clothing, or for any of the other necessities of life that men toil to obtain or construct through their industry. As a powerful emperor likes to have in his palace not only fair and noble maidens but also princes, dukes, soldiers, and others always ready to serve him, each group in its own way in various kinds of business, so I too take pleasure not only in the interior delights of contemplatives. It is also the various kinds of useful employments, which are carried out for my honor and love, which draw me to abide and to dwell with delight among the children of men. For in these kinds of occupations do they find more opportunity to exercise the virtues of charity, patience, humility, and so on."

Then she saw the principal administrator of the monastery prostrated in the Lord's presence, leaning on his left side and rising at intervals with the greatest difficulty to offer to the Lord, with his left hand, on which he was leaning, a gold coin embellished with a precious stone. And the Lord said to her: "Behold: If I were to alleviate this trouble about which you are praying, then I should be deprived of the fine gem which is so pleasing to me in this coin; and he who offers it would be deprived of his reward, because he would then be offering me with his right hand a coin with no gem. For he who strives to do the will of God in everything, yet without suffering any adversity, is like a man who offers me a plain coin; but a man who always meets with adversity in all he does, and yet conforms his will to the will of God is like a man who offers God a gold coin set with a gem of great price."

Nevertheless, she did not give up, but prayed the more earnestly that the Lord would hear her and help the administrators of the monastery in the grave difficulty we have mentioned. The Lord answered: "Why do you find it so hard when someone suffers tribulation for my sake, since I am the only friend whose fidelity is never altered by the passage of time?" For instance, if a man has reached such extremity that he is beyond all human help and consolation, then a person who is aware of having been shown fidelity by that man will experience great distress. And yet I, the only true friend, come to his desolate soul in his dire necessity, bringing with me, evergreen and flourishing, all the good works, whether of thought, word, or deed, ever done by this man in his lifetime; they flower like roses and lilies, sprinkled over my garments. And the living beauty of my divine presence revives in his soul the hope of the eternal life to which he knows he is called to be rewarded for all his works. Through the joy that will give him, he will become able, once he is freed from his body, to receive the gift of everlasting felicity and, in the words of Genesis he can exclaim in joy and praise: 'Behold, the smell of my beloved is as the smell of a plentiful field' (cf. Gen. 27:27). For, as the body consists of various members bound together, so the soul consists of various affections, namely fear, sorrow, joy, love, hope, hatred, and modest shame. In the measure in which each of these is used by a man for my glory, that man will find in me joy, ineffable and sure delight in proportion, to prepare him for eternal blessedness. In the resurrection to come, when this mortal body will put on incorruption (1 Cor. 15:13), each of his bodily members will receive a particular reward for each of the works done in my name and for love of me. But an incomparably greater reward will be given to his soul for each action stemming from the holy affections, whether done for my love or out of compunction or simply in order to preserve the life of the body."

Later, in compassion for the faithful administrator of the monastery, she continued to pray frequently to the Lord that he would reward him for the trying work he so often had to do in managing the temporal affairs of the community. The Lord replied: "His body, which becomes so weary for my sake in all these works, is for me like a treasury into which I put as many pieces of silver as he performs bodily actions to obtain what is necessary. And his heart is to me like a coffer, in which I know, with joy, that I have as many pieces of gold as the thoughts he has given to providing with care for those entrusted to him, for my greater glory."

Then she said to the Lord in wonder: "Lord, it does not seem to me that his man is so perfect that everything he does is done purely for your greater glory. Rather, I think very often he is led by other motives, such as temporal gain, and, consequently, his body's comfort. And how can you, O God of unmixed sweetness, find such delight in his heart and his body as you say you do?" To this the Lord, with the greatest kindness replied: "It is because his will is so conformed to my divine will that I am always the chief motive of all he does. Therefore, he will derive inestimable profit from every single one of his thoughts, words, and deeds. Nevertheless, if he were to strive to do all his business with purer and more devout intentions, then that business and all his works would have more value, even as gold is more valuable than silver. Again, if he were to strive to direct all his thoughts and cares toward me with a purer and more devout intention, they would be rendered as much more valuable as the best and purest gold is finer and more valuable than gold which is old and has lost its brilliance."

Chapter 69. The Merit of Patience

It happened one day that a person was accidentally injured whilst at work and badly hurt. Gertrude felt very sorry for this person and prayed to the Lord for her, asking that he would not allow the member of the community who which had been injured in the course of legitimate work to perish. Kindly, the Lord replied: "There is no danger of that, but in return for her pain she will receive a reward of infinite value. And in addition, every member of the community who is moved to wait on this member to relieve and cure her pain will receive a similar reward in eternity. When a piece of cloth is being dyed yellow, anything else which falls into the dye is also stained with the same color; just so, when one member suffers, all the other members who wait on her shall receive with her a reward in everlasting glory" (cf. 1 Cor. 12:26).

She asked: "My Lord, how is it that those who wait on another receive such a great reward, since they do this not so that the injured person may be willing to suffer more, or more patiently, for love of you, but simply in order to relieve her pain?" To which the Lord of ineffable consolations gave this answer: "When a man bears patiently, for love of me, suffering for which there is no further human remedy and which he is not able to heal by his own efforts, I will sanctify the suffering with the words which in my extreme agony I addressed to my Father in prayer: 'My Father, if it be possible, let this chalice pass from me,'[100] which will gain for that person an incomparable reward and merit."

She asked: "Is it not more pleasing to you, my God, if someone suffers whatever happens to him with patience for love of you, rather than if he is patient only in suffering which he cannot avoid?" He replied: "This is a secret which lies hidden in the abyss of my divine counsels and surpasses all human understanding. But, humanly speaking, there is the same difference between these two kinds of suffering as there is between two colors, both perfect and both considered so beautiful that it is hard to know which to choose." Then she desired the Lord to grant to the injured person to receive the full force of the consolation contained in these words, when she should hear them. He replied: "No. But rest assured that I omit to do this out of a secret disposition of my divine wisdom, so that she may be further tried and commended to me especially by three virtues; namely, patience, faith, and humility. Patience, because if she were to feel in these words the consolation which you feel in them, all her sufferings would be at an end and the merit of her patience would be diminished. Faith, in that she may rather rely on what another says than on what she herself feels, since, according to Gregory, there is no merit in faith in something that is demonstrated by human reason.[101] And humility, because she will realize that others surpass her in that they know by divine inspiration what she has not been found worthy to know."

Chapter 70. The Profession of God's Benefits

Gertrude was praying for someone whom she pitied because she had heard that she had spoken impatiently, asking God why he sent her trials which she considered unsuitable for her. The Lord said to her: "Ask her what kind of trials would suit her, and tell her that, since she cannot enter the kingdom of God without at least some trials, she should now choose the ones she thinks would suit her; and when they come to her, let her be patient." By these words of the Lord, Gertrude understood how very dangerous it is to imagine that one would be patient under certain circumstances of one's own choosing, but not in those which the Lord sends one. Whereas, on the contrary, one should always be quite sure that what God sends is the best, and if one fails to be patient, that should be a source of humiliation.

And the Lord added, in tones of coaxing love: "And what do you think about it? Aren't the trials I send you most unsuitable?" She rejoined: "O my Lord, not at all! Rather, I profess, and to my last breath I shall profess it, that both in body and soul, in everything, whether in prosperity or adversity, you provide for me in the way that is most suitable; and that no wisdom from the beginning of the world until the end could ever have been able to do it, save only yours, the one and uncreated wisdom, my sweetest God, reaching from end to end mightily and ordering all things sweetly!"[102]

Then the Son, tenderly lifting her up, took her to God the Father, asking her to make her profession to him. She said: "I give you thanks with all my strength, holy Father, through him who is seated at your right hand, for the more than magnificent gifts which I have received of your bounteous generosity. For I surely know that I could never have received them from any other power save only your divine power, which governs and gives life to all creation." Then he took her to the Holy Spirit that she might also profess his goodness. She said: "I give you thanks, Holy Spirit, Paraclete, through him who, cooperating with you, took on human nature in the Virgin's womb, for continually coming to meet me, in spite of my unworthiness, with the gentle blessings of your gratuitous sweetness in all things. For I am certain that no other goodness but yours could ever have done this, nothing but your ineffable sweetness, in which is hidden, from which proceeds, and with which are received all good things."

Then the Son of God, lovingly embracing and kissing her, said: "After this profession of yours, I shall receive you into my special care;[103] care greater than that which I owe to any creature, either as their creator, or as their redeemer, or as the one who has made special choice of them."

She understood this to mean that when anyone makes profession of the goodness of God and then abandons himself with trust and gratitude to his providence, then the Lord takes him in a special way into his care, just as a prelate more specially watches over those whose vows he has himself received.

Chapter 74. Of Various Persons in the Same Order[104]

When she was praying for someone who was filled with ardent desire, she received this answer: "Tell him from me that if he wishes to be united to me in a more intimate union of love, he must try, like a noble bird, to make his nest at my feet, a nest constructed of the dried stalks of his own wretchedness and the branches of my greatness, where he may rest in continual remembrance of his own wretchedness, for mortal man is always of himself inclined to evil and slow to do good, unless he be forestalled by my grace. Let him often reflect on my mercy, remembering how, like a father, I am prompt to receive penitents who turn to me again after they have fallen. When he wants to fly away from the nest to find food, let him wing his flight to my bosom, where, in loving gratitude, he may reflect on the many and varied gifts which I have freely heaped upon him in the overflowing bounty of my love. If he wishes to stretch still wider the wings of his desire and to ascend still higher, let him soar aloft with the eagle's swift flight by contemplation of heavenly things above himself, hovering with outspread wings before my face; raised on seraph's wings in the audacity of his love, let him contemplate the king in his glory with the clear gaze of the spirit.

But since no one in this present life can continue long on the heights of contemplation (to which, as Bernard says, one can hardly attain to in this life, and then only rarely and for a short time,[105] let him fold his wings again and, remembering his own wretchedness, quickly drop down to his nest, resting there for a time before he flies upward once more through an act of thanksgiving toward pastures of delectable pleasure, and so goes out of himself in ecstasy to attain to the heights of divine contemplation. And so, by these constantly alternating dispositions, either returning to the consideration of his own frailty, or going forth by meditating on the gifts he has received, or else raised aloft by the contemplation of heavenly things, he will always experience the delight of supernatural joys."

She also remembered someone who had been devoutly recommended to her who, after having spent the first flower of his youth in the world, had at length renounced it and vowed himself to the service of God in the religious life. Turning to the Lord, she offered him her heart, desiring that he should fulfil now the promise which has been related above, to his greater glory and to the consolation and profit of this person; that is, that through it would flow, as through a channel, his divine consolations to anyone who humbly asked her for this. Straightway she saw her heart like a channel raised up and applied to the honey-sweet heart of the most loving Jesus, the Son of God, who appeared to her seated on his royal throne.

Then she saw the person for whom she was praying come and kneel reverently before the Lord. The Lord graciously held out his left hand and said: "In my incomprehensible omnipotence, and my inscrutable wisdom, and my sweetest goodness, I will receive him." At the same time, she saw the Lord hold out to this person three fingers of his left hand, that is, the forefinger, the middle, and the ring finger; for his part, the person dextrously placed the same fingers of his own left hand on top, his forefinger on the Lord's forefinger, his middle finger on the Lord's middle finger, and his ring finger on the Lord's, so that they fitted beautifully together. This done, the Lord turned over his blessed hand so that the aforesaid person's fingers appeared underneath while the Lord's were uppermost. In this way the Lord made it known that this person should try to regulate his life in three ways.

First, whenever he wanted to undertake any work, he should place himself under the protection of the divine omnipotence, acknowledging himself to be a worthless servant who had consumed the strength of his youth in vain, unmindful of the Lord God who had

created and loved him, and desiring and praying that the divine omnipotence would give him the strength to do his work well. Second, he
should protest before the inscrutable wisdom of God that he is quite
unworthy to receive the influx of supernatural knowledge, because
from childhood he had never accustomed himself to use his faculties
for studying divine realities, but had used them rather for purposes of
human pride or vainglory. And so, after plunging himself into the
deepest valley of humility, he should strive with a supreme effort to
detach himself from everything earthly and apply himself to divine
contemplation. And when God, in his generosity, filled his soul with
an overflowing abundance of riches, he should not fail to communicate
it in charity to others, according to the circumstances of time and
place. Third, he should receive with great gratitude the gift of the good
will which the Lord had freely given him in his love and which would
enable him to carry out the two preceding counsels.

It seemed to her then that the Lord had on his left hand a ring
made of some common material set with a precious stone of a fiery red.
Then she understood that the ring denoted the worthless life of this
person, which he had offered to the Lord when he had renounced the
world and vowed himself to fight in the army of the Lord.[106] The
precious stone she understood to signify the generosity of divine love
which moved the Lord to grant, from that same free generosity of
divine love, the gift of the good will which made his works perfect in
the sight of God. That is why the voice—that is, the intention—of this
person should be used for nothing but praise and thanksgiving for such
a magnificent gift of divine liberality. Then she understood that whenever, with the Lord's help, this person did some good work, the Lord
would place it on his right hand like a precious ring and would show it
to the whole court of heaven, as though it gave him glory to receive
such a gift from his spouse, that is, the soul of this person. This would
call forth from all the citizens of heaven as much affection for that
person as ever princes show for the bride of the king, declaring that
they have for her as much fidelity and devotion as it befits princes to
show toward the chosen bride of their lord. And these blessed ones
will give this person all the help which the church triumphant in
heaven has the power and duty to give to the church still militant here
on earth, as often as God calls them to do so and in the way that has
just been related.

Again, while she was devoutly praying for another person, she
was taught how that person should regulate the conduct of his whole

life, in this manner: He should build his nest in the hollow of the wall (Song 2:14), that is, in the most sacred side of the Lord Jesus, and, resting in this deep abyss, he should suck honey from the rock (cf. Deut. 32:13), that is, the sweetness of the aspirations of the divine heart of Jesus. And then he should meditate diligently on what the Holy Scriptures are able to reveal to him about Christ's holy life on earth and try to follow his example in all things, but in three things in particular. The first is that the Lord often spent the night in prayer, so he, in all his trials and adversities, should ever seek help and take refuge in prayer. The second is that as the Lord went about preaching in the towns and villages, so he should endeavour to edify others not only in words but also in all his actions, gestures, and general comportment. The third is that as Christ the Lord bestowed all kinds of benefits on the needy, so he should communicate the following blessing through all his words and actions. Whenever he was about to do or to say anything, he should begin with the intention of recommending it to the Lord in union with his divine will and for the salvation of the world. Then, having completed it, he should offer it again, in union with the same, to the Son of God, that he may deign to correct it and make it worthy of being presented to God the Father, to his eternal glory.

Gertrude also understood that whenever this person desired to come forth from his nest, he must make use of three supports to lean on: on one he should place his feet, and should support himself on the right and the left with the others. The first support should be ardent charity inspiring him with the desire to draw all men to God, with all his might, for love of God, and to be of use to them for the glory of God, in union with that love through which the Lord wrought the salvation of the whole human race. The second support, which he was to use on the right, was a humble subjection, by which he was to submit himself to everybody for God's sake, carefully taking heed that no one, neither superiors or inferiors, should ever find in his words or actions a cause for disedification. The third support, which was to sustain him on the left, should be the watchful custody of himself by means of which he should endeavour to preserve himself and to avoid the stains which he might contract by thoughts, words, or actions, and which could be the means of incurring the slightest divine displeasure.

Once she was praying for another person, the state of whose life was depicted to her in this way. He appeared to be building for himself before God's throne a magnificent throne of cut and polished gems, and, for cement, he was using pure gold. Sometimes he seemed to be resting, seated on the throne which he was building, and sometimes he got up and continued to strive to build it up higher. Gertrude realized that the gems signified various afflictions whereby the gift of God had been preserved and enhanced in the soul of this person, for the Lord prepares for his elect a hard way in this life, lest pleasures along the way might make them forgetful of those pleasures which are in their true fatherland. As for the gold cementing the gems together, it represented the habitual supernatural grace possessed by this soul which he should not fail to make use of with full and firm confidence to join together all his adversities and afflictions, whether interior or exterior, for the good of his salvation. If sometimes he sat resting on his throne, this showed that at times he enjoyed divine consolations. And when at length he got up to resume his building, it symbolized the continuous perseverance in good works whereby a person advances day by day toward perfection.

When she was praying for another person, this is how his state was revealed to her. She beheld before the glorious throne of the divine majesty a very beautiful tree, with trunk and branches flourishing in the glad green of spring and leaves shining with the splendor of gold. The person for whom she was praying climbed up into the tree and began to cut off with a tool some of the little branches which were beginning to wither. For each branch that was cut off, he was immediately handed other branches from the throne of God which seemed to be closely surrounded on all sides by branches of the same color. These branches he grafted on the tree in place of the ones which had been cut away and, at once regaining their vigor, she saw them produce fruit of a red color, which this person gathered and offered to the Lord; and the Lord was marvelously pleased with it.

Now, the tree signified the religious life which the person for whom she was praying had entered to serve God. The golden leaves signified the good works he had performed in the Order to which he belonged. These works, through the merits of a relative of his, who had led him to the Order and had commended him to the Lord with fervent desires and prayers, were given a value as much greater as gold has greater value than other metals. As for the tool he was using for cutting away the withered branches, it signified the consideration of his own defects, which he cut away by penance as soon as he recognized them. The branch which was handed to him from the throne of God to replace the branch which had been cut away signified the

240

perfection of the most holy life of Jesus Christ who, through the merits
and prayers of the near relation already mentioned, was always more
than ready to supply for the person's defects. By the fruit which he
gathered and offered to the Lord is signified the good will with which
he corrected his faults. That is always very pleasing to the Lord, for
the good will of a sincere heart is much more acceptable to him than
great works done without a pure intention.

Praying for two other people who had devoutly recommended
themselves to her, but of whose state she knew nothing, she said to the
Lord: "Lord, to you all hearts are known; graciously deign to reveal to
me, in spite of my great unworthiness, something about these two
persons which may be according to your will and profitable for their
salvation."

Then the Lord kindly reminded her of two other revelations
which she had been given a short time before concerning two different
people for whom she had been praying, of whom one was learned and
the other illiterate, although she was no less turned toward God than
was the first. He said that the revelations which had been made about
them could well be used for the instruction of these persons. He added:
"The five preceding revelations and the two following could well be
used for the instruction of anyone, whether in a religious order or any
other profession."

The revelation concerning the learned person is as follows. When
she was praying for her, the Lord said: "I have taken her up with the
apostles into the mountain of new light. Therefore let this person try to
regulate her life according to the interpretation of the names of the
apostles on Mount Thabor (Mk. 9:1f). Now 'Peter' is to be interpreted
'he who recognizes.'[107] Therefore she should try in everything she
reads to consider carefully, to investigate, and so to know herself. For
instance, when she reads anything about vices or virtues, she should
carefully consider and try to ascertain whether any vice still remains in
her and how much progress she is making in virtue. After she has
acquired a more perfect knowledge of herself, she should try, according
to the interpretation of the name 'James' the supplanter (Gen. 27:26),[108]
to overcome herself, fighting vigorously against all vices, and by constant effort, to acquire the perfection of the virtues in which she is
deficient. Then, as the name 'John' is to be interpreted as 'in whom is
grace,'[109] she should try to give one hour, at the most convenient time
every day, whether daytime or nighttime, morning or evening, to
detach herself from all exterior things, in order to withdraw into her-

self and, attending only to me, to see what is my will. And then, in whatever way I inspire her, she should either give me praise, or give me thanks for benefits bestowed on her personally or in general, or pray for sinners or for souls in purgatory; and she should devote herself entirely to doing this during the time she has determined for herself."

The revelation for the illiterate person was this. Gertrude had pitied her, seeing her perplexed and troubled because she felt she was prevented from praying by the various duties she had to perform. Then, when she prayed for her, she received this answer from the Lord: "I have not chosen her to serve me for one hour only, but rather that she should be with me all day long without a break; that is, that she should carry out all her work for my praise, with the same intention that she would have if she were praying. She could also add this devotion: to desire that all who profit physically from her labors should not only be refreshed in body but should make progress in my love and be confirmed in all that is good. And whenever she does this it will seem to me as if each of her works and labors were a dish which she is seasoning for me with some particularly tasty sauce."

NOTES

Note that the translation of Book III of the *Legatus* omits a number of brief chapters, specifically 3, 8, 12, 13, 15, 21, 24, 27, 29, 31, 37, 39, 45, 47, 49, 54, 58, 62, 66, 71, 72, 73, and 75–90.

1. This is presumably another nun of Helfta, and almost certainly the confidant mentioned in the Prologue. It is not unlikely that, as Dom Pierre Doyère believes (cf. vol. 3 of the *Sources Chrétiennes* edition of St. Gertrude, p. 15, footnote), she is also the author of Book I.
2. Gertrude seems to be referring to Proverb 25:2, which, however, says the precise opposite: "It is the glory of God to conceal the word, and the glory of kings to search out the speech." This error is to be found already in St. Bernard, *Song* 65,3. Doyère (p. 17, footnote) suggests that there is some confusion between the text of Proverbs cited above and Tobit 12:7: "It is good to hide the secret of a king; but honorable to reveal and confess the words of God."
3. The first part of the third antiphon of the Office of St. Agnes, used also in the ceremony of the Solemn Profession and Consecration of Virgins: "*Anulo suo subarrhavit me Dominus meus Jesus Christus.*" The

antiphon is now also used in the Office of St. Gertrude herself, with the variation suggested by Bk. II, ch. 20: "My Lord Jesus Christ has espoused me with seven rings."

4. The second part of the antiphon mentioned in note 3 above: ". . . et tamquam sponsam decoravit me corona."

5. St. Bartholomew, Apostle: feast-day August 24.

6. *Stella Maris Maria:* This antiphon has not survived. It has been suggested that the reference is to the *Ave Maris Stella,* but that is not an antiphon but a hymn, and it is not likely that such a familiar chant would be so inaccurately described. The phrase "*stella maris*" does occur in the antiphon *Alma Redemptoris Mater,* but the same difficulty applies.

7. In speaking of the gardens Gertrude may be thinking of the little garden tended by the nuns in their cloister and which might absorb too much of their time. Nothing spiritual is here intended by the symbol of the garden, and there is no reference to the *hortus conclusus* ("enclosed garden") and its traditional interpretations. On the contrary, Gertrude is using the similitude of the gardens to symbolize temptations which might distract the soul from God. With her usual good sense, she recognizes and makes clear that while physical temptations may have a certain attraction they are not of any real interest or danger to one who has attained to any knowledge of God; the same is not true of spiritual or intellectual temptations: the garden representing honor and one's own will was attractive enough for Gertrude to reject it at least partly because of its size rather than its nature.

8. St. Matthew, Apostle: feast-day September 21.

9. Cf. Responsory nine at Matins for the Sundays in November: "*Laudabilis populus quem Dominus exercituum benedixit dicens: Opus manuum mearum tu es, hereditas mea Israel*" ("Praiseworthy is the people which the Lord of hosts has blessed, saying: 'You are the work of my hands, Israel my inheritance' ").

10. St. Maurice: feast-day September 22.

11. Feast of the Holy Innocents: December 28.

12. By an advocate in the body of the Lord St. Gertrude means the Sacred Heart.

13. Doyère traces this quotation, which does not in fact follow the words of Job, to an ancient Office of November 2 (All Souls) found in a few MSS (pp. 30–31, note).

14. St. Mary Magdalen: feast-day July 22.

15. This is not the place to discuss in detail the question of the

identification of Mary Magdalen "of whom seven devils had gone out" (Lk. 8:2), and who was present at the crucifixion (Matt. 27:56) and was the first to see the risen Christ (Jn. 20: 11–18) with the sinner who anointed Jesus' feet (Lk. 7:37). The identification goes back at least to St. Gregory the Great and was generally accepted in the Latin though not the Greek church.

16. Cf. *Rule* of St. Benedict, ch. 5 (quoting 2 Cor. 9:7): "God loves a cheerful giver."

17. Cf. Exod. 19:9. "From early times the cloud into which Moses entered on the mount has been interpreted as a symbol of contemplation. . . . The contemplative, enveloped by the cloud, is in touch with the divine, and during the time of contemplation withdrawn from human companionship" (Hilda Graef, *The Light and the Rainbow* [London, 1959], p. 15).

18. "The admirable and ineffable condescension of God's love" ("*mira et ineffabili dignatione divina pietas*"): cf. *Exsultet*, chant in praise of the Paschal Candle, Easter Vigil Mass: "*O mira circa nos tuae pietatis dignatio! O inaestimabilis dilectio caritatis!*" ("O admirable condescension of your love toward us! O inestimable love and affection!").

19. The mode of expression of this passage is not clear and might give rise to a certain confusion. It must therefore be stressed that the souls for whom the Lord encouraged Gertrude to pray were not souls already in hell, but souls still living in this world in a condition which would lead eventually to their damnation. The Latin phrase *in statu damnationis* could refer to either of these categories of souls. The meaning here is made clear by the phrases "those who were *destined to be* damned" and "might . . . be recalled to a better way of life." Gertrude's first hesitation to pray for such souls stems from her strong belief in predestination: she feels it is not right for her to pray for souls who might be predestined to damnation, as if she were trying to alter the divine plan. We have chosen to make the whole passage unambiguous by rendering *in statu damnationis* as "in a state of mortal sin."

20. "With a serene countenance": *sereno vultu*. In the context of the Eucharistic Prayer ("the time was approaching when she was to go to communion") this is probably an echo of the prayer *Supra quae*, which follows the Consecration in the Roman Canon: "*Supra quae propitio ac sereno vultu respicere digneris*" ("Deign to look upon (the offerings) with a favorable and serene countenance").

21. St. Matthias, Apostle: feast-day May 14.

22. Esther 2:13. The rest of this chapter contains many references to the book of Esther.

23. A reminiscence may be intended of the incident in the life of St. Benedict recounted by Gregory the Great in Book II of the *Dialogues* 2,4: Benedict, attacked by a violent carnal temptation, threw himself into a patch of nettles, rolled in them, and was thenceforth never troubled by such temptations. A similar story is told of Francis of Assisi.

24. *"Salve Sancta Parens, enixa puerpera Regem qui caelum terramque regit in saecula saeculorum"* ("Hail, holy Mother, who bore the King who rules over heaven and earth for ever and ever"). Introit, by Sedulius (fifth century), from the Common of Our Lady.

25. This interdict is also mentioned by Mechthild (*Book of Special Grace* 3,16). It was imposed shortly before 1296, during the vacancy of the episcopal see, by the cathedral chapter of Halberstadt because of a legal dispute over a debt incurred by the monastery of Helfta.

26. Cf. Gregory the Great, *Dialogues* II, 21,4. Speaking of Elijah and indirectly of St. Benedict, Gregory says: *"Quod omnipotens Deus ex magnae pietatis dispensatione disponit, quia dum prophetiae spiritum aliquando dat et aliquando subtrahit, prophetantium mentes et elevat in celsitudine et custodit in humilitate, ut et accipientes spiritum inveniant quid de Deo sint, et rursum prophetiae spiritum non habentes cognoscant quid sint de semetipsis"* ("God arranges this out of the great love of his Providence; for sometimes he grants the spirit of prophecy, and sometimes he withdraws it, thus raising the minds of the prophets to the heights and also preserving their humility; so that in receiving the spirit they may find out what they are by God's grace, and again, when they do not have the spirit of prophecy they may know what they are of themselves").

27. *"Recordare, Virgo Mater, in conspectu Dei, ut loquaris pro nobis bona, et ut avertat indignationem suam a nobis"* ("Remember, O Virgin Mother, to speak good for us in the sight of God, and to turn away his indignation from us"). Offertory from the Common of Our Lady, based on Jeremiah 18:20.

28. "Love compels me": *Amor coegit me.* The phrase itself is found in the much later hymn *Auctor beate saeculi,* but the idea is there in germ in the hymn *Iesu nostra redemptio* (see note 45 below): *"Quae te vicit clementia ut ferres nostra crimina . . . ? Ipsa te cogat pietas ut mala nostra superes"* ("What mercy overcame you and made you bear our sins . . . ? May that same love compel you to overcome our evils").

29. Lanspergius in his edition of the *Legatus* suggests this is a Mass celebrated in the parish church; but it is unlikely that the nuns would have left the abbey, or, if they had, that they would have been unable to receive communion. It is more probable that this is a Mass celebrated at the abbey for those layfolk who regularly came to the abbey Mass. A marginal note in several MSS explains that the interdict did not affect the parishioners. They, then, would have been permitted to communicate at the abbey, though that was forbidden to the nuns.

30. Feast of the Assumption, August 15.

31. Feast of St. Lawrence, August 10.

32. Cf. Introit for the first Sunday after Epiphany (now used during the first week of Ordinary Time): "*In excelso throno vidi sedere virum, quem adorat multitudo angelorum*" ("Upon a high throne I saw a man seated who was adored by a multitude of angels").

33. This is probably an allusion to the verse of the fourth Responsory at Matins of the feast of the Assumption in the monastic Breviary: "*Gaudent chori angelorum, consortes et concives nostri*" ("The choirs of angels, our companions and fellow-citizens, rejoice"). Angels are traditionally seen as the fellow-citizens of monks and nuns.

34. This refers to a text common in the liturgy of Paschaltide: "*Gaude et laetare, Virgo Maria, alleluia; quia surrexit Dominus vere, alleluia*" ("Rejoice and be glad, Virgin Mary, alleluia; for the Lord is risen indeed, alleluia").

35. Holy, holy, holy: cf. Is. 6:3, Rev. 4:8. It has been traditional from the earliest Christian centuries to see each "holy" as applying to one of the Persons of the Blessed Trinity, Father, Son, and Holy Spirit respectively.

36. Almighty power, wisdom, and goodness (or loving kindness) are the three particular attributes of the three Persons of the Blessed Trinity and recur frequently in the works of Gertrude.

37. The fleur-de-lys is the symbol of the Blessed Trinity, and also of a virgin, the virgin Mary in particular.

38. Cf. *Rule* of St. Benedict, ch. 9: "*Omnes de sedilibus suis surgant ob honorem et reverentiam Sanctae Trinitatis*" ("Let all rise from their seats to show honor and reverence to the blessed Trinity").

39. This paragraph is constructed largely from references to two of Jesus' parables: the Wise and Foolish Virgins (Matt. 25:1ff) and the Prodigal Son (Lk. 15:11ff).

40. The pelican is depicted in church art and in heraldry as it is here described by Gertrude, "in her piety," that is, wounding her breast

with her beak in order to feed her young (or raise them from the dead) with her blood. This legend, which arose from the red tip on the pelican's beak and its posture when feeding its young from the "bag" which forms part of the beak, has led the pelican to become the symbol of Christ's charity and his saving death, especially as mediated through the eucharist. The sixth verse of Thomas Aquinas' *Adoro Te* runs: "*Pie pellicane, Iesu Domine, Me immundum munda tuo sanguine; cuius una stilla salvum facere, totum mundum quit ab omni scelere*" ("Pelican of mercy, Jesu Lord and God, Cleanse me, wretched sinner, in thy precious blood; Blood whereof one drop for humankind outpoured Might from all transgression have the world restored"). An interesting point is that Gertrude says "Blood from the *father's* heart" (ex sanguine cordis *paterni*). That is probably to emphasize the parallel with Christ, but it is always the female pelican which is depicted as feeding or reviving her young with her blood. Indeed some versions of the legend claim the father pelican as the cause of the children's death!

41. "Sleeves turned back": cf. *Ceremonial for Bishops*, Book II, ch. 8: "The Bishop vests in a chasuble, carefully turning back the sleeves so as not to be impeded in the sacred function."

42. Gertrude here quotes verbatim from an ancient Responsory, preserved in the liturgy of the Premonstratensians: "*Invitatus ad convivium venio gratias agens quia dignatus es, Domine Jesu, ad tuas epulas invitare, sciens quod ex toto corde meo desiderabam te*" ("I was invited to your banquet and I came giving thanks that you, Lord Jesus, deigned to invite [me] to your feast, knowing that I desired you with my whole heart"). The Lord answers her in the words of the second part of the Responsory.

43. The possibility of breaking up the sacred species in the mouth (cf. the reference above to "breaking up the host with my teeth") suggests that the custom of having large and thick hosts, which had in general disappeared by Gertrude's time, still survived at Helfta.

44. "*Felix anima, quae in Christi recumbit pectore, et inter Verbi brachia requiescit*" ("Blessed is the soul which reclines upon Christ's breast, and rests between the arms of the Word"): Bernard, *Song* 51,5.

45. "*Iesu nostra redemptio*" ("Jesus our redemption"): Vespers hymn for the feast of the Ascension (anonymous, ninth century).

46. St. Paul remarks that Christ is the "firstborn among many brethren" (Rom. 8:29). This idea is suggested by Gertrude here since she is speaking of Christ's Incarnation from the blessed Virgin, but the source for this surprising appellation is more probably the Song of

Songs, for example 4:9: "Thou hast wounded my heart, my sister, my spouse." Gertrude is the spouse of Christ and so his sister; he is therefore her brother. Compare chapter 23 below.

47. The feast of the Annunciation of the Lord: March 25.

48. These blessings and remissions come to nine, the same number as there are invocations in the *Kyrie eleison: Kyrie eleison* ("Lord have mercy")—three times; *Christe eleison* ("Christ have mercy")—three times; *Kyrie eleison*—three times. Originally all nine invocations were understood to be addressed to the Lord Jesus Christ, but soon (and evidently Gertrude assumes this) they were interpreted as a triple invocation of each of the three Persons of the blessed Trinity.

49. The reference, again, to the attributes of the blessed Trinity serve to emphasize that the heart of Jesus, though belonging strictly to the Son incarnate, contains all the virtues of the divinity; it is the instrument, as Gertrude puts it, through which the Trinity operates in its relations with humankind.

50. One manner of receiving the blood of Christ under the species of wine, recorded as early as the eighth century in Rome, and certainly in use in the thirteenth century, is by sucking it from the chalice through a metal tube like a drinking-straw. That is what Gertrude seems to have in mind as she describes Christ's gifts coming to her from his heart through a sort of golden tube.

51. On the spiritual senses, see notes 60 and 105 to Book II above.

52. "*Vidi aquam egredientem de templo a latere dextro*" ("I saw water coming forth from the temple, on the right side"). Today this antiphon, taken from Ezekiel 47, is used only at the Asperges in Paschaltide. It is possible that Gertrude means simply that this took place during the Easter season "when the *Vidi Aquam* is sung," and not that it was actually sung at Vespers; or perhaps this text was once used as a Vespers antiphon that has not survived.

53. "Places": The word is *officinas*, literally "workshops," but Gertrude's response shows her to have understood it in a much broader sense.

54. The spiritual cloister is a recurring theme in the twelfth and thirteenth centuries. Sometimes the authors describe the monastery itself, and all its regular places, from the point of view of their utility for the soul; sometimes the soul is seen as the cloister; sometimes (an example is to be found in Mechthild of Magdeburg's *Flowing Light of Divinity* 7,36) the officials of the monastery are compared to the virtues

that should reside in the soul. Gertrude is unusual in describing the Lord himself as her cloister.

55. See B1. Jordan of Saxony, *Life of St. Dominic*, 4.

56. *"Veni et ostende nobis faciem tuam, Domine, qui sedes super Cherubim, et salvi erimus"* ("Come and show us your face, O Lord, who are seated above the Cherubim, and we shall be saved"). Introit for Saturday of the third week of Advent (now for the last Tuesday in Advent). The texts cited in the first part of this chapter are used in the liturgy of Advent and Christmas.

57. Cf. Wisd. 18:14; this text is frequently used in the Christmas liturgy.

58. Cf. Bk. III, ch. 26, and note 50 above.

59. *"Ecce veniet Dominus protector noster, sanctus Israel"* ("See, the Lord our protector comes, the Holy One of Israel"): fifth Responsory at Matins of the second Sunday of Advent.

60. *"Sanctificamini, filii Israel, dicit Dominus"* ("Sanctify yourselves, children of Israel, says the Lord"): third Responsory at Matins of the Vigil of Christmas.

61. Cf. Ps. 109:3. It is the text of the communion antiphon of Midnight Mass of Christmas.

62. Cf. 1 Jn. 1:5; it is worth noting that *lux divinitatis* (the phrase translated by "the light of the divinity") is the Latin title given to the revelations of Mechthild of Magdeburg. The original Low German version was known as *Das fliessende Licht der Gottheit*.

63. Cf. Matt. 16:24. Gertrude, as so often, quotes not the scriptural text but the liturgical one; this is the opening of the Magnificat antiphon for second Vespers of one martyr. Another example of this is in Book III, chapter 13, in which she quotes not the text of Matthew 25:40 but the antiphon (Magnificat antiphon of the first Monday in Lent) based upon it.

64. *"Viri sancti gloriosum sanguinem fuderunt pro Domino"* ("The holy men shed their glorious blood for the Lord"); second Responsory at Matins of martyrs.

65. From an old Responsory for the feast of St. John the evangelist (December 27), taken from his *Life* by Abdias. This refers to the ancient legend that John the evangelist, ordered to drink poison by the emperor Domitian, did so without suffering any ill effects.

66. Versicle, taken from the hymn *Te Deum*, formerly used after the absolution at Prime: "℣. *Dignare, Domine, die isto* ℟. *Sine peccato nos*

custodire" ("℣. Vouchsafe, O Lord, this day ℟. To keep us without sin").

67. The text of this Responsory, formerly the ninth at Matins of Sexagesima Sunday, has been replaced by the similar "*Benedixit Deus Noe et filii eius*" ("God blessed Noah and his sons").

68. Genesis 4:9. This passage (verses 1–16) is used as a lesson at Matins of Thursday after Septuagesima Sunday.

69. "*Induit me Dominus vestimentis salutis et indumento laetitiae cir-cumdedit me, et tamquam sponsam decoravit me corona*" ("The Lord has clothed me with the garments of salvation, and with the robe of joy he has covered me; and as a bride he has decked me with a crown."): eleventh Responsory at Matins of Virgins, taken from Isaiah 61:10, to which Gertrude also refers in the following lines.

70. "*Vocavit Angelus Domini Abraham*" ("The angel of the Lord called Abraham"): fifth Responsory at Matins for Quinquagesima Sunday.

71. Is. 66:13, taken from the passage used as the third canticle at Christmas Matins.

72. Dom Cuthbert Butler, in his *Western Mysticism* (New York, 1923), p. 115, notes: "It was St. Gregory's experience, as we have seen it to be St. Augustine's, that the soul can maintain itself in the act of contemplation only for a brief moment, and then, exhausted by the effort, it falls back to its normal state. This recoil is graphically and eloquently described in various passages . . . for example St. Gregory, *Hom. in Ez* 2,2,12; *Moralia* viii, 50; xxiii, 43."

73. This Tract, based on Psalm 41:2,4, is now used in the Office of Holy Saturday; it was sung in some places during the Middle Ages at Masses for the Dead.

74. We are not to understand that members of the community were permitted to communicate twice in one day, but rather that there were two Masses celebrated, at either of which one might communicate.

75. "His own adorable hand": The Latin words are *manu sua veneranda*, which recall the words of the Institution in the first Eucharistic Prayer (the Roman Canon): "*Accepit panem in sanctas ac venerabiles manus suas*" ("He took the bread in his holy and venerable hands").

76. Literally, "for love of my love." The phrase probably originates in Augustine's "for love of your love" (*Confessions*, Bk. 2, ch. 1).

77. Cf. Bernard, *Song* 15,6: "*Jesus mel in ore, in aure melos, in corde iubilus*" ("Jesus is honey in the mouth, music in the ear, gladness in the heart"). The phrase is frequently quoted not only by Gertrude but by

many other writers including, for example, the Englishman Richard Rolle.

78. It may be surprising to see the words "he . . . abides between my breasts" on the lips of the Lord. The word *ubera* is used only of female breasts in normal Latin. It is worth noting, however, that on the first verse of the Song of Songs St. Bernard (*Song* 9, 5–6) does speak of the breasts of the spouse (Jesus), saying that they are his willingness to forgive, and his patience, and that grace flows from them. Compare also Rev. 1:13: "One like to a Son of man . . . girt about the paps [again a word used only of a woman's breasts, *mastos* in Greek, *mamilla* in Latin] with a golden girdle."

79. "Heart": literally, *iecur*, "liver." The liver was considered in antiquity to be the seat of the passions. It is quite likely that not only was Gertrude's heart (or liver) metaphorically inflamed with passionate love in meditating on the passion of the Lord, but that she was suffering from some physical infirmity in that region as well.

80. "Her Hours": The Little Hours or Little Office of Our Lady, recited, not of obligation, by some religious who are not bound to recite the Divine Office, and also by several of the contemplative orders as a matter of devotion, after the Office of obligation has been recited. It is a short Office, consisting of psalms and Marian hymns and antiphons in which the Hail Mary is frequently used. Gertrude was clearly unwell, since she was to recite Matins of the Divine Office in private and not in Choir; that Office, of obligation, would have taken precedence over the Little Office.

81. Magnificat antiphon of the first Vespers of the Feast of the Purification: "*virgo peperit, et post partum virgo permansit*" ("a virgin bore him, and remained a virgin after childbirth"). Used frequently, with some variations, in the Office of Our Lady.

82. This part of the chapter is very reminiscent of Book I, chapter 2 of St. Mechthild's *Book of Special Grace*, which is, however, considerably shorter.

83. The reference is to Pontius Pilate who was, of course, a pagan, though of a somewhat different type. Gertrude is writing soon after the crusade against the Saracens led by St. Louis in 1270, in which he lost his life. These events were no doubt fresh in her mind.

84. This was probably the army of King Adolphus who in the year 1294 occupied the region around Eisleben while marching against the sons of Duke Albert.

85. *"O lux beatissima, reple cordis intima tuorum fidelium"* ("O most blessed Light, fill the depths of the hearts of your faithful people"): the fifth verse of the sequence *Veni Sancte Spiritus* ("Come, Holy Spirit") for Pentecost Sunday, composed by Stephen Langton, Cardinal Archbishop of Canterbury (d. 1228).

86. *"Veni Sancte Spiritus, reple tuorum corda fidelium, et tui amoris in eis ignem accende"* ("Come, Holy Spirit, fill the hearts of your faithful, and kindle within them the fire of your love").

87. This is a reminiscence of the fifth verse of the hymn *Veni creator Spiritus* ("Come, Creator Spirit"), perhaps by Rhabanus Maurus of Fulda (776–856), which runs, *"Hostem repellas longius, pacemque dones protinus . . ."* ("Drive the enemy far away, and grant peace").

88. This phrase is perhaps not immediately clear, but it is theologically accurate: The point is that God's will is all-powerful; if he desires that something should take place, within or outside himself, there is nothing that can prevent it.

89. The theme of the heartbeats of the Lord can be found also, for example, in St. Mechthild's *Book of Special Grace* (Bk I ch. 5 and Bk. V ch. 32). While Gertrude describes the Lord's heartbeats as normal, however, Mechthild describes them as unique, consisting not of two pulsations but of three strong ones (representing his divine love) and one weaker one (representing his human love).

90. "Come, my chosen one": These are the opening words of the fourth antiphon of the Common of Virgins: *"Veni, electa mea, et ponam in te thronum meum"* ("Come, my chosen one, and I shall place my throne in you"). The same text is used as a Responsory in the ceremony of monastic profession.

91. "Takes hold of patience": The phrase appears in the *Rule* of St. Benedict on the fourth degree of humility (ch. 7).

92. "Note": literally *"neum,"* the term used for a group of notes forming one melodic unit in Gregorian Chant.

93. It is worth noting that the Lord replaces priestly ordination with consecration; the reference is presumably to the Consecration of Virgins which, while not a sacrament, is a sacramental which Gertrude could (and would) have received, and which would correspond as nearly as possible to priestly ordination, which she could not. This seems to give further support to the contention (see Bk. 2, note 94 above) that Gertrude never considered herself to have a sacramental capacity to absolve from sin.

94. There is no trace or record of this foundation, which seems to have come to nothing.

95. "Surrounded by fresh spring flowers, roses and lilies": The Latin is "*Circumdatus vernantibus floribus rosarum et liliorum.*" Gertrude seems here to be conflating two liturgical texts: the Responsory now used at first Vespers of the Assumption of Mary—"*Sicut dies verni circumdabant eam flores rosarum et lilia convallium*" ("blossoming roses and lilies-of-the-valley surrounded her like a spring day")—and the antiphon now used at Vespers of the feast of the Rosary—"*Viderunt eam filiae Sion vernantem in floribus rosarum*" ("The daughters of Sion saw her, spring-like, among the blossoming roses"). It is interesting that both these texts refer to our Lady and not to our Lord.

96. These words of the Lord are to be found in the Prologue to the whole work, which demonstrates, first, that the Prologue must be considered as an integral part of the work, and, second, that the Lord wishes to be considered as the principal author of the whole work.

97. The phrase is taken from the Collect for the Requiem Mass: "*Deus, cui proprium est misereri semper et parcere.*"

98. The monastery of Helfta seems often to have been in danger and to have suffered depredations. See, for example, Mechthild's *Book of Special Grace* 4, 11–12.

99. This is probably a reference to Ghebhard von Mansfeld, who attacked the monastery in 1284 and was excommunicated for this.

100. Again, the quotation is not biblical but liturgical; the text follows not Matthew 26:39 but the Responsory *In monte Oliveti*, then used at Matins of Maundy Thursday (now Good Friday).

101. Gregory the Great, *Homilies on the Gospels*, 26. The text is taken from the twelfth lesson of Matins of the Octave of Easter.

102. Gertrude is quoting, inaccurately and probably from memory, not Wisdom 8:1, but the antiphon *O Sapientia* of Vespers of December 17.

103. The word rendered here as "receive" is *suscipio*. Gertrude (or the Lord) surely intends a reference to the ceremony of monastic profession, in which the professed sings three times: "*Suscipe me Domine*" ("Receive me, O Lord"). This reminiscence is probably intended to extend throughout the chapter, which is why we have chosen to render *profiteor* and *professio* throughout as "profess," "profession," even where "confess" might perhaps be more natural English.

104. In this chapter, as elsewhere, it is not always easy (sometimes it

is impossible) to tell the sex of the person under discussion. This may have been intentional and done for reasons of discretion, the people in question being still alive; compare the habit of Mechthild of Magdeburg of referring to herself with masculine pronouns to disguise her identity. However, it may simply be due to the fact that the Latin word for "person" (*persona*) is feminine, with the result that it is possible to speak of a man in grammatically feminine terms. The same applies to the word for soul (*anima*), whose feminine gender means that the phrase "bride of Christ" can be used with no incongruity of a man's soul. We have chosen in general to employ the feminine, and sometimes the neutral "they"; this chapter is an exception as there seems to be an intentional distinction between the persons with whom the chapter directly deals and the two unquestionably female persons mentioned at the end.

105. Bernard, *Song* 23,15.

106. Cf. *Rule* of St. Benedict, prologue: "*Abrenuntians propriis voluntatibus, Domino Christo vero Regi militaturus*" ("renouncing his own will to fight in the army of Christ, the true King").

107. The etymology applies to the name Simon, not Peter. This, probably incorrect, interpretation is also found in the *Life of Christ* II,3 by Ludolph the Carthusian. The name is more likely to be, like Simeon, a form of a name meaning "God has heard."

108. The English names James and Jacob represent a single name in Hebrew, Greek, and Latin. This etymology (of Jacob), which may well be correct, is found at Genesis 27:36.

109. Again the etymology is not entirely accurate; the name John (*Johanan*) probably means "Yahweh has been gracious."

Select Bibliography

1. TEXTS

Sanctae Gertrudis Magnae, Virginis Ordinis Sancti Benedicti, Legatus Divinae Pietatis. Accedunt eiusdem Exercitia Spiritualia. Ed. D. Paquelin. Paris: Oudin, 1875. (Includes the *Epistola Apologetica* of Lanspergius, Gertrude's first editor. Cologne, 1536.)

Gertrude d'Helfta, *Oeuvres Spirituelles* (Latin—French); I: *Les Exercices;* II–V: *Le Héraut.* Paris: Editions du Cerf, 1967–1986 (*Sources Chrétiennes* 127, 139, 143, 255, 331). Ed. P. Doyère et al.

The Life and Revelations of St. Gertrude by a Nun of Kenmare. Kenmare, 1952. (A biography based on Book 1 of the *Legatus*, followed by an English translation of Books 2–5.)

Gertrude the Great of Helfta, *Spiritual Exercises.* Tr. G. Jaron and J. Lewis. Kalamazoo: Cistercian Publications, 1989. (CF49)

Bernard of Clairvaux, *On the Song of Songs* I–IV. Tr. K. Walsh, et al. Kalamazoo: Cistercian Publications 1971–1980. (Cf. 4,7,31,41)

Sanctae Mechtildis, Virgins Ordinis Sancti Benedicti, Liber Specialis Gratiae. Ed. D. Paquelin. Paris: Oudin, 1875.

Le Livre de la Grâce Spéciale, révélations de Ste Mechtilde, vierge de l'Ordre de S. Benoît. Paris: Oudin, 1878 (complete).

SELECT BIBLIOGRAPHY

Select Revelations of St. Mechthild, Virgin. Tr. by a secular priest. London: Thomas Richardson and Sons, 1875.

The Revelations of Mechthild of Magdeburg. Tr. L. Menzies. London: Longmans Green and Co., 1953 (with some omissions).

2. BACKGROUND READING

Bynum, C. W. *Jesus as Mother: Studies in the Spirituality of the High Middle Ages.* Berkeley: University of California, 1982.

Gilson, E. *The Mystical Theology of St. Bernard.* Tr. A. H. C. Downes. Kalamazoo: Cistercian Publications, 1990.

Guéranger, P. *The Liturgical Year.* Tr. L. Shepherd. London: Burns and Oates, 1904.

Jédin, H., ed. *History of the Church.* Vol. 4: *From the High Middle Ages to the Eve of the Reformation.* New York: Seabury, 1980.

Knowles, D. *What is Mysticism?* London: Burns and Oates, 1967.

Leclercq, J. *The Love of Learning and the Desire for God.* Tr. C. Misrahi. New York: Fordham University Press, 1961.

McCann, J. *The Rule of St. Benedict.* London: Burns and Oates, 1952.

Pius XII. Encyclical Letter *Haurietis Aquas.* London: Catholic Truth Society no. 62 (AAS vol. 48, 1956).

Podhradsky, G. *New Dictionary of the Liturgy.* London: Geoffrey Chapman, 1967.

Vagaggini, C. *Theological Dimensions of the Liturgy.* Tr. L. J. Doyle and W. A. Jurgens. Collegeville: The Liturgical Press, 1976. (See especially chapter 22, pp. 740–803: "The Example of a Mystic: St. Gertrude and Liturgical Spirituality)."

Index

INDEX

Other Volumes in this Series

Fakhruddin Iraqi • DIVINE FLASHES
Menahem Nahum of Chernobyl • THE LIGHT OF THE EYES
Early Dominicans • SELECTED WRITINGS
John Climacus • THE LADDER OF DIVINE ASCENT
Francis and Clare • THE COMPLETE WORKS
Gregory Palamas • THE TRIADS
Pietists • SELECTED WRITINGS
The Shakers • TWO CENTURIES OF SPIRITUAL REFLECTION
Zohar • THE BOOK OF ENLIGHTENMENT
Luis de León • THE NAMES OF CHRIST
Quaker Spirituality • SELECTED WRITINGS
Emanuel Swedenborg • THE UNIVERSAL HUMAN AND SOUL-BODY INTERACTION
Augustine of Hippo • SELECTED WRITINGS
Safed Spirituality • RULES OF MYSTICAL PIETY, THE BEGINNING OF WISDOM
Maximus Confessor • SELECTED WRITINGS
John Cassian • CONFERENCES
Johannes Tauler • SERMONS
John Ruusbroec • THE SPIRITUAL ESPOUSALS AND OTHER WORKS
Ibn ʿAbbād of Ronda • LETTERS ON THE SŪFĪPATH
Angelus Silesius • THE CHERUBINIC WANDERER
The Early Kabbalah
Meister Eckhart • TEACHER AND PREACHER
John of the Cross • SELECTED WRITINGS
Pseudo-Dionysius • THE COMPLETE WORKS
Bernard of Clairvaux • SELECTED WORKS
Devotio Moderna • BASIC WRITINGS
The Pursuit of Wisdom • AND OTHER WORKS BY THE AUTHOR OF THE CLOUD OF UNKNOWING
Richard Rolle • THE ENGLISH WRITINGS
Francis de Sales, Jane de Chantal • LETTERS OF SPIRITUAL DIRECTION
Albert and Thomas • SELECTED WRITINGS
Robert Bellarmine • SPIRITUAL WRITINGS
Nicodemos of the Holy Mountain • A HANDBOOK OF SPIRITUAL COUNSEL
Henry Suso • THE EXEMPLAR, WITH TWO GERMAN SERMONS
Bérulle and the French School • SELECTED WRITINGS
The Talmud • SELECTED WRITINGS
Ephrem the Syrian • HYMNS
Hildegard of Bingen • SCIVIAS
Birgitta of Sweden • LIFE AND SELECTED REVELATIONS
John Donne • SELECTIONS FROM *DIVINE POEMS*, SERMONS, *DEVOTIONS AND PRAYERS*
Jeremy Taylor • SELECTED WORKS
Walter Hilton • *SCALE OF PERFECTION*